Instant Vortex Air Fryer R

250+ Quick And Tasty Recipes From Breakfast To Dessert That Your Family Will Love

Samantha Baker

BREAKFAST

Cajun Breakfast Muffins

Intermediate Recipe Preparation Time: 10 minutes **Cooking Time:** 10 minutes **Serving**: 6

INGREDIENTS:

- Olive oil
- 4 eggs, beaten
- 2¼ cups frozen hash browns, thawed
- 1 cup diced ham
- ½ cup shredded Cheddar cheese
- ½ teaspoon Cajun seasoning

DIRECTIONS:

1. Lightly spray 12 silicone muffin cups with olive oil.
2. In a medium bowl, mix together the eggs, hash browns, ham, Cheddar cheese, and Cajun seasoning in a medium bowl.
3. Spoon a heaping 1½ tablespoons of hash brown mixture into each muffin cup.
4. Place the muffin cups in the fryer basket.
5. Air fry until the muffins are golden brown on top and the center has set up, 8 to 10 minutes
6. Make It Even Lower Calorie: Reduce or eliminate the cheese.

NUTRITION: Calories 178 Fat 9g Saturated Fat 4gCholesterol 145mg Carbs 13g Protein 11g Fiber 2g Sodium: 467mg

Hearty Blueberry Oatmeal

Intermediate Recipe Preparation Time: 10 minutes **Cooking Time:** 25 minutes **Serving**: 6

INGREDIENTS:

- 1½ cups quick oats
- 1¼ teaspoons ground cinnamon, divided
- ½ teaspoon baking powder
- Pinch salt
- 1 cup unsweetened vanilla almond milk
- ¼ cup honey
- 1 teaspoon vanilla extract
- 1 egg, beaten
- 2 cups blueberries
- Olive oil
- 1½ teaspoons sugar, divided
- 6 tablespoons low-fat whipped topping (optional)

DIRECTIONS:

1. In a large bowl, mix together the oats, 1 teaspoon of cinnamon, baking powder, and salt.
2. In a medium bowl, whisk together the almond milk, honey, vanilla and egg.
3. Pour the liquid ingredients into the oats mixture and stir to combine. Fold in the blueberries.
4. Lightly spray a round air fryer–friendly pan with oil.
5. Add half the blueberry mixture to the pan.
6. Sprinkle ⅛ teaspoon of cinnamon and ½ teaspoon sugar over the top.
7. Cover the pan with aluminum foil and place gently in the fryer basket. Air fry for 20 minutes remove the foil and air fry for an additional 5 minutes Transfer the mixture to a shallow bowl.
8. Repeat with the remaining blueberry mixture, ½ teaspoon of sugar, and ⅛ teaspoon of cinnamon.
9. To serve, spoon into bowls and top with whipped topping.

NUTRITION: Calories 170 Fat 3g Saturated Fat 1g Cholesterol 97mg Carbs 34g Protein 4g Fiber 4g Sodium: 97mg

Banana Bread Pudding

Intermediate Recipe Preparation Time: 10 minutes **Cooking Time:** 20 minutes

Serving: 4

INGREDIENTS:

- Olive oil
- 2 medium ripe bananas, mashed
- ½ cup low-fat milk
- 2 tablespoons peanut butter
- 2 tablespoons maple syrup
- 1 teaspoon ground cinnamon
- 1 teaspoon vanilla extract
- 2 slices whole-grain bread, torn into bite-sized pieces
- ¼ cup quick oats

DIRECTIONS:

1. Lightly spray four individual ramekins or one air fryer–safe baking dish with olive oil.
2. In a large mixing bowl, combine the bananas, milk, peanut butter, maple syrup, cinnamon, and vanilla. Using an electric mixer or whisk, mix until fully combined.
3. Add the bread pieces and stir to coat in the liquid mixture.
4. Add the oats and stir until everything is combined.
5. Transfer the mixture to the baking dish or divide between the ramekins. Cover with aluminum foil.
6. Place 2 ramekins in the fryer basket and air fry until heated through, 10 to 12 minutes
7. Remove the foil and cook for 6 to 8 more minutes
8. Repeat with the remaining 2 ramekins. Make It Even Lower Calorie: Reduce the calories by using sugar-free maple syrup or by replacing the peanut butter with PB2 (powdered peanut butter). Combine 4 tablespoons of powdered peanut butter with 2 tablespoons of water to equal 2 tablespoons of peanut butter.

NUTRITION: Calories 212 Fat 6g Saturated Fat 2g Carbs 38g Protein 6g Sodium: 112mg

Air fried German Pancakes

Basic Recipe
Preparation Time: 5 minutes **Cooking Time:** 8 Minutes **Serving**: 5
INGREDIENTS:

- Serving size: 1/2 cup batter
- 3 Full eggs
- Whole wheat flour: 1 cup
- Almond milk: 1 cup
- A pinch of salt
- Apple sauce: 2 heaping tablespoons (optional but recommended to replace the need for added oil or butter)
- For Garnishing:
- Berries
- Greek yogurt
- Confectioner sugar
- Maple syrup (optional)

DIRECTIONS:

1. Set the air fryer temperature to 390°F/199°C. Inside the air fryer, set the cast iron tray or ramekin as it heats. Take the blender and add all the batter ingredients to it, and combine until smooth. If the batter is too thick, simply add milk or applesauce tablespoons to smooth out. Use nonstick baking spray and spray the cast iron tray or ramekin, and then dump in a batter serving.
2. Air fry the batter for 6-8 minutes
3. Do not worry if top gets hard to touch. This is the advantage of using the air fryer – it provides the pancake with a good firm outer coating/edges that softens as it cools. Place the remaining batter in the refrigerator in an airtight container to freshen it up every morning.
4. Garnish, and serve.

NUTRITION: Calories 139 Protein 8 g Fat 4 g Carbs 18 g
Fiber 3 g Sugar 1 g

Air-Fried Flax Seed French toast Sticks with Berries

Intermediate Recipe Preparation Time: 25 minutes **Cooking Time:** 35 minutes
Serving: 4
INGREDIENTS:

- Whole-grain bread: 4 slices (1 1/2-oz.)
- 2 Big Eggs
- 1/4 cup 2% reduced-fat milk
- Vanilla extract: 1 teaspoon
- Ground cinnamon: ½ teaspoon
- 1/4 cup of light brown sugar, split,
- 2/3 cup flax seed cooking spray
- 2 Cups of fresh-cut strawberries
- Maple syrup: 8 teaspoons
- Powdered sugar: 1 teaspoon

DIRECTIONS:

1. Cut each of the bread slices into four long sticks. In a shallow dish, whisk together eggs, milk, cinnamon, vanilla extract, and 1 tablespoon brown sugar. In a second, shallow dish, combine flaxseed meal and remaining 3 tablespoons of brown sugar.
2. Dip the pieces of bread in a mixture of eggs, soak them slightly, and allow any excess to drip away. Dredge each piece in a mixture of flax seeds and coat on all sides. Cover the bits of bread with cooking oil.
3. Place pieces of bread in a single layer in the air fryer basket, leave room between each piece and cook at 375 ° F in batches until golden brown and crunchy,
   10 minutes, turn slices over halfway through cooking. Place 4 sticks of French toast on each plate to serve. Finish with 1/2 cup of strawberries, 2 teaspoons of maple syrup, and a powdered sugar layer. Serve right now.

NUTRITION: Calories 361 Fat 10g Saturated Fat 1g Unsaturated Fat 7g Protein 14g Carbs 56g Fiber 10g Sugars: 30g Sodium: 218mg

Breakfast Frittatas

Basic Recipe
Preparation Time: 15 minutes **Cooking Time:** 20 minutes **Serving:** 2
INGREDIENTS:

- Breakfast sausage: ¼ pound, completely cooked and crumbled
- Eggs: 4, lightly beaten
- Shredded cheddar cheese: ½ cup
- Red pepper: 2 tablespoons, chopped
- Green onion: 1 chopped
- Cayenne pepper: 1 pinch
- Cooking spray

DIRECTIONS:

1. Combine the sausage, eggs, cheddar cheese, onion, bell pepper, and cayenne in a bowl and blend. Set the temperature of the air-fryer to 360°F (180°C). Sprinkle a 6x2-inch non-stick cake pan with a cooking spray.
2. Put the mixture of the eggs in the prepared cake pan. Cook in the air fryer for 18 to 20 minutes until the frittata is set.

NUTRITION: Calories 379.8 Protein 31.2g Carbs 2.9g Cholesterol 443mg Sodium: 693.5mg

Air-Fried Breakfast Bombs

Basic Recipe
Preparation Time: 20 minutes **Cooking Time:** 5 minutes **Serving:** 2
INGREDIENTS:

- Bacon: 3 slices, center-cut
- 3 Big, lightly beaten eggs
- 1 1/3-ounce fat cream cheese, softened
- Fresh chives: 1 tablespoon, chopped
- 4 Ounces of new whole wheat flour pizza dough

- Cooking spray

DIRECTIONS:

1. Cook the bacon over medium to very crisp in a medium skillet, around 10 minutes Take bacon off the pan. In a pan, add eggs to the bacon drippings; cook for about 1 minute, frequently stirring, until almost set, but still loose. Transfer eggs to a bowl; add cream cheese, chives, and crumbled bacon to taste.
2. Divide the dough into four pieces equal to each. Roll each piece into a 5-inch circle onto a lightly floured surface— place one-fourth of each dough circle in the middle of the egg mixture. Brush the outside edge of the dough with water; wrap the dough around the mixture of the eggs to form a bag, pinch the dough at the seams together.
3. In air fryer tray, put dough bags in a single layer; coat thoroughly with cooking spray. Cook for 5 to 6 minutes at 350 ° F until golden brown, then test for 4 minutes

Nutrition: Calories 305 Fat 15g Saturated fat 5g Unsaturated fat 8g Protein 19g Sodium 548mg Calcium 5% DV Potassium 2% DV

Carbs 26g Fiber 2g Sugars 1g Added sugars 0g

Banana Bread

Basic Recipe
Preparation Time: 5 minutes **Cooking Time:** 30 minutes **Serving:** 4
Ingredients:

- Banana: 1, ripe and mashed
- 1 egg
- Brown sugar: 2-3 tablespoons
- Canola oil: 2 tablespoons
- Milk: 1/4 cup
- Plain flour: ¾ cup mixed with 1/2 tablespoon baking soda

DIRECTIONS:
1. Whisk the egg into the mashed banana in a small bowl. Add the sugar, butter, and milk and whisk again.
2. Add the flour and baking soda in the mixture and blend until mixed.
3. If using an air fryer, preheat for 3 minutes to 320°F/160°C.
4. Pour the batter into the dish of air fryer (apply a little butter on the basket) and cook for 32 to 35 minutes, or until a toothpick inserted into the cake's bottom comes out clean. A touch of stickiness is all right.
5. Let the tin/dish cool for 10 minutes, then transfer to a wire rack to cool down.

NUTRITION: Calories 233 kcal Carbs 34g Sugar: 13g Vitamin A: 105IU Cholesterol 42mg Sodium: 25mg Protein 5g Fat 9g Saturated Fat 1g Potassium: 178mg Fiber 1g Vitamin C: 2.6mg Calcium: 34mg Iron: 1.4m

Scrambled Eggs

Basic Recipe
Preparation Time: 4Minutes **Cooking Time:** 10 minutes **Serving:** 2
Ingredients:

- Unsalted butter: 1/3 tablespoon
- 2 Eggs
- Milk: 2 tablespoons
- Salt and black pepper to try
- Cheddar cheese: 1/8 cup

DIRECTIONS:

1. Place fresh butter in a fryer-safe oven/air saucepan and place it inside the fryer. Cook, about 2 minutes, at 300 degrees until fresh butter get melted.
2. Whisk the milk and eggs all together then add some pepper and salt for taste. Cook for 3-4 minutes at 300 degrees, then put eggs to the inside of the fry pan and stir.
3. Cook for another 2-3 minutes, then add (cheddar) cheese and stir the eggs once more. Cook another 2 minutes. Remove that pan from air fryer and instantly serve.

NUTRITION: Calories 126 kcal Fat 9g Cholesterol 200mg Carbs 1g Protein 9g Sugar: 0g

Bacon and Eggs

Basic Recipe
Preparation Time: 4 minutes **Cooking Time:** 10 minutes **Serving:** 3
INGREDIENTS:

- 6 nitrate-free bacon strips
- Eggs: 6
- Spinach: 6 cups
- Olive oil: ½ tablespoon

DIRECTIONS:

1. Place the eggs on top of the second air fryer rack. Set the temperature at 270 degrees F. Air fry in hard-boiled for 15 minutes, for medium-boiled for 12 minutes and for soft boiled for 10 minutes Lift for 2 minutes and put in the ice water bath and peel shell.
2. Place bacon in the lower rack. Set temperature for 12-14 minutes at 375°F and cook. 14 minutes are preferable to get extra crispy bacon. Serve with sautéed cooked spinach in olive oil.

NUTRITION: Calories 427 Fat 29g Saturated Fat 9.3g Trans Fat 0g

Sausage Breakfast Casserole

Intermediate Recipe Preparation Time: 10 minutes **Cooking Time:** 20 minutes
Serving: 6

INGREDIENTS:

- Hash browns: 1 Lb.
- Breakfast Sausage: 1 lb.
- Eggs: 4
- Green Bell Pepper: 1, diced
    - Red Bell Pepper: 1, diced
    - Yellow Bell Pepper: 1, diced
    - Sweet onion: ¼ cup, diced

DIRECTIONS:

1. Cover the air fryer basket lined with foil. Put the hash browns on the bottom basket of the air fryer.
2. Place the uncooked sausage over it.
3. Place the peppers and the onions evenly on top.
4. Cook it 10 minutes on 355°F.
5. When needed, open the air fryer and mix the casserole up a bit.
6. Whisk each egg in a bowl, and then pour right over the saucepan.
7. Cook another 10 minutes on 355°F.
8. Serve with a sprinkle of salt and pepper. **NUTRITION:** Calories 517 Fat 37g Saturated Fat 10g Trans Fat 0g Unsaturated Fat 25g Cholesterol 189mg Sodium: 1092mg Carbs 27g Fiber 3g Sugar: 4g Protein 21g

Breakfast Burritos

Basic Recipe
Preparation Time: 20 minutes **Cooking Time:** 3Minutes **Serving:** 8
INGREDIENTS:

- Breakfast sausage: 1 pound
- 1 Chopped bell pepper
- Eggs: 12, lightly beaten
- Black pepper: ½ teaspoon
- Sea salt: 1 teaspoon
- Flour tortillas: 8 (burrito style)
- Shredded cheddar cheese: 2 cups

DIRECTIONS:

1. Crumble and cook the sausage until brown in a large skillet. Add chopped peppers. Dry out grease put the sausage on a towel-lined sheet of paper, cover, and set aside.
2. Melt 1 spoonful of butter in a large saucepan, add eggs, salt, and pepper and cook over medium heat, stirring continuously until almost set and no longer runny.
3. Remove from heat and whisk in cooked sausage.
4. In the center of a tortilla, add some of the egg and sausage mixtures, top with some of the bacon, fold sides, and roll-up. Preheat the fryer until 390 degrees.
5. Spray burritos gently with a drop of olive oil. Place as many burritos as fit into the air fryer and cook for 3 minutes at 390 degrees, rotating trays halfway through. Cook extra for 3 minutes for crispier burritos Immediately remove and serve, or allow cooling slightly, then wrapping well and freezing for meal preparation.

NUTRITION: Calories 283kcal Carbs 16g Protein 16g Fat 17g

Baked Bacon Egg Cups

Intermediate Recipe Preparation Time: 10 minutes

Cooking Time: 12 Minutes **Serving:** 2 **INGREDIENTS:**

- 2 eggs
- 1 tablespoon chives, fresh, chopped
- ½ teaspoon paprika
- ½ teaspoon cayenne pepper
- 3-ounces cheddar cheese, shredded
- ½ teaspoon butter
- ¼ teaspoon salt
- 4-ounces bacon, cut into tiny pieces

DIRECTIONS:

1. Slice bacon into tiny pieces and sprinkle it with cayenne pepper, salt, and paprika. Mix the chopped bacon. Spread butter in bottom of ramekin dishes and beat the eggs there. Add the chives and shredded cheese. Add the chopped bacon over egg mixture in ramekin dishes. Place the ramekins in your air fryer basket. Preheat your air fryer to 360°Fahrenheit. Place the air fryer basket in your air fryer and cook for 12-minutes. When the cook time is completed, remove the ramekins from air fryer and serve warm.

NUTRITION: Calories 553 Fat 43.3g Carbs 2.3g Protein 37.3g

Breakfast Chicken Strips

Intermediate Recipe Preparation Time: 10 minutes **Cooking Time:** 12 minutes
Serving: 4
INGREDIENTS:

- 1 teaspoon paprika
- 1 tablespoon cream
- 1 lb. chicken fillet
- ½ teaspoon salt
- ½ teaspoon black pepper

DIRECTIONS:

1. Cut the chicken fillet into strips. Sprinkle the chicken fillets with salt and pepper. Preheat the air fryer to 365°Fahrenheit. Place the butter in the air basket tray and add the chicken strips. Cook the chicken strips for 6-minutes Turn the chicken strips to the other side and cook them for an additional 5- minute after strips are cooked, sprinkle them with cream and paprika, then transfer them to serving plates. Serve warm.

NUTRITION: Calories 245 Fat 11.5g Carbs 0.6g Protein 33g

No-Bun Breakfast Bacon Burger

Intermediate Recipe Preparation Time: 10 minutes **Cooking Time:** 8 minutes
Serving: 2
INGREDIENTS:

- 8-ounces ground beef
- 2-ounces lettuce leaves

- ½ teaspoon minced garlic
- 1 teaspoon olive oil
- ½ teaspoon sea salt
- 1 teaspoon ground black pepper
- 1 teaspoon butter
- 4-ounces bacon, cooked
- 1 egg
- ½ yellow onion, diced
- ½ cucumber, slice finely
- ½ tomato, slice finely

DIRECTIONS:

1. Begin by whisking the egg in a bowl, then add the ground beef and combine well. Add cooked, chopped bacon to the ground beef mixture. Add butter, ground black pepper, minced garlic, and salt. Mix and make burgers. Preheat your air fryer to 370°Fahrenheit. Spray the air fryer basket with olive oil and place the burgers inside of it. Cook the burgers for 8-minutes on each side. Meanwhile, slice the cucumber, onion, and tomato finely. Place the tomato, onion, and cucumber onto the lettuce leaves. When the burgers are cooked, allow them to chill at room temperature, and place them over the vegetables and serve.

NUTRITION: Calories 618 Fat 37.8g Carbs 8.6g Protein 59.4g

Breakfast Coconut Porridge

Intermediate Recipe Preparation Time: 5 minutes **Cooking Time:** 7 minutes **Serving:** 4

INGREDIENTS:

- 1 cup coconut milk
- 3 tablespoons blackberries
- 2 tablespoons walnuts
- 1 teaspoon butter
- 1 teaspoon ground cinnamon
- 5 tablespoons chia seeds
- 3 tablespoons coconut flakes
- ¼ teaspoon salt

DIRECTIONS:

1. Pour the coconut milk into the air fryer basket tray. Add the coconut, salt, chia seeds, ground cinnamon, and butter. Ground up the walnuts and add them to the air fryer basket tray. Sprinkle the mixture with salt. Mash the blackberries with a fork and add them also to the air fryer basket tray. Cook the porridge at 375°Fahrenheit for 7-minutes when the cook time is over, remove the air fryer basket from air fryer and allow sitting and resting for 5- minutes Stir porridge with a wooden spoon and serve warm.

NUTRITION: Calories 169 Fat 18.2g Carbs 9.3g Protein 4.2g

Morning Time Sausages

Intermediate Recipe

Preparation Time: 10 minutes **Cooking Time:** 12 minutes **Serving:** 6

INGREDIENTS:

- 7-ounces ground chicken
- 7-ounces ground pork
- 1 teaspoon ground coriander
- 1 teaspoon basil, dried
- ½ teaspoon nutmeg
- 1 teaspoon olive oil
- 1 teaspoon minced garlic
- 1 tablespoon coconut flour
- 1 egg
- 1 teaspoon soy sauce
- 1 teaspoon sea salt
- ½ teaspoon ground black pepper

DIRECTIONS:

1. Combine the ground pork, chicken, soy sauce, ground black pepper, garlic, basil, coriander, nutmeg, sea salt, and egg. Add the coconut flour and mix the mixture well to combine. Preheat your air fryer to 360°Fahrenheit. Make medium-sized sausages with the ground meat mixture. Spray the inside of the air fryer basket tray with the olive oil. Place prepared sausages into the air fryer basket and place inside of air fryer. Cook the sausages for 6-minutes. Turn the sausages over and cook for 6- minutes more. When the cook time is completed, let the sausages chill for a little bit. Serve warm.

NUTRITION: Calories 156 Fat 7.5g Carbs 1.3g Protein 20.2g

Scrambled Pancake Hash

Intermediate Recipe Preparation Time: 10 minutes **Cooking Time:** 9Minutes
Serving: 6
INGREDIENTS:

- 1 egg
- ¼ cup heavy cream
- 5 tablespoons butter
- 1 cup coconut flour
- 1 teaspoon ground ginger
- 1 teaspoon salt
- 1 tablespoon apple cider vinegar
- 1 teaspoon baking soda

DIRECTIONS:

1. Combine the salt, baking soda, ground ginger and flour in a mixing bowl. In a separate bowl, crack the egg into it. Add butter and heavy cream. Mix well using a hand mixer. Combine the liquid and dry mixtures and stir until smooth. Preheat your air fryer to 400°Fahrenheit. Pour the pancake mixture into the air fryer basket tray. Cook the pancake hash for 4-minutes. After this, scramble the pancake hash well and continue to cook for another 5-minute more. When dish is cooked, transfer it to serving plates, and serve hot!

   NUTRITION: Calories 178 Fat 13.3g Carbs 10.7g Protein 4.4g

Breakfast Meatloaf Slices

Intermediate Recipe Preparation Time: 10 minutes **Cooking Time:** 20 minutes
Serving: 6
INGREDIENTS:

- 8-ounces ground pork
- 7-ounces ground beef
- 1 teaspoon olive oil
- 1 teaspoon butter
- 1 tablespoon oregano, dried
- 1 teaspoon cayenne pepper
- 1 teaspoon salt
- 1 tablespoon chives
- 1 tablespoon almond flour
- 1 egg
- 1 onion, diced

DIRECTIONS:

1. Beat egg in a bowl. Add the ground beef and ground pork. Add the chives, almond flour, cayenne pepper, salt, dried oregano, and butter. Add diced onion to ground beef mixture. Use hands to shape a meatloaf mixture. Preheat the air fryer to 350°Fahrenheit. Spray the inside of the air fryer basket with olive oil and place the meatloaf inside it. Cook the meatloaf for 20-minutes. When the meatloaf has cooked, allow it to chill for a bit. Slice and serve it.

NUTRITION: Calories 176 Fat 6.2g Carbs 3.4g Protein 22.2g

Seed Porridge

Basic Recipe
Preparation Time: 10 minutes **Cooking Time:** 12 minutes **Serving:** 3
INGREDIENTS:

- 1 tablespoon butter
- ¼ teaspoon nutmeg
- 1/3 cup heavy cream
- 1 egg
- ¼ teaspoon salt
- 3 tablespoons sesame seeds
- 3 tablespoons chia seeds

DIRECTIONS:

1. Place the butter in your air fryer basket tray. Add the chia seeds, sesame seeds, heavy cream, nutmeg, and salt. Stir gently. Beat the egg in a cup and whisk it with a fork. Add the whisked egg to air fryer basket tray. Stir the mixture with a wooden spatula. Preheat your air fryer to 375°Fahrenheit. Place the air fryer basket tray into air fryer and cook the porridge for 12-minutes stir it about 3 times during the cooking process. Remove

   the porridge from air fryer basket tray immediately and serve hot!

NUTRITION: Calories 275 Fat 22.5g Carbs 13.2g Protein 7.9g

Kale Breakfast Fritters

Intermediate Recipe Preparation Time: 8 minutes **Cooking Time:** 8 minutes
Serving: 8 **INGREDIENTS:**

- 12-ounces kale, chopped
- 1 teaspoon oil
- 1 tablespoon cream
- 1 teaspoon paprika
- ½ teaspoon sea salt
- 2 tablespoons almond flour
- 1 egg
- 1 tablespoon butter
- ½ yellow onion, diced

DIRECTIONS:

1. Wash and chop the kale. Add the chopped kale to blender and blend it until smooth. Dice up the yellow onion. Beat the egg and whisk it in a mixing bowl. Add the almond flour, paprika, cream and salt into bowl with whisked egg and stir. Add the diced onion and blended kale to mixing bowl and mix until you get fritter dough. Preheat your air fryer to 360°Fahrenheit. Spray the inside of the air fryer basket with olive oil. Make medium-sized fritters with prepared mixture and place them into air fryer basket. Cook the kale fritters 4-minutes on each side. Once they are cooked, allow them to chill then serve.

NUTRITION: Calories 86 Fat 5.6g Carbs 6.8g Protein 3.6g

Keto Air Bread

Intermediate Recipe Preparation Time: 10 minutes **Cooking Time:** 25 minutes
Serving: 19 **INGREDIENTS:**

- 1 cup almond flour
- ¼ sea salt
- 1 teaspoon baking powder
- ¼ cup butter
- 3 eggs

DIRECTIONS:

1. Crack the eggs into a bowl then using a hand blender mix them up. Melt the butter at room temperature. Take the melted butter and add it to the egg mixture. Add the salt, baking powder and almond flour to egg mixture and knead the dough. Cover the prepared dough with a towel for 10-minutes to rest. Meanwhile, preheat your air fryer to 360°Fahrenheit. Place the prepared dough in the air fryer tin and cook the bread for 10-

minutes. Then reduce the heat to 350°Fahrenheit and cook the bread for additional 15-minutes you can use a toothpick to check to make sure the bread is cooked. Transfer the bread to a wooden board to allow it to chill. Once the bread has chilled, then slice and serve it.

NUTRITION: Calories 40 Fat 3.9g Carbs 0.5g Protein 1.2g

Herbed Breakfast Eggs

Intermediate Recipe Preparation Time: 10 minutes **Cooking Time:** 17 minutes **Serving:** 2

INGREDIENTS:

- 4 eggs
- 1 teaspoon oregano
- 1 teaspoon parsley, dried
- ½ teaspoon sea salt
- 1 tablespoon chives, chopped
- 1 tablespoon cream
- 1 teaspoon paprika

DIRECTIONS:

1. Place the eggs in the air fryer basket and cook them for 17-minutes at 320°Fahrenheit. Meanwhile, combine the parsley, oregano, cream, and salt in shallow bowl. Chop the chives and add them to cream mixture. When the eggs are cooked, place them in cold water and allow them to chill. After this, peel the eggs and cut them into halves. Remove the egg yolks and add yolks to cream mixture and mash to blend well with a fork. Then fill the egg whites with the cream-egg yolk mixture. Serve immediately.

NUTRITION: Calories 136 Fat 9.3g Carbs 2.1g Protein 11.4g

Eggs in Zucchini Nests

Basic Recipe
Preparation Time: 10 minutes **Cooking Time:** 7 minutes **Serving:** 2
INGREDIENTS:

- 4 teaspoons butter
- ½ teaspoon paprika
- ½ teaspoon black pepper
- ¼ teaspoon sea salt
- 4-ounces cheddar cheese, shredded
- 4 eggs
- 8-ounces zucchini, grated

DIRECTIONS:

1. Grate the zucchini and place the butter in ramekins. Add the grated zucchini in ramekins in the shape of nests. Sprinkle the zucchini nests with salt, pepper, and paprika. Beat the eggs and pour over zucchini nests.

2. Top egg mixture with shredded cheddar cheese. Preheat the air fryer basket and cook the dish for 7-minutes. When the zucchini nests are cooked, chill them for 3-minutes and serve them in the ramekins.

NUTRITION: Calories 221 Fat 17.7g Carbs 2.9g Protein 13.4g

Breakfast Liver Pate

Intermediate Recipe Preparation Time: 5 minutes **Cooking Time:** 10 minutes
Serving: 7 **INGREDIENTS:**

- 1 lb. chicken liver
- 1 teaspoon salt
- ½ teaspoon cilantro, dried
- 1 yellow onion, diced
- 1 teaspoon ground black pepper
- 1 cup water
- 4 tablespoons butter

DIRECTIONS:

1. Chop the chicken liver roughly and place it in the air fryer basket tray. Add water to air fryer basket tray and add diced onion. Preheat your air fryer to 360°Fahrenheit and cook chicken liver for 10- minutes. Dry out the chicken liver when it is finished cooking.
2. Transfer the chicken liver to blender, add butter, ground black pepper and dried cilantro and blend. Once you get a pate texture, transfer to liver pate bowl and serve immediately or keep in the fridge for later.

NUTRITION: Calories 173 Fat 10.8g Carbs 2.2g Protein 16.1g

Keto Bread-Free Breakfast Sandwich

Intermediate Recipe Preparation Time: 10 minutes **Cooking Time:** 10 minutes
Serving: 2
INGREDIENTS:

- 6-ounces ground chicken
- 2 slices of cheddar cheese
- 2 lettuce leaves
- 1 tablespoon dill, dried
- ½ teaspoon sea salt
- 1 egg
- 1 teaspoon cayenne pepper
- 1 teaspoon tomato puree

DIRECTIONS:

1. Combine the ground chicken with the pepper and sea salt. Add the dried dill and stir. Beat the egg into the ground chicken mixture. Make 2 medium- sized burgers from the ground chicken mixture. Preheat your air fryer to 380°Fahrenheit. Spray the air fryer basket tray with olive oil and place the ground chicken burgers inside of it. Cook the chicken burgers for 10-minutes Flip over burgers and cook for an additional 6-minutes. When the

    burgers are cooked, transfer them to the lettuce leaves. Sprinkle the top of them with tomato puree and with a slice of cheddar cheese. Serve immediately!

    NUTRITION: Calories 324 Fat 19.2g Carbs 2.3g Protein 34.8g

Egg Butter

Basic Recipe
Preparation Time: 5 minutes **Cooking Time:** 17 minutes **Serving:** 2
INGREDIENTS:

- 4 eggs
- 4 tablespoons butter
- 1 teaspoon salt

DIRECTIONS:

1. Cover the air fryer basket with foil and place the eggs there. Transfer the air fryer basket into the air fryer and cook the eggs for 17 minutes at 320°Fahrenheit. When the time is over, remove the eggs from the air fryer basket and put them in cold water to chill them. After this, peel the eggs and chop them up finely. Combine the chopped eggs with butter and add salt. Mix it until you get the spread texture. Serve the egg butter with the keto almond bread.

NUTRITION: Calories 164 Fat 8.5g Carbs 2.67g Protein 3g

Awesome Lemon Bell Peppers

Intermediate Recipe Preparation Time: 10 minutes **Cooking Time:** 5 minutes
Serving: 4
INGREDIENTS:

- 4 bell peppers
- 1 teaspoon olive oil
- 1 tablespoon lemon juice
- 1/4 teaspoon garlic, minced
- 1 teaspoon parsley, chopped
- 1 pinch sea salt
- Pinch of pepper

DIRECTIONS:

1. Preheat your Air Fryer to 390 degrees F in —AIR FRY‖ mode
2. Add bell pepper in the Air fryer
3. Drizzle with it with the olive oil and air fry for 5 minutes
4. Take a serving plate and transfer it
5. Take a small bowl and add garlic, parsley, lemon juice, salt, and pepper
6. Mix them well and Drizzle with the mixture over the peppers
7. Serve and enjoy!

NUTRITION: Calories 59 kcal Carbs 6g Fat 4g Protein 2g

Avocado Rolls

Intermediate Recipe

Preparation Time: 10 minutes **Cooking Time:** 25 minutes **Serving:** 4

INGREDIENTS:

- 10 Dr. Sebi friendly wrappers
- 3 avocados, sliced
- 1 tomato, diced
- Salt and pepper to taste
- 1 tablespoon olive oil
- 4 tablespoon peppers
- 2 tablespoons date sugar
- 1 tablespoon hemp seed oil
- 1 tablespoon alkaline vinegar

DIRECTIONS:

1. Take a bowl and mash avocados
2. Stir in tomatoes, salt, and pepper, mix well
3. Arrange wrappers and scoop mix on top
4. Roll and seal edges
5. Cook in your Air fryer for 5 minutes at 350 degrees F
6. Take a bowl and mix remaining ingredients, serve with sauce
7. Enjoy!

NUTRITION: Calories 422 kcal Carbs 38 g Fat 15 g

Portobello Hearty Mushroom Burgers

Intermediate Recipe Preparation Time: 10 minutes **Cooking Time:** 20 minutes
Serving: 4

INGREDIENTS:

- 2 cups Portobello mushroom caps
- 1 avocado, sliced
- 1 plum tomato, sliced
- 1 cup torn lettuce
- 1 cup purslane
- 1/2 teaspoon cayenne
- 1 teaspoon oregano
- 2 teaspoons basil
- 3 tablespoons olive oil

DIRECTIONS:

1. Remove mushroom stems and cut off ½ inch slices from top slice
2. Take a bowl and mix in onion powder, cayenne, oregano, olive oil, and basil
3. Cover Air Fryer basket with a baking sheet, brush grape seed oil
4. Put caps on baking sheet
5. Pour mixture on top and let them sit for 10 minutes
6. Preheat your Air Fryer 400 degrees F and transfer to Fryer, bake it for 8 minutes, flip and Bake it for 8 minutes more
7. Lay caps on serving dish, layer sliced avocado, tomato, lettuce, purslane
8. Cover with another mushroom cap
9. Serve and enjoy!

NUTRITION: Calories 358 kcal Carbs 49 g Fat 13 g Protein 15g

Crazy Mac and Cheese

Intermediate Recipe Preparation Time: 10 minutes **Cooking Time:** 20 minutes **Serving:** 4

INGREDIENTS:

- 12 ounces alkaline pasta
- 1/4 cup chickpea flour
- 1 cup raw Brazilnut
- 1/2 teaspoon onion powder
- 1 teaspoon salt
- 2 teaspoons grape seed oil
- 1 cup hemp seed milk
- 1 cup of water
- 1/2 key lime, juiced

DIRECTIONS:

1. Take a bowl and add nuts, soak overnight. Cook pasta according to package Preheat your Air Fryer to 325 degrees F. Transfer cooked pasta to a baking dish and Drizzle with oil, add remaining ingredients to a blender and blend until smooth
2. Pour mix over mac and mix
3. Transfer to Air Fryer and Bake it for 25 minutes
4. Serve and enjoy!

NUTRITION: Calories 255 kcal Carbs 1 g Fat 23 g Protein 12 g

Zucchini Noodles with Avocado Sauce

Basic Recipe
Preparation Time: 10 minutes **Cooking Time:** 15 minutes **Serving:** 4
INGREDIENTS:

- 3 medium zucchinis
- 1 and 1/2 cup cherry tomatoes
- 1 avocado
- 2 green onions, sliced
- 1 garlic clove
- 3 tablespoons olive oil
- Juice of 1 key lemon
- 1 tablespoon spring water
- Salt and cayenne to taste

DIRECTIONS:

1. Preheat your Air Fryer to 385 degrees F
2. Take your Air Fryer cooking basket and cover with parchment paper
3. Put tomatoes and Drizzle with olive oil, season with salt and cayenne
4. Transfer to your Fryer and cook for 10-15 minutes until starting to split
5. Add quartered avocado, parsley, sliced green onion, garlic, spring water, lemon juice, 1/2 teaspoon salt to a food processor
6. Blend until creamy
7. Cut zucchini ends using use spiralizer to turn into zoodles
8. Mix zoodles with sauce
9. Divide into 3 bowls and serve with tomatoes
10. Enjoy!

NUTRITION: Calories 180 kcal Carbs 14 g Fat 14 g Protein 2g

Candied Walnut and Strawberry

Intermediate Recipe Preparation Time: 10 minutes **Cooking Time:** 10 minutes
Serving: 4
INGREDIENTS:

- 1/2 cup walnuts, chopped
- 1 tablespoon raw agave nectar
- 1/4 teaspoon salt
- Dressing
- 1/2 cup strawberries, sliced
- 2 tablespoons shallots
- 1/2 cup grape seed oil
- 2 teaspoons raw agave nectar
- 1 and 1/2 teaspoon lime juice
- 1 teaspoon onion powder
- 1/2 teaspoon ginger
- 1/4 teaspoon dill
- 1/4 teaspoon salt

DIRECTIONS:

1. Coat walnuts with agave and salt
2. Transfer to a cooking basket lined with parchment
3. Preheat your Air Fryer to 300 degrees F roast for 6- 8 minuteslet them cool. Add dressing ingredients to a bowl, blend for half a minute
4. Add walnuts. Mix and enjoy!

NUTRITION: Calories 260 kcal Carbs 28 g Fat 16 g Protein 4g

Blueberry Spelt Pancakes

Intermediate Recipe Preparation Time: 10 minutes **Cooking Time:** 10 minutes
Serving: 4
INGREDIENTS:

- 2 cups spelt flour
- 1 cup hemp milk
- 1/2 cup spring water
- 2 tablespoons grape seed
- 1/2 cup Agave
- 1/2 cup blueberries
- 1/4 teaspoon Sea Moss
- 2 tablespoons Hemp Seeds
- Grape seed oil

DIRECTIONS:

1. Place Moss, agave, hemp seeds, grape seed oil, spelt in a large bowl
2. Mix well

   3. Add milk and water, mix until you have your desired consistency
   4. Toss in blueberries and toss well
   5. Preheat your Air Fryer to 325 degrees F
   6. Transfer batter to Air Fryer basket lined with parchment paper
   7. Cook for 3-4 minutes, flip and cook for 3 minutes more until golden on both side
   8. Serve and enjoy!

NUTRITION: Calories 276 kcal Carbs 36 g Fat 11 g Protein 9g

Good Morning Energy Crackers

Intermediate Recipe Preparation Time: 10 minutes **Cooking Time:** 25 minutes
Serving: 4
INGREDIENTS:

- 1/2 cup hemp seeds
- 1/2 cup quinoa
- 1/2 cup sunflower seeds
- 1/2 cup sesame seeds
- 1 garlic clove, crushed
- 1/2 teaspoon cayenne pepper
- Salt and pepper to taste
- 1 and 1/4 cup spring water

DIRECTIONS:

1. Preheat your oven to 280 degrees F
2. Take a bowl and mix everything, spread the mix in your cooking basket lined with baking sheet
3. Bake it for 20-25 minutes
4. Break into pieces and serve
5. Enjoy!

NUTRITION: Calories 148 kcal Carbs 1.4 g Fat 1.6 g Protein 4.8g

Masala Quinoa Meal

Intermediate Recipe Preparation Time: 10 minutes **Cooking Time:** 45 minutes
Serving: 4
INGREDIENTS:

- 1/2 white onion, chopped
- Pinch of salt
- 1 red bell pepper, chopped
- 1/2 jalapeno pepper, seeded and chopped
- 2 tablespoons ginger, peeled and grated
- 1 tablespoon masala powder
- 1 cup quinoa
- 2 cups Sebi friendly vegetable stock
- 1/2 lemon, juiced

DIRECTIONS:

1. Preheat your Air Fryer to 350 degrees F
2. Take a large skillet and place it over medium heat, add onion and salt, Sauté for 3 minutes
3. Add pepper, jalapeno, ginger, garam masala and Sauté for 1 minute
4. Add quinoa to the stock, stir
5. Transfer mix to Air Fryer cooking basket
6. Cook for about 3-40 minutes until fluffy
7. Add lemon juice and fluff more
8. Adjust the seasoning accordingly and serve
9. Enjoy!

NUTRITION: Calories 503 kcal Carbs 103 g Fat 3 g Protein 32g

Toasted Quinoa Chunks

Basic Recipe
Preparation Time: 10 minutes **Cooking Time:** 15 minutes **Serving:** 4
INGREDIENTS:

- 8 ounces walnuts
- 1/2 cup uncooked quinoa
- 1 teaspoon salt
- 1 tablespoon olive oil
- 1 teaspoon ground onion powder
- 1 teaspoon paprika powder

DIRECTIONS:

1. Preheat your Air Fryer to 400 degrees F
2. Take a bowl and mix everything
3. Transfer mixture to Air Fryer cooking basket lined with parchment paper
4. Bake it for 10 minutes
5. Break into pieces and serve
6. Enjoy!

NUTRITION: Calories 187 kcal Carbs 6 g Fat 3 g Protein 5 g

Lime and Cumin Quinoa

Intermediate Recipe Preparation Time: 10 minutes **Cooking Time:** 30 minutes
Serving: 4
INGREDIENTS:

- 2 tablespoons avocado oil
- 1/4 white onion, chopped
- Pinch of salt
- 2 garlic cloves, minced
- 1 cup quinoa
- 1/2 lime, juiced
- 1 tablespoon onion powder
- 1 teaspoon chili powder
- 1/4 teaspoon paprika
- 2 cups Sebi friendly vegetable stock

DIRECTIONS:

1. Preheat your Air Fryer to 300 degrees F
2. Take a pan and place it over medium heat
3. Add onion and salt, Sauté for 3 minutes
4. Add garlic, quinoa, lime, cumin, chili, paprika and Sauté for 2 minutes
5. Transfer mix to Air Fryer cooking basket
6. Add stock and cook for 20-25 minutes
7. Serve and enjoy

NUTRITION: Calories 266 kcal Carbs 40g Fat 8g Protein 9g

Fancy Breakfast Quinoa

Basic Recipe

Preparation Time: 10 minutes **Cooking Time:** 3Minutes **Serving:** 4

INGREDIENTS:

- 1/2 cup walnuts, soaked and chopped
- 4 ounces sesame seeds, soaked
- 2 ounces hemp seeds, soaked overnight
- 1 teaspoon date sugar
- 1/2 teaspoon ground cinnamon
- 5 ounces quinoa puff
- 1 teaspoon hemp seed oil
- 1 cup of coconut milk

DIRECTIONS:

1. Take a bowl and mix in all the seeds and spices
2. Add hemp seed oil
3. Stir well until the mixture is thick
4. Flatten mixture on your cooking basket
5. Preheat your Air Fryer to 330 degrees F
6. Transfer to your Air fryer and cook for 2-3 minutes until light brown
7. Transfer mix to a serving bowl
8. Add quinoa puff, stir well and add coconut milk stir again
9. Serve and enjoy

NUTRITION: Calories 510 kcal Carbs 50 g Fat 8 g Protein 21g

Dr. Sebi Kamut Puff Cereal

Basic Recipe

Preparation Time: 10 minutes **Cooking Time:** 12 minutes **Serving:** 4

INGREDIENTS:

- Agave nectar
- 6 ounces bag of Kamut puff

DIRECTIONS:

1. Begin by spreading Kamut Puffs over your Air Fryer cooking basket, Drizzle with agave nectar on top
2. Stir well
3. Transfer to Air Fryer and cook for 8-12 minutes
4. Let the puffs cool for 10-15 minutes
5. Enjoy with coconut milk and use it as needed! **NUTRITION:** Calories 196 kcal Carbs 29 g Fat 8 g Protein 2g

Fresh Sautéed Apple

Basic Recipe
Preparation Time: 10 minutes **Cooking Time:** 10 minutes **Serving:** 4
INGREDIENTS:

- 2 tablespoons olive oil
- 3 apples, peeled, cored and sliced
- 1 tablespoon garlic clove, grated
- 1 tablespoon date sugar
- Pinch of salt

Directions:

1. Preheat your Air Fryer 300 degrees F. Add coconut oil to the cooking basket, add remaining ingredients and stir well.
2. Transfer to Air Fryer, cook for 5-10 minutes, making sure to shake the basket occasionally until golden. Serve and enjoy!

NUTRITION: Calories 32 kcal Carbs 32g Fat 9g Protein 3g

Perfect Vegetable Roast

Basic Recipe
Preparation Time: 10 minutes **Cooking Time:** 10 minutes **Serving:** 4
INGREDIENTS:

- 2 cups Roma tomatoes
- 1/2 cup mushrooms halved
- 1 red bell pepper, seeded and cut into bite-sized portions
- 1 tablespoon coconut oil
- 1 tablespoon garlic powder
- 1 teaspoon salt

DIRECTIONS:

1. Preheat your Air Fryer 400 degrees F
2. Take a bowl and add mushrooms, Roma tomatoes, bell pepper, oil, salt, garlic powder and mix well
3. Transfer to Air Fryer cooking basket
4. Cook for 12-15 minutes, making sure to shake occasionally
5. Serve and enjoy once crispy!

NUTRITION: Calories 19 kcal Carbs 19 g Fat 16 g Protein 7g

Herb Frittata

Preparation Time: 10 minutes **Cooking Time:** 25 minutes **Servings:** 4

INGREDIENTS:

- 2 tablespoons chopped green scallions
- 1/2 teaspoon ground black pepper
- 2 tablespoons chopped cilantro
- 1/2 teaspoon salt
- 2 tablespoons chopped parsley
- 1/2 cup half and half, reduced-fat
- 4 eggs, pastured
- 1/3 cup shredded cheddar cheese, reduced-fat

DIRECTION:

1. Switch on the air fryer, insert fryer basket, grease it with olive oil, then shut with its lid, set the fryer at 330 degrees F and preheat for 10 minutes.
2. Meanwhile, take a round heatproof pan that fits into the fryer basket, grease it well with oil and set aside until required.
3. Crack the eggs in a bowl, beat in half-and-half, then add remaining ingredients, beat until well mixed and pour the mixture into prepared pan.
4. Open the fryer, place the pan in it, close with its lid and cook for 15 minutes at the 330 degrees F until its top is nicely golden, frittata has set and inserted toothpick into the frittata slides out clean.
5. When air fryer beeps, open its lid, take out the pan, then transfer frittata onto a serving plate, cut it into pieces and serve.

NUTRITION: Calories 141 Cal Carbs 2 g Fat 10 g Protein 8 g Fiber 0 g

Pancakes

Preparation Time: 5 minutes **Cooking Time:** 29 minutes **Servings:** 4

INGREDIENTS:

- 1 1/2 cup coconut flour
- 1 teaspoon salt
- 3 1/2 teaspoons baking powder
- 1 tablespoon erythritol sweetener
- 1 1/2 teaspoon baking soda
- 3 tablespoons melted butter
- 1 1/4 cups milk, unsweetened, reduced-fat
- 1 egg, pastured

DIRECTION:

1. Switch on the air fryer, insert fryer pan, grease it with olive oil, then shut with its lid, set the fryer at 220 degrees F and preheat for 5 minutes.
2. Meanwhile, take a medium bowl, add all the ingredients in it, whisk until well blended and then let the mixture rest for 5 minutes.
3. Open the fryer, pour in some of the pancake mixture as thin as possible, close with its lid and cook for 6 minutes until nicely golden, turning the pancake halfway through the frying.
4. When air fryer beeps, open its lid, transfer pancake onto a serving plate and use the remaining batter for cooking more pancakes in the same manner.
5. Serve straight away with fresh fruits slices. **NUTRITION:** Calories 237.7 Cal Carbs 39.2 g Fat 10.2   g Protein 6.3 g Fiber 1.3 g

Zucchini Bread

Preparation Time: 25 minutes **Cooking Time:** 40 minutes **Servings:** 8

INGREDIENTS:

- ¾ cup shredded zucchini
- 1/2 cup almond flour
- 1/4 teaspoon salt
- 1/4 cup cocoa powder, unsweetened
- 1/2 cup chocolate chips, unsweetened, divided
- 6 tablespoons erythritol sweetener
- 1/2 teaspoon baking soda
- 2 tablespoons olive oil
- 1/2 teaspoon vanilla extract, unsweetened
- 2 tablespoons butter, unsalted, melted
- 1 egg, pastured

DIRECTION:

1. Switch on the air fryer, insert fryer basket, grease it with olive oil, then shut with its lid, set the fryer at 310 degrees F and preheat for 10 minutes.
2. Meanwhile, place flour in a bowl, add salt, cocoa powder, and baking soda and stir until mixed.
3. Crack the eggs in another bowl, whisk in sweetener, egg, oil, butter, and vanilla until smooth and then slowly whisk in flour mixture until incorporated.
4. Add zucchini along with 1/3 cup chocolate chips and then fold until just mixed.
5. Take a mini loaf pan that fits into the air fryer, grease it with olive oil, then pour in the prepared batter and sprinkle remaining chocolate chips on top.
6. Open the fryer, place the loaf pan in it, close with its lid and cook for 30 minutes at the 310 degrees F until inserted toothpick into the bread slides out clean.
7. When air fryer beeps, open its lid, remove the loaf pan, then place it on a wire rack and let the bread cool in it for 20 minutes.
8. Take out the bread, let it cool completely, then cut it into slices and serve.

NUTRITION: Calories 356 Cal Carbs 49 g Fat 17   g Protein 5.1 g Fiber 2.5 g

Blueberry Muffins

Preparation Time: 10 minutes **Cooking Time:** 30 minutes **Servings:** 14

INGREDIENTS:

- 1 cup almond flour
- 1 cup frozen blueberries
- 2 teaspoons baking powder
- 1/3 cup erythritol sweetener
- 1 teaspoon vanilla extract, unsweetened
- ½ teaspoon salt
- ¼ cups melted coconut oil
- 1 egg, pastured
- ¼ cup applesauce, unsweetened
- ¼ cup almond milk, unsweetened

DIRECTION:

1. Switch on the air fryer, insert fryer basket, grease it with olive oil, then shut with its lid, set the fryer at 360 degrees F and preheat for 10 minutes.
2. Meanwhile, place flour in a large bowl, add berries, salt, sweetener, and baking powder and stir until well combined.
3. Crack the eggs in another bowl, whisk in vanilla, milk, and applesauce until combined and then slowly whisk in flour mixture until incorporated.
4. Take fourteen silicone muffin cups, grease them with oil, and then evenly fill them with the prepared batter.
5. Open the fryer; stack muffin cups in it, close with its lid and cook for 10 minutes until muffins are nicely golden brown and set.
6. When air fryer beeps, open its lid, transfer muffins onto a serving plate and then remaining muffins in the same manner.
7. Serve straight away.

NUTRITION: Calories 201 Cal Carbs 27.3g Fat 8.8 g Protein 3g Fiber 1.2g

Baked Eggs

Preparation Time: 5 minutes **Cooking Time:** 17 minutes **Servings:** 2 **INGREDIENTS:**

- 2 tablespoons frozen spinach, thawed
- ½ teaspoon salt
- ¼ teaspoon ground black pepper
- 2 eggs, pastured
- 3 teaspoons grated parmesan cheese, reduced-fat
- 2 tablespoons milk, unsweetened, reduced-fat

DIRECTION:

1. Switch on the air fryer, insert fryer basket, grease it with olive oil, then shut with its lid, set the fryer at 330 degrees F and preheat for 5 minutes.
2. Meanwhile, take two silicon muffin cups, grease them with oil, then crack an egg into each cup and evenly add cheese, spinach, and milk.
3. Season the egg with salt and black pepper and gently stir the ingredients, without breaking the egg yolk.
4. Open the fryer, add muffin cups in it, close with its lid and cook for 8 to 12 minutes until eggs have cooked to desired doneness.
5. When air fryer beeps, open its lid, take out the muffin cups and serve.

NUTRITION: Calories 161 Cal Carbs 3 g Fat 11.4 g Protein 12.1 g Fiber 1.1 g

Bagels

Preparation Time: 10 minutes **Cooking Time:** 20 minutes **Servings:** 6 **INGREDIENTS:**

- 2 cups almond flour
- 2 cups shredded mozzarella cheese, low-fat
- 2 tablespoons butter, unsalted
- 1 1/2 teaspoon baking powder
- 1 teaspoon apple cider vinegar
- 1 egg, pastured
- For Egg Wash:
- 1 egg, pastured
- 1 teaspoon butter, unsalted, melted

DIRECTION:

1. Place flour in a heatproof bowl, add cheese and butter, then stir well and microwave for 90 seconds until butter and cheese has melted.
2. Then stir the mixture until well combined, let it cool for 5 minutes and whisk in the egg, baking powder, and vinegar until incorporated and dough comes together.
3. Let the dough cool for 10 minutes, then divide the dough into six pieces, shape each piece into a bagel and let the bagels rest for 5 minutes.
4. Prepare the egg wash and for this, place the melted butter in a bowl, whisk in the egg until blended and then brush the mixture generously on top of each bagel.
5. Take a fryer basket, line it with parchment paper and then place prepared bagels in it in a single layer.
6. Switch on the air fryer, insert fryer, then shut with its lid, set the fryer at 350 degrees F and cook for 10 minutes at the 350 degrees F until bagels are nicely golden and thoroughly cooked, turning the bagels halfway through the frying.
7. When air fryer beeps, open its lid, transfer bagels to a serving plate and cook the remaining bagels in the same manner.
8. Serve straight away.

NUTRITION: Calories 408.7 Cal   Carbs 8.3 g   Fat 33.5 g Protein 20.3g Fiber 4g

Cauliflower Hash Browns

Preparation Time: 10 minutes **Cooking Time:** 25 minutes **Servings:** 6

INGREDIENTS:

- 1/4 cup chickpea flour
- 4 cups cauliflower rice
- 1/2 medium white onion, peeled and chopped
- 1/2 teaspoon garlic powder
- 1 tablespoon xanthan gum
- 1/2 teaspoon salt
- 1 tablespoon nutritional yeast flakes
- 1 teaspoon ground paprika

DIRECTION:

1. Switch on the air fryer, insert fryer basket, grease it with olive oil, then shut with its lid, set the fryer at 375 degrees F and preheat for 10 minutes.
2. Meanwhile, place all the ingredients in a bowl, stir until well mixed and then shape the mixture into six rectangular disks, each about ½-inch thick.
3. Open the fryer, add hash browns in it in a single layer, close with its lid and cook for 25 minutes at the 375 degrees F until nicely golden and crispy, turning halfway through the frying.
4. When air fryer beeps, open its lid, transfer hash browns to a serving plate and serve.

NUTRITION: Calories 115.2 Cal Carbs 6.2 g Fat 7.3 g Protein 7.4 g Fiber 2.2 g

SNACK

Parmesan Zucchini Chips

Basic Recipe

Preparation Time: 15 minutes **Cooking Time:** 10 minutes **Servings:** 4 **INGREDIENTS:**

- Salt to taste
- 3 medium zucchinis
- 1 cup grated Parmesan cheese

DIRECTIONS:

1. Preheat the oven in Air Fryer mode at 110 F for 2 to 3 minutes Use a mandolin slicer to very finely slice the zucchinis, season with salt, and coat well with the Parmesan cheese. In batches, arrange as lots of zucchini pieces as possible in a single layer on the cooking tray. When the device is ready, move the cooking tray onto the leading rack of the oven and close the oven. Set the timer to 7 minutes and press Start. Cook till the cheese melts while turning the midway. Transfer the chips to serving bowls to cool and make the remaining. Serve warm.

NUTRITION: Calories 107 Fat 6.99 g Carbs 3.73 g Protein 7.33 g

Cattle Ranch Garlic Pretzels

Basic Recipe

Preparation Time: 10 minutes **Cooking Time:** 15 minutes **Servings:** 4 **INGREDIENTS:**

- ½ tsp garlic powder
- 2 cups pretzels
- 1 ½ tsp ranch dressing mix
- 1 tbsp melted butter

DIRECTIONS:

2. Preheat the oven in Air Fryer mode at 270 F for 2 to 3 minutes. In a medium bowl, blend all the ingredients up until well-integrated, pour into the rotisserie basket and near to seal. Repair the basket onto the lever in the oven and close the oven. Set the timer to 15 minutes, press Start and cook until the pretzels are gently browner. After, open the oven, secure the basket utilizing the rotisserie lift and transfer the snack into serving bowls. Permit cooling and delight in.

NUTRITION: Calories 35 Fat 3.72 g Carbs 0.4 g Protein 0.12 g

Herby Sweet Potato Chips

Basic Recipe
Preparation Time: 10 minutes **Cooking Time:** 10 minutes **Servings:** 4 **INGREDIENTS:**

- 1 tsp dried mixed herbs
- 2 medium sweet potatoes, peeled
- 1 tbsp olive oil

DIRECTIONS:

3. Pre-heat the oven in Air Fry mode at 375 F for 2 to 3 minutes. On the other hand, utilize a mandolin slicer to thinly slice the sweet potatoes, transfer to a medium bowl and blend well with the herbs and olive oil till well coated. In batches, organize as numerous sweet potato pieces as possible in a single layer on the cooking tray. When the device is ready, slide the cooking tray onto the top rack of the oven and close the oven. Set the timer to 7 minutes and press Start. Cook till the sweet potatoes are crispy while turning midway. Transfer the chips to serving bowls when prepared and make the remaining in the same manner. Delight in.

NUTRITION: Calories 87 Fat 3.48 g Carbs 13.38 g
Protein 1.03 g

Cumin Tortilla Chips with Guacamole

Basic Recipe
Preparation Time: 5 minutes **Cooking Time:** 15 minutes **Servings:** 4
INGREDIENTS:

- For the tortilla chips:
- 2 tablespoon olive oil
- 12 corn tortillas
- 1 tbsp paprika powder
- 1 tbsp cumin powder
- Salt and black pepper to taste
- For the guacamole:
- 1 little company tomato, sliced
- A pinch dried parsley
- 1 big avocado, pitted and peeled

DIRECTIONS:

4. Preheat the oven in Air Fry mode at 375 F for 2 to 3 minutes in a medium bowl, mix all the ingredients for the tortilla chips well and put the mix into the rotisserie basket. Close to seal. Fix the basket onto the lever in the oven and close the oven. Set the timer to 15 minutes, press Start and cook until the tortillas are golden brown.
5. After, open the oven, take out the basket using the rotisserie lift and transfer the chips to serving bowls.Meanwhile, as the chips cooked, in a little bowl, mash the avocados and blend with the tomato and parsley up until well combined.
6. Serve the tortilla chips with the guacamole. **NUTRITION:** Calories 159 Fat 14.74 g Carbs 7.82 g Protein 1.94 g

Oven-Dried Strawberries

Basic Recipe
Preparation Time: 10 minutes **Cooking Time:** 10 minutes **Servings:** 4
INGREDIENTS:

- 1-poundlarge strawberries

DIRECTIONS:

7. Pre-heat the air fryer in Dehydrate mode at 110 F for 2 to 3 minutes Use a mandolin slicer to thinly slice the strawberries. In batches, arrange a few of the strawberry pieces in a single layer on the cooking tray.
8. When the device is ready, move the cooking tray onto the top rack of the oven and close the oven
9. Set the timer to 7 minutes and press Start. Cook until the fruits are crispy.
10. Transfer the fruit chips to serving bowls when all set and make the remaining in the same manner. Delight in.

NUTRITION: Calories 36 Fat 0.34 g Carbs 8.71 g Protein 0.76 g

Chili Cheese Toasts

Basic Recipe
Preparation Time: 5 minutes **Cooking Time:** 10 minutes **Servings:** 4
INGREDIENTS:

- 1 tsp garlic powder
- 1 tsp red chili flakes
- 6 pieces sandwich bread
- 4 tablespoon butter
- 1 cup grated cheddar cheese
- 2 little fresh red chilies, deseeded and minced
- ½ tsp salt
- 1 tablespoon sliced fresh parsley

DIRECTIONS:

11. Pre-heat the oven in Broil mode at 375 F for 2 to 3 minutes Spread the butter on one side of each bread pieces and lay on a tidy, flat surface. Divide the cheddar cheese on top and followed with the remaining ingredients. Lay 3 pieces of the bread on the cooking tray, slide the tray onto the middle rack of the oven, and close the oven. Set the timer for 3 to 4 minutes and press Start. Cook till the cheese melts and is golden brown on top. Remove the first batch when ready and prepare the other three bread pieces. Slice them into triangle halves and serve immediately.

NUTRITION: Calories 105 Fat 11.53 g Carbs 0.68 g
Protein 0.29 g

Cheese Sticks

Basic Recipe
Preparation Time: 10 minutes **Cooking Time:** 10 minutes **Servings:** 6
INGREDIENTS:

- 1 teaspoon garlic powder
- 1 teaspoon of Italian spices
- ¼ teaspoon rosemary, ground
- 2 eggs
- 1 cheese sticks
- ¼ cup parmesan cheese, grated
- ¼ cup whole-wheat flour

DIRECTIONS:

12. Unwraps the cheese sticks. Keep aside. Beat the eggs into a bowl. Mix the cheese, flavorings, and flour in another bowl. Now roll the sticks in the egg and then into the batter. Coat well. Keep them in your air fryer basket. Cook for 7 minutes at 370 degrees F. Serve hot.

NUTRITION: Calories 76 Carbs 5g Fat 4g Protein 5g

Blended Veggie Chips

Basic Recipe
Preparation Time: 20 minutes **Cooking Time:** 10 minutes **Servings:** 4
INGREDIENTS:

- 1 big carrot
- 1 tsp salt
- 1 tsp Italian spices
- 1 zucchini
- 1 sweet potato peeled
- ½ tsp pepper
- 1 red beet, peeled
- A pinch cumin powders

DIRECTIONS:

13. Preheat the air fryer in Dehydrate mode at 110 F for 2 to 3 minutes
14. Utilize a mandolin slicer to thinly slice all the vegetables and transfer to a medium bowl. Season it with salt, Italian spices, and cumin powder. In batches, organize some of the veggies in a single layer on the cooking tray.
15. When the device is ready, move the cooking tray onto the top rack of the oven and close the oven then set the timer to 7 or 9 minutes and press Start.Cook up until the veggies are crispy. Transfer the vegetables to serving bowls when all set and make the staying in the same manner. Delight in.

NUTRITION: Calories 84 Fat 0.15 g Carbs 18.88 g Protein 2.25 g

Sweet Apple and Pear Chips

Basic Recipe
Preparation Time: 15 minutes **Cooking Time:** 10 minutes **Servings:** 4
INGREDIENTS:

- 6 pears, peeled
- 6 Honey crisp apples

DIRECTIONS:

16. Pre-heat the air fryer in Dehydrate mode at 110 F for 2 to 3 minutes. On the other hand, utilize a mandolin slicer to very finely slice the apples and pears. In batches, set up a few of the fruit slices in a single layer on the cooking tray.
17. When the device is ready, move the cooking tray onto the top rack of the oven and close the oven
18. Set the timer to 7 minutes and press Start. Cook till the fruits are crispy. Transfer the fruit chips to

serving bowls when all set and make the staying in the same manner. Take pleasure in.

NUTRITION: Calories 142 Fat 0.46 g Carbs 37.7g Protein 0.71g

Cocoa Banana Chips

Basic Recipe
Preparation Time: 5 minutes **Cooking Time:** 7 minutes **Servings:** 4 **INGREDIENTS:**

- ¼ tsp cocoa powder
- 5 large firm bananas, peeled
- A pinch of cinnamon powder

DIRECTIONS:

19. Preheat the air fryer in Dehydrate mode at 110 F for 2 to 3 minutes. On the other hand, utilize a mandolin slicer to very finely slice the bananas, and coat well with the cocoa powder and the cinnamon powder. In batches, organize as many banana pieces as possible in a single layer on the cooking tray.
20. When the device is ready, slide the cooking tray onto the top rack of the oven and close the oven set the timer to 7 minutes and press Start. Cook until the banana pieces are crispy. Transfer the chips to serving bowls when all set and make the remaining in the same manner. Take pleasure in.

NUTRITION: Calories 152 Fat 0.57 g Carbs 38.89 g
Protein 1.87 g

Coriander Roasted Chickpeas

Basic Recipe

Preparation Time: 10 minutes **Cooking Time:** 45minutes **Servings:** 2 **INGREDIENTS:**

- ¼ tsp garlic powder
- 1 (15 oz) can chickpeas, Dry-out pipes
- ¼ tsp ground coriander
- 1/8 tsp salt
- ¼ tsp chili pepper powder
- ¼ tsp curry powder
- ¼ tsp ground cumin
- ¼ tsp paprika
- Olive oil for spraying

DIRECTIONS:

21. Pre-heat the oven in Air Fryer mode at 375 F for 2 to 3 minutes in a medium bowl, mix the chickpeas with all the spices until well-integrated and pour into the rotisserie basket. Grease lightly with olive oil, shake the basket, and close the seal. Fix the basket onto the lever in the oven and close the oven. Set the timer to 35 or 45 minutes, press Start and cook up until the chickpeas are golden brown. After, open the oven, take out the basket utilizing the rotisserie lift and transfer the treat into serving bowls. Allow cooling and delight in.

NUTRITION: Calories 91 Fat 1.82 g Carbs 14.87 g Protein 4.61 g

Corn Nuts

Basic Recipe
Preparation Time: 10 minutes **Cooking Time:** 20 minutes **Servings:** 8
INGREDIENTS:

- 3 tablespoons of vegetable oil
- 1 oz. white corn
- 1-½ teaspoons salt

DIRECTIONS:

22. Cover the corn with water in a bowl. Keep aside. Dry out the corn. Spread it on a flat pan and use paper towels to pat dry.
23. Pre-heat your air fryer to 400 degrees F. Transfer the corn to a bowl then include salt and oil. Stir to coat uniformly.
24. Keep the corn in your air fryer basket. Cook for 8 minutes Shake the basket and cook for 10 minutes more. Transfer to a plate lined with a paper towel. Set aside to cool.

NUTRITION: Calories 240 Fat 8g Carbs 36g Protein 6g

Baked Potatoes

Intermediate Recipe Preparation Time: 10 minutes **Cooking Time:** 1hour
Servings: 2 **INGREDIENTS:**

- ½ teaspoon of coarse sea salt
- 1 tablespoon peanut oil
- 2 large potatoes, scrubbed

DIRECTIONS:

25. Pre-heat your air fryer to 400 degrees F. Brush peanut oil on your potatoes and sprinkle some salt. Then keep them in the basket of your air fryer.
26. Cook the potatoes for an hour. Serve hot.

NUTRITION: Calories 360 Carbs 64g Fat 8g Protein 8g

Coconut Chicken Bites

Basic Recipe
Preparation Time: 10 minutes **Cooking Time:** 15 minutes **Servings:** 4
INGREDIENTS:

- 2 teaspoons garlic powder
- 2 eggs
- Salt and black pepper to the taste
- ¾ cup panko bread crumbs
- ¾ cup coconut, shredded
- Cooking spray
- 8 chicken tenders

DIRECTIONS:

1. Using a bucket, mix pepper, salt and eggs with garlic powder and whisk well.
2. In another bowl, mix coconut with panko and stir well.
3. Dip the chicken tenders in eggs mix and then coat in coconut one well.

   4. Spray chicken bites with cooking spray, place them in your air fryer's basket and cook them at 350 degrees F for 10 minutes
   5. Serve.
   6. Enjoy!

   NUTRITION: Calories 252 Fat 4 Carbs 14 Protein 24

Buffalo Cauliflower Snack

Basic Recipe
Preparation Time: 10 minutes **Cooking Time:** 15 minutes **Servings:** 4
INGREDIENTS:

- 4 cups cauliflower florets
- 1 cup panko bread crumbs
- ¼ cup butter, melted
- ¼ cup buffalo sauce
- Mayonnaise for serving

DIRECTIONS:

1. In a bowl, mix the buffalo sauce and butter and beat well. Soak cauliflower florets in this mix and coat with breadcrumbs. Put them in the air fryer basket and cook at 350 degrees Fahrenheit for 15 minutes. Arrange them on a platter and serve with mayo on the side. Enjoy!

NUTRITION: Calories 241 Fat 4 Carbs 8 Protein 4

Banana Snack

Basic Recipe

Preparation Time: 10 minutes **Cooking Time:** 5 minutes **Servings:** 8

INGREDIENTS:

- 16 baking cups crust
- ¼ cup peanut butter
- ¾ cup chocolate chips
- 1 banana, peeled and sliced into 16 pieces
- 1 tablespoon vegetable oil

DIRECTIONS:

2. Put chocolate chips in a small pot, heat up over low heat, stir until it melts and take off heat.
3. In a bowl, mix peanut butter with coconut oil and whisk well.
4. Spoon 1 teaspoon chocolates mix in a cup, add 1 banana slice and top with 1 teaspoon butter mix
5. Repeat with the rest of the cups, place them all into a dish that fits your air fryer, cook at 320 degrees F for 5 minutes, transfer to a freezer and keep there until you serve them as a snack.
6. Enjoy!

NUTRITION: Calories 70 Fat 4 Carbs 10 Protein 1

Potato Spread

Basic Recipe
Preparation Time: 10 minutes **Cooking Time:** 10 minutes **Servings:** 10
INGREDIENTS:

- 19 ounces canned garbanzo beans, Dried
- 1 cup sweet potatoes, peeled and chopped
- ¼ cup tahini
- 2 tablespoons lemon juice
- 1 tablespoon olive oil
- 5 garlic cloves, minced
- ½ teaspoon cumin, ground
- 2 tablespoons water
- A pinch of salt and white pepper

DIRECTIONS:

1. Put potatoes in your air fryer's basket, cook them at 360 degrees F for 15 minutes, cool them down, peel, put them in your food processor and pulse well. Basket, add sesame paste, garlic, beans, lemon juice, cumin, water and oil and pulse really well. Add salt and pepper, pulse again, divide into bowls and serve.
2. Enjoy!

NUTRITION: Calories 200 Fat 3 Carbs 20 Protein 11

Mexican Apple Snack

Basic Recipe
Preparation Time: 10 minutes **Cooking Time:** 5 minutes **Servings:** 4
INGREDIENTS:

- 3 big apples, cored, peeled and cubed
- 2 teaspoons lemon juice
- ¼ cup pecans, chopped
- ½ cup dark chocolate chips
- ½ cup clean caramel sauce

DIRECTIONS:

1. In a bowl, mix apples with lemon juice, stir and transfer to a pan that fits your air fryer.
2. Add chocolate chips, pecans, Drizzle with the caramel sauce, toss, introduce in your air fryer and cook at 320 degrees F for 5 minutes
3. Toss gently, divide into small bowls and serve right away as a snack.
4. Enjoy!

NUTRITION: Calories 200 Fat 4 Carbs 20 Protein 3

Shrimp Muffins

Basic Recipe
Preparation Time: 10 minutes **Cooking Time:** 26minutes **Servings:** 6
INGREDIENTS:

- 1 spaghetti squash, peeled and halved
- 2 tablespoons mayonnaise
- 1 cup mozzarella, shredded
- 8 ounces shrimp, peeled, cooked and chopped
- 1 and ½ cups panko
- 1 teaspoon parsley flakes
- 1 garlic clove, minced
- Salt and black pepper to the taste
- Cooking spray

DIRECTIONS:

1. Put squash halves in your air fryer, cook at 350 degrees F for 16 minutes, leave aside to cool down and scrape flesh into a bowl. Add salt, pepper, parsley flakes, panko, shrimp, mayo and mozzarella and stir well.
2. Spray a muffin tray that fits your air fryer with cooking spray and divide squash and shrimp mix in each cup. Introduce in the fryer and cook at 360 degrees F for 10 minutes
3. Arrange muffins on a platter and serve as a snack.
4. Enjoy!

NUTRITION: Calories 60 Fat 2g Carbs 4g Protein 4g

Zucchini Cakes

Basic Recipe
Preparation Time: 10 minutes **Cooking Time:** 12 minutes **Servings:** 8 **INGREDIENTS:**

- Cooking spray
- ½ cup dill, chopped
- 1 egg
- ½ cup whole wheat flour
- Salt and black pepper to the taste
- 1 yellow onion, chopped
- 2 garlic cloves, minced
- 3 zucchinis, grated

DIRECTIONS:

1. In a bowl, mix zucchinis with garlic, onion, flour, salt, pepper, egg and dill, stir well, shape small patties out of this mix, spray them with cooking spray, place them in the air fryer's basket and boil at 370 degrees F for 6 minutes on each side.
2. Serve them as a snack right away.
3. Enjoy!

NUTRITION: Calories 60 Fat 1g Carbs 6g Protein 2g

Cauliflower Bars

Basic Recipe

Preparation Time: 10 minutes **Cooking Time:** 25 minutes **Servings**: 12 **INGREDIENTS:**

- 1 big cauliflower head, florets separated
- ½ cup mozzarella, shredded
- ¼ cup egg whites
- 1 teaspoon Italian seasoning
- Salt and black pepper to the taste

DIRECTIONS:

1. Put cauliflower florets in your food processor, pulse well, spread on a lined baking sheet that fits your air fryer, introduce in the fryer and cook at 360 degrees F for 10 minutes
2. Transfer cauliflower to a bowl, add salt, pepper, cheese, egg whites and Italian seasoning, stir really well, spread this into a rectangle pan that fits your air fryer, press well, introduce in the fryer and cook at 360 degrees F for 15 minutes more. Cut into 12 bars, arrange them on a platter and serve as a snack
3. Enjoy!

NUTRITION: Calories 50 Fat 1g Carbs 3g Protein 3 g

Pesto Crackers

Basic Recipe
Preparation Time: 10 minutes **Cooking Time:** 17 minutes **Servings:** 6
INGREDIENTS:

- ½ teaspoon baking powder
- Salt and black pepper to the taste
- 1 and ¼ cups flour
- ¼ teaspoon basil, dried
- 1 garlic clove, minced
- 2 tablespoons basil pesto
- 3 tablespoons butter

DIRECTIONS:

4. In a bowl, mix salt, pepper, baking powder, flour, garlic, cayenne, basil, pesto and butter and stir until you obtain a dough.
5. Spread this dough on a lined baking sheet that fits your air fryer, introduce in the fryer at 325 degrees F and Bake it for 17 minutes
6. Leave aside to cool down, cut crackers and serve them as a snack.
7. Enjoy!

NUTRITION: Calories 200 Fat 20 Carbs 4 Protein 7

Pumpkin Muffins

Basic Recipe
Preparation Time: 10 minutes **Cooking Time:** 15 minutes **Servings:** 8
INGREDIENTS:

- ¼ cup butter
- ¾ cup pumpkin puree
- 2 tablespoons flaxseed meal
- ¼ cup flour
- ½ cup sugar
- ½ teaspoon nutmeg, ground
- 1 teaspoon cinnamon powder
- ½ teaspoon baking soda
- 1 egg
- ½ teaspoon baking powder

DIRECTIONS:

8. In a bowl, mix butter with pumpkin puree and egg and blend well.
9. Add flaxseed meal, flour, sugar, baking soda, baking powder, nutmeg and cinnamon and stir well.
10. Spoon this into a muffin pan that fits your fryer introduces in the fryer at 350 degrees F and Bake it for 15 minutes
11. Serve muffins cold as a snack.
12. Enjoy!

NUTRITION: Calories 50 Fat 3 Carbs 2 Protein 2

Zucchini Chips

Basic Recipe

Preparation Time: 10 minutes **Cooking Time:** 1hour **Servings**: 6 **INGREDIENTS:**

- 3 zucchinis, thinly sliced
- Salt and black pepper to the taste
- 2 tablespoons olive oil
- 2 tablespoons balsamic vinegar

DIRECTIONS:

13. Using a bucket, mix vinegar with oil adding pepper with salt and stir well.
14. Add zucchini slices, toss to coat well, introduce in your air fryer and cook at 200 degrees F for 1 hour.
15. Serve zucchini chips cold as a snack.
16. Enjoy!

NUTRITION: Calories 40 Fat 3 Carbs 3 Protein 7

Beef Jerky Snack

Intermediate Recipe Preparation Time: 2 hours
Cooking Time: 1hour and 30 minutes
Servings: 6
INGREDIENTS:

- 2 cups soy sauce
- ½ cup Worcestershire sauce
- 2 tablespoons black peppercorns
- 2 tablespoons black pepper
- 2 pounds beef round, sliced

DIRECTIONS:

17. In a bowl, mix soy sauce with black peppercorns, black pepper and Worcestershire sauce and whisk well.
18. Add beef slices, toss to coat and leave aside in the fridge for 6 hours.
19. Introduce beef rounds in your air fryer and cook them at 370 degrees F for 1 hour and 30 minutes
20. Transfer to a bowl and serve cold.
21. Enjoy!

NUTRITION: Calories 300 Fat 12 Carbs 3 Protein 8 g

Honey Party Wings

Intermediate Recipe
Preparation Time: 1hour and 12 minutes
Cooking Time: 10 minutes **Servings:** 8 **INGREDIENTS:**

- 16 chicken wings
- 2 tablespoons soy sauce
- 2 tablespoons of honey
- Salt and black pepper taste to taste
- 2 tablespoons lime juice

DIRECTIONS:

22. In a bowl, mix the wings with soy sauce, honey, salt, pepper and lime juice, mix well and put in the refrigerator for 1 hour. Transfer the wings to an air fryer, cook at 360 degrees F for 12 minutes, and turn it over halfway.
23. Serve on a plate and serve as an appetizer. Enjoy!

NUTRITION: Calories 211 Fat 4 Carbs 14 Protein 3

Salmon Party Patties

Basic Recipe
Preparation Time: 10 minutes **Cooking Time:** 22 minutes **Servings:** 4
INGREDIENTS:

- 3 big potatoes, boiled, Dried and mashed
- 1 big salmon fillet, skinless, boneless
- 2 tablespoons parsley, chopped
- 2 tablespoon dill, chopped
- Salt and black pepper to the taste
- 1 egg
- 2 tablespoons bread crumbs
- Cooking spray

DIRECTIONS:

24. Place salmon in your air fryer's basket and cook for 10 minutes at 360 degrees F. Transfer salmon to a cutting board, cool it down, flake it and put it in a bowl. Add mashed potatoes, salt, pepper, dill, parsley, egg and bread crumbs, stir well and shape 8 patties out of this mix. Place salmon patties in your air fryer's basket, spry them with cooking oil, and for 12 minutes cook at 360 degrees F, flipping them halfway, transfer them to a platter and serve as an appetizer. Enjoy!

NUTRITION: Calories 231 Fat 3 Carbs 14 Protein 4

Banana Chips

Basic Recipe
Preparation Time: 10 minutes **Cooking Time:** 15 minutes **Servings:** 4
INGREDIENTS:

- 4 bananas, peeled and sliced
- A pinch of salt
- ½ teaspoon turmeric powder
- ½ teaspoon chaat masala
- 1 teaspoon olive oil

DIRECTIONS:

25. In a bowl, mix banana slices with salt, turmeric, chaat masala and oil, toss and leave aside for 10 minutes Transfer banana slices to your preheated air fryer at 360 degrees F and cook them for 15 minutes flipping them once.
26. Serve as a snack.
27. Enjoy!

NUTRITION: Calories 121 Fat 1 Carbs 3 Protein 3

Sesame Tofu Cubes

Basic Recipe
Preparation Time: 20 minutes **Cooking Time:** 20 minutes **Servings:** 2
INGREDIENTS:

- 8 oz tofu
- 1 teaspoon cornstarch

- 1 teaspoon scallions, chopped
- 1 teaspoon rice vinegar
- 1 teaspoon sesame oil
- 1 teaspoon soy sauce

DIRECTIONS:

1. Cut the tofu into the cubes.
2. Put the tofu cubes in the bowl and sprinkle with the rice vinegar, sesame oil, and soy sauce.
3. Shake the mixture.
4. Leave the tofu for 10 minutes to marinate.
5. Preheat the air fryer to 370 F.
6. Sprinkle the marinated tofu with the cornstarch and put in the air fryer basket.
7. Cook tofu for 20 minutes
8. Shake the tofu after 11 minutes of cooking.
9. Then chill the tofu gently and sprinkle with the chopped scallions.
10. Enjoy!

NUTRITION: Calories 108 Fat 7 Carbs 3.4 Protein 9.5

Thyme Salty Tomatoes

Basic Recipe

Preparation Time: 10 minutes **Cooking Time:** 10 minutes **Servings:** 2 **INGREDIENTS:**

- 2 tomatoes
- 1 tablespoon thyme
- 1 pinch salt
- 1 teaspoon olive oil

DIRECTIONS:

1. Preheat the air fryer to 375 F.
2. Slice the tomatoes.
3. Then combine together thyme and salt. Shake the mixture.
4. Sprinkle the sliced tomatoes with the thyme mixture. Place the sliced tomatoes in the air fryer and spray with the olive oil.
5. Cook the tomatoes for 10 minutes
6. When the tomatoes are cooked – they should have tender and little bit dry texture.
7. Enjoy!

NUTRITION: Calories 46 Fat 2.7 Carbs 5.6 Protein 1.2

Creamy Chicken Liver

Basic Recipe

Preparation Time: 10 minutes **Cooking Time:** 10 minutes **Servings:** 2 **INGREDIENTS:**

- 7 oz chicken liver
- ¼ cup water
- 1 tablespoon butter
- 2 teaspoon cream
- 1 tablespoon fresh dill, chopped
- 1 pinch salt

DIRECTIONS:

1. Preheat the air fryer to 390 F.
2. Combine together water, chicken liver, and salt.
3. Mix the mixture and place it in the air fryer basket.
4. Cook the chicken liver for 10 minutes
5. Stir it after 5 minutes of cooking.
6. Then transfer the cooked chicken liver to the bowl.
7. Add cream and butter.
8. Blend the mixture until smooth.
9. After this, add chopped fresh dill and stir gently.
10. Serve the meal and enjoy!

NUTRITION: Calories 223 Fat 12.5 Carbs 1.9 Protein 24

Catfish Sticks

Basic Recipe
Preparation Time: 10 minutes **Cooking Time:** 10 minutes **Servings:** 2
INGREDIENTS:

- 8 oz catfish fillet
- ½ teaspoon salt
- ½ teaspoon ground black pepper
- ¼ cup panko breadcrumbs
- 1 egg
- ½ teaspoon olive oil

DIRECTIONS:

1. Cut the catfish fillet into 2 medium pieces (sticks).
2. Then sprinkle the catfish with the salt and ground black pepper.
3. Beat the egg in the bowl and whisk it.
4. Dip the catfish fillets in the whisked egg.
5. After this, coat the fish in the panko breadcrumbs.
6. Preheat the air fryer to 380 F.
7. Put the fish sticks in the air fryer basket and spray with the olive oil.
8. Cook the fish sticks for 10 minutes
9. Flip the sticks into another side after 10 minutes of cooking.
10. When the fish sticks are cooked – let them chill gently.
11. Serve the meal!

NUTRITION: Calories 231 Fat 12.2 Carbs 8 Protein 21.5

Honey Banana Chips

Basic Recipe
Preparation Time: 10 minutes **Cooking Time**: 6 minutes **Servings:** 2
INGREDIENTS:

- 2 bananas
- 1 teaspoon honey
- 1 pinch white pepper
- ½ teaspoon olive oil

DIRECTIONS:

1. Peel the bananas and slice them into the chip's pieces. Then sprinkle the bananas with the honey and white pepper.
2. Spray the olive oil over the bananas and mix them gently with the help of the hands.
3. Preheat the air fryer to 320 F. Put the banana chips in the air fryer basket and cook for 6 minutes

4. Serve the cooked banana chips immediately.
5. Enjoy!

NUTRITION: Calories 126 Fat 1.6 Carbs 29.9 Protein 1.3

Ginger Apple Chips

Basic Recipe
Preparation Time: 10 minutes **Cooking Time:** 10 minutes **Servings:** 2
INGREDIENTS:

- ½ teaspoon olive oil
- 3 apples
- 1 pinch ground ginger

DIRECTIONS:

1. Peel the apples and remove the seeds. Slice the apples and sprinkle them with the ground ginger and olive oil.
2. Preheat the air fryer to 400 F.
3. Place the apple slices on the air fryer rack.
4. Cook the apple chips for 10 minutes
5. Shake the apple chips carefully after 4 minutes of cooking.
6. Then chill the apple chips carefully.
7. Serve the meal immediately or keep it in the paper bag in the dry place.
8. Enjoy!

NUTRITION: Calories 184 Fat 1.8 Fiber 8.1 Carbs 46.3

Protein 0.9

Maple Carrot Fries

Basic Recipe
Preparation Time: 5 minutes **Cooking Time**: 10 minutes **Servings:** 2
INGREDIENTS:

- 1 cup baby carrot
- ¼ cup maple syrup
- 1 pinch salt
- ½ teaspoon thyme
- ½ teaspoon ground black pepper
- 1 teaspoon dried oregano
- 1 tablespoon olive oil

DIRECTIONS:

1. Preheat the air fryer to 410 F.
2. Place the baby carrot in the air fryer basket.
3. Sprinkle the baby carrot with the thyme, salt, ground black pepper, and dried oregano.
4. Then spray the olive oil over the baby carrot and shake it well.
5. Cook the baby carrot fries for 10 minutes
6. Shake the carrot fries after 6 minutes of cooking.
7. Chill the cooked meal for 5 minutes
8. Enjoy!

NUTRITION: Calories 197 Fat 7.3 Carbs 34.4 Protein 0.7

Sweet Potato Fries

Basic Recipe
Preparation Time: 10 minutes
Cooking Time: 15 minutes

Servings: 2
INGREDIENTS:

- 2 sweet potatoes
- 1 tablespoon coconut oil
- 1/3 teaspoon salt
- ½ teaspoon ground black pepper
- ½ teaspoon onion powder

DIRECTIONS:

1. Preheat the air fryer to 370 F.
2. Peel the sweet potatoes and cut them into the fries.
3. Sprinkle the vegetables with the salt, ground black pepper, and onion powder.
4. Shake the sweet potatoes and sprinkle with the coconut oil.
5. Put the uncooked sweet potato fries in the air fryer basket and cook for 15 minutes
6. Shake the sweet potato fries every 5 minutes
7. When the sweet potato fries are cooked – let them chill gently
8. Serve the meal!

NUTRITION: Calories 225 Fat 6.8 Carbs 42.1 Protein 2.6

Squid Rings

Basic Recipe
Preparation Time: 10 minutes **Cooking Time**: 4 minutes **Servings:** 2
INGREDIENTS:

- 2 squid tubes
- 2 eggs
- 1/3 cup flour
- ¼ teaspoon salt
- ½ teaspoon onion powder
- ½ teaspoon garlic powder

DIRECTIONS:

1. Wash and peel the squid cubes carefully. Then slice the squid cubes into the rings.
2. Beat the eggs in the bowl and whisk them.
3. Then dip the squid rings in the whisked eggs.
4. Combine together flour, salt, onion powder, and garlic powder. Stir the mixture with the help of the fork.
5. Then coat the squid rings with the flour mixture.
6. Preheat the air fryer to 400 F.
7. Put the squid rings onto the air fryer rack.
8. Cook the squid rings for 4 minutes
9. Shake the squid rings after 3 minutes of cooking.
10. When the squid rings are cooked – let them chill till the room temperature
11. Enjoy!

NUTRITION: Calories 383 Fat 10.5 Carbs 17.2 Protein 55.8

Carrot Chips

Basic Recipe
Preparation Time: 10 minutes **Cooking Time:** 20 minutes **Servings:** 2
INGREDIENTS:

- 3 carrots
- ½ teaspoon salt
- ½ teaspoon ground black pepper
- 1 tablespoon canola oil

DIRECTIONS:

1. Peel the carrot and slice into the chips.
2. Then sprinkle the uncooked carrot chips with the salt, ground black pepper, and canola oil.
3. Shake the carrot chips carefully.
4. Preheat the air fryer to 360 F.
5. Put the carrot chips in the air fryer basket.
6. Shake the carrot chips in halfway.
7. Check the doneness of the carrot chips while cooking.
8. Chill the carrot chips and serve.
9. Enjoy!

NUTRITION: Calories 101 Fat 7 Carbs 9.3 Protein 0.8

Corn Okra Bites

Basic Recipe
Preparation Time: 10 minutes **Cooking Time**: 4 minutes **Servings:** 2 **INGREDIENTS:**

- 4 tablespoon corn flakes, crushed
- 9 oz okra
- 1 egg
- ½ teaspoon salt
- 1 teaspoon olive oil

DIRECTIONS:

1. Preheat the air fryer to 400 F.
2. Chop the okra roughly.
3. Combine together the corn flakes and salt.
4. Crack the egg into the bowl and whisk it.
5. Toss the chopped okra in the whisked egg.
6. Then coat the chopped okra with the corn flakes.
7. Put the chopped okra in the air fryer basket and sprinkle with the olive oil.
8. Cook the okra for 4 minutes
9. Shake the okra after 2 minutes of cooking.
10. When the okra is cooked – let it chill gently.
11. Enjoy!

NUTRITION: Calories 115 Fat 4.8 Carbs 12.7 Protein 5.2

Salty Potato Chips

Basic Recipe

Preparation Time: 10 minutes **Cooking Time**: 19 minutes **Servings:** 2 **INGREDIENTS:**

- 3 potatoes
- 1 tablespoon canola oil
- ½ teaspoon salt

DIRECTIONS:

1. Wash the potatoes carefully and do not peel them. Slice the potatoes into the chips.
2. Sprinkle the potato chips with the olive oil and salt. Mix the potatoes carefully.
3. Preheat the air fryer to 400 F. Put the potato chips in the air fryer basket and cook for 19 minutes
4. Shake the potato chips every 3 minutes
5. When the potato chips are cooked – chill them well.
6. Enjoy!

NUTRITION: Calories 282 Fat 7.3 Carbs 50.2 Protein 5.4

Corn & Beans Fries

Basic Recipe
Preparation Time: 10 minutes **Cooking Time:** 10 minutes **Servings:** 2
INGREDIENTS:

- ¼ cup corn flakes crumbs
- 1 egg
- 10 oz green beans
- 1 tablespoon canola oil
- ½ teaspoon salt
- 1 teaspoon garlic powder

DIRECTIONS:

1. Preheat the air fryer to 400 F.
2. Put the green beans in the bowl.
3. Beat the egg in the green beans and stir carefully until homogenous.
4. Then sprinkle the green beans with the salt and garlic powder.
5. Shake gently.
6. Then coat the green beans in the corn flakes crumbs well.
7. Put the green beans in the air fryer basket in one layer.
8. Cook the green beans for 7 minutes
9. Shake the green beans twice during the cooking.
10. When the green beans are cooked – let them chill and serve.
11. Enjoy!

NUTRITION: Calories 182 Fat 9.4 Carbs 21 Protein 6.3

Sugary Apple Fritters

Basic Recipe
Preparation Time: 10 minutes **Cooking Time:** 10 minutes **Servings:** 2
INGREDIENTS:

- 2 red apples
- 1 teaspoon sugar
- 1 tablespoon flour
- 1 tablespoon semolina
- 1 teaspoon lemon juice
- ½ teaspoon ground cinnamon
- 1 teaspoon butter
- 1 egg

DIRECTIONS:

1. Peel the apples and grate them.
2. Sprinkle the grated apples with the lemon juice.
3. Then add sugar, flour, semolina, and ground cinnamon.
4. Mix the mixture and crack the egg.
5. Mix the apple mixture carefully.
6. Preheat the air fryer to 370 F.
7. Toss the butter in the air fryer basket and melt it.
8. When the butter is melted – make the medium fritters from the apple mixture. Use 2 spoons for this step.
9. Place the fritters in the air fryer basket and cook for 6 minutes
10. After this, flip the fritters to another side and cook for 2 minutes more.
11. Dry the cooked fritters with the help of the paper towel and serve.
12. Enjoy!

NUTRITION: Calories 207 Fat 4.6 Carbs 40.3 Protein 4.5

Oregano Onion Rings

Basic Recipe

Preparation Time: 14 minutes **Cooking Time:** 10 minutes **Servings:** 2

INGREDIENTS:

- 1 tablespoon oregano
- 1 tablespoon flour
- ½ teaspoon cornstarch
- 1 egg
- ½ teaspoon salt
- 2 white onions, peeled
- 1 tablespoon olive oil

DIRECTIONS:

1. Crack the egg into the bowl and whisk it. Combine together the flour and cornstarch in the separate bowl.
2. Add oregano and salt. Shake the mixture gently. Peel the onions and slice them to get the —rings‖.
3. Then dip the onion rings in the whisked egg. After this, coat the onion rings in the flour mixture.
4. Preheat the air fryer to 365 F.
5. Spray the air fryer basket with the olive oil inside. Then place the onion rings in the air fryer and cook for 8 minutes
6. Shake the onion rings after 4 minutes of cooking. Let the cooked meal chill gently.
7. Serve it!

NUTRITION: Calories 159 Fat 9.6 Carbs 15.5 Protein 4.6

Cinnamon Mixed Nuts

Basic Recipe
Preparation Time: 5 minutes **Cooking Time:** 20 minutes **Servings**: 5
INGREDIENTS:

- ½ cup pecans
- ½ cup walnuts
- ½ cup almonds
- A pinch of cayenne pepper
- 2 tbsp sugar
- 2 tbsp egg whites
- 2 tsp cinnamon

DIRECTIONS

1. Add the pepper, sugar, and cinnamon to a bowl and mix them well; set aside. In another bowl, mix in the pecans, walnuts, almonds, and egg whites. Add the spice mixture to the nuts and give it a good mix. Lightly grease the frying basket with cooking spray. Pour in the nuts, and cook them for 10 minutes on Air Fry function at 350 F. Stir the nuts using a wooden vessel, and cook for further for 10 minutes Pour the nuts in the bowl. Let cool.

NUTRITION: Calories 180 Fat 12g Carbs 13g Protein 6g

Apple & Cinnamon Chips

Basic Recipe

Preparation Time: 15 minutes **Cooking Time:** 10 minutes **Servings:** 2

INGREDIENTS:

- 1 tsp sugar
- 1 tsp salt
- 1 whole apple, sliced
- ½ tsp cinnamon
- Confectioners' sugar for serving

DIRECTIONS:

2. Preheat your Air Fryer to 400 F. In a bowl, mix cinnamon, salt and sugar; add the apple slices. Place the prepared apple spices in the cooking basket and cook for 10 minutes on Bake function. Dust with sugar and serve.

NUTRITION: Calories 110 Fat 0g Carbs 27g Protein 1g

Sesame Cabbage & Prawns Egg Roll Wraps

Basic Recipe
Preparation Time: 32 minutes **Cooking Time**: 18 minutes **Servings:** 4
INGREDIENTS:

- 2 tbsp vegetable oil
- 1-inch piece fresh ginger, grated
- 1 tbsp minced garlic
- 1 carrot, cut into strips
- ¼ cup chicken broth
- 2 tbsp reduced-sodium soy sauce
- 1 tbsp sugar
- 1 cup shredded Napa cabbage
- 1 tbsp sesame oil
- 8 cooked prawns, minced
- 1 egg
- 8 egg roll wrappers

DIRECTIONS

3. In a skillet over high heat, heat vegetable oil, and cook ginger and garlic for 40 seconds, until fragrant. Stir in carrot and cook for another 2 minutes Pour in chicken broth, soy sauce, and sugar and bring to a boil.

4. Add cabbage and let simmer until softened, for 4 minutes Remove skillet from the heat and stir in

sesame oil. Let cool for 15 minutes Strain cabbage mixture, and fold in minced prawns. Whisk an egg in a small bowl. Fill each egg roll wrapper with prawn mixture, arranging the mixture just below the center of the wrapper.

5. Fold the bottom part over the filling and tuck under. Fold in both sides and tightly roll up. Use the whisked egg to seal the wrapper. Place the rolls into a greased frying basket, spray with oil and cook for 12 minutes at 370 F on Air Fry function, turning once halfway through.

NUTRITION: Calories 149.3 Fat 3.5g Carbs 20g Protein8.8 g

Rosemary Potatoes

Basic Recipe

Preparation Time: 10 minutes **Cooking Time:** 25 minutes **Servings:** 2 **INGREDIENTS:**

- 1.5 pounds potatoes, halved
- 2 tbsp olive oil
- 3 garlic cloves, grated
- 1 tbsp minced fresh rosemary
- 1 tsp salt
- ¼ tsp freshly ground black pepper

DIRECTIONS:

6. In a bowl, mix potatoes, olive oil, garlic, rosemary, salt, and pepper, until they are well-coated. Arrange the potatoes in the basket and cook t 360 F on Air Fry function for 25 minutes, shaking twice during the cooking. Cook until crispy on the outside and tender on the inside.

NUTRITION: Calories 132 Fats: 2.5g Carbs 18.3g Protein 9.5g

Crunchy Mozzarella Sticks with Sweet Thai Sauce

Intermediate Recipe Preparation Time: 2 hours **Cooking Time:** 20 minutes **Servings:** 2 **INGREDIENTS:**

- 12 mozzarella string cheese
- 2 cups breadcrumbs
- 3 eggs
- 1 cup sweet Thai sauce
- 4 tbsp skimmed milk

DIRECTIONS

7. Pour the crumbs in a bowl. Crack the eggs into another bowl and beat with the milk. One after the other, dip each cheese sticks in the egg mixture, in the crumbs, then egg mixture again and then in the crumbs again.

8. Place the coated cheese sticks on a cookie sheet and freeze for 1 to 2 hours. Preheat Air Fry function to 380 F. Arrange the sticks in the frying basket without overcrowding. Cook for 8 minutes, flipping them halfway through cooking to brown evenly. Cook in batches. Serve with a sweet Thai sauce.

NUTRITION: Calories 173 Fat 5.6g Carbs 27g Protein 3.3g

Chili Cheese Crisps

Basic Recipe
Preparation Time: 17 minutes **Cooking Time:** 10 minutes **Servings**: 3
INGREDIENTS:

- 4 tbsp grated cheese + extra for rolling
- 1 cup flour + extra for kneading
- ¼ tsp chili powder
- ½ tsp baking powder
- 3 tsp butter
- A pinch of salt

DIRECTIONS

9. In a bowl, mix in the cheese, flour, baking powder, chili powder, butter, and salt. The mixture should be crusty. Add some drops of water and mix well to get dough. Remove the dough on a flat surface.
10. Rub some extra flour in your palms and on the surface, and knead the dough for a while. Using a rolling pin, roll the dough out into a thin sheet.
11. With a pastry cutter, cut the dough into your desired lings' shape. Add the cheese lings to the basket, and cook for 8 minutes at 350 F on Air Fry function, flipping once halfway through.

NUTRITION: Calories 1085 Fat 71g Carbs 64g Protein 55g

Parmesan Baked Tomatoes

Basic Recipe
Preparation Time: 10 minutes **Cooking Time:** 10 minutes **Servings:** 4
INGREDIENTS:

- 1 cup grated mozzarella cheese
- 1 cup grated Parmesan cheese
- ½ cup chopped basil
- Olive oil
- 4 tomatoes, halved

DIRECTIONS:

12. Grease a baking pan with some cooking spray. Place tomato halves over the pan; stuff with cheese and basil.
13. Place Instant Vortex over the kitchen platform. Arrange to drip pan in the lower position. Press —Bake,‖ set timer to 10 minutes, and set the temperature to 400°F.
14. When Instant Vortex is pre-heated, it will display —Add Food‖ on its screen. Open the door, and take out the middle roasting tray.
15. Place the pan over the tray and push it back; close door and cooking will start. Midway, it will display —Turn Food‖ on its screen; ignore it, and it will continue to cook after 10 seconds. Cook until cheese is bubbly.

    16. Open the door after the cooking cycle is over; serve warm.

NUTRITION: Calories 486 Fat 7.5g Carbs 11g Protein 17.5g

Gingered Scallops

Basic Recipe
Preparation Time: 10 minutes **Cooking Time:** 15 minutes **Servings:** 4-6
INGREDIENTS:

- 6 very large sea scallops
- ¼ cup tamarind sauce
- 1 tablespoon dark brown sugar
- 6 slices bacon, cut in half crosswise
- 1 ½ teaspoon minced ginger

DIRECTIONS:

17. In a mixing bowl, add tamarind sauce, brown sugar, ginger, and scallops. Combine the ingredients to mix well with each other. Set aside for 15-20 minutes
18. Then, wrap each scallop with two bacon slices. Secure using toothpicks.
19. Grease a baking pan with some cooking spray. Place scallops over the pan.
20. Place the air fryer over the kitchen platform. Arrange to drip pan in the lower position. Press —Air Fry,‖ set the timer to 15 minutes, and set the temperature to 350°F.
21. When the air fryer is pre-heated, it will display —Add Food‖ on its screen. Open the door, and take out the middle roasting tray.
22. Place the pan over the tray and push it back; close door and cooking will start. Midway, it will display —Turn Food‖ on its screen; flip scallops and close door. Cook until bacon is crispy and brown.
23. Open the door after the cooking cycle is over; serve warm.

NUTRITION: Calories 173 Fat 14g Carbs 3g Protein 5.5g

Baked Bacon Potatoes

Basic Recipe
Preparation Time: 5 minutes **Cooking Time:** 10 minutes **Servings:** 4
INGREDIENTS:

- ¼ cup chopped scallions
- 1 cup grated cheddar cheese
- 3 russet potatoes, cleaned and cut into 1-inch rounds
- ¼ cup butter
- 3 tablespoon bacon bits, cooked and crumbled

DIRECTIONS:

24. Grease a baking pan with some cooking spray. Place potato over the pan; brush with butter and top with scallions and cheese.

25. Place Instant Vortex over the kitchen platform. Arrange to drip pan in the lower position. Press

    ―Bake,‖ set timer to 15 minutes, and set the temperature to 400°F. Instant Vortex will start pre- heating.

26. When Instant Vortex is pre-heated, it will display

    ―Add Food‖ on its screen. Open the door, and take out the middle roasting tray.

27. Place the pan over the tray and push it back; close door and cooking will start. Midway, it will display
    ―Turn Food‖ on its screen; ignore it, and it will continue to cook after 10 seconds. Cook until cheese is bubbly.

28. Open the door after the cooking cycle is over; serve warm with bacon on top.

NUTRITION: Calories 330 Fat 12g Carbs 48g Protein 7.5g

Coconut Shrimps

Basic Recipe
Preparation Time: 10 minutes **Cooking Time**: 12 minutes **Servings:** 4
INGREDIENTS:

- 8 ounces coconut milk
- ½ cup panko breadcrumbs
- 8 large shrimp, peeled and deveined
- Salt and ground black pepper, to taste
- ½ teaspoon cayenne pepper

DIRECTIONS:

29. In a mixing bowl, add salt, black pepper, and coconut milk. Combine the ingredients to mix well with each other.

30. In another bowl, add breadcrumbs, cayenne pepper, Ground black pepper, and salt. Combine the ingredients to mix well with each other. Coat the shrimps evenly with first coconut mixture and then with crumbs. Grease a baking pan with some cooking spray. Place shrimps over the pan.

31. Place Instant Vortex over the kitchen platform. Arrange to drip pan in the lower position. Press —Air Fry, set the timer to 15 minutes, and set the temperature to 350°F.

32. When air Fryer is pre-heated, it will display —Add Food on its screen. Open the door, and take out the middle roasting tray. Place the pan over the tray and push it back; close door and cooking will start. Midway, it will display —Turn Food on its screen; flip shrimps and close door.

33. Open the door after the cooking cycle is over; serve warm.

NUTRITION: Calories 209 Fat 15g Carbs 6g Protein 4.5g

Guacamole Tortilla Chips

Basic Recipe
Preparation Time: 10 minutes **Cooking Time:** 15 minutes **Servings:** 4
INGREDIENTS:

- Chips:
- 1 tablespoon cumin powder

- 1 tablespoon paprika powder
- 12 corn tortillas
- 2 tablespoon olive oil
- Ground black pepper and salt to taste
- Guacamole:
- 1 small firm tomato, chopped
- 1 large avocado, pitted, peeled and mashed
- A pinch dried parsley

DIRECTIONS:

1. In a mixing bowl, add all chips ingredients. Combine the ingredients to mix well with each other. In another bowl, add guacamole ingredients. Combine the ingredients to mix well with each other.
2. Place Instant Vortex over the kitchen platform. Arrange to drip pan in the lower position.
3. Press —Air Fry,‖ set the timer to 15 minutes, and set the temperature to 375°F.
4. In the rotisserie basket, add chips mixture.
5. When the air fryer is pre-heated, it will display —Add Food‖ on its screen. Open the door and lock the basket. Press the red lever and arrange the basket on the left side; now, just simply rest the basket rod over the right side.
6. Close door and press —Rotate‖; cooking will start. Cook until chips are evenly golden.
7. Open the door after the cooking cycle is over; serve chips with guacamole.

NUTRITION: Calories 140 Fat 13g Carbs 11g Protein 2.5g

Roasted Chickpeas

Intermediate Recipe Preparation Time: 10 minutes **Cooking Time**: 45 minutes **Servings:**
2 **INGREDIENTS:**

- 1 (15 ounces) can chickpeas, Dry outed
- 1/4 teaspoon garlic powder
- 1/4 teaspoon ground cumin
- 1/4 teaspoon ground coriander
- 1/4 teaspoon curry powder
- 1/8 teaspoon salt
- 1/4 teaspoon chili pepper powder
- 1/4 teaspoon paprika
- Olive oil

DIRECTIONS:

1. In a mixing bowl, add chickpeas and spices. Combine the ingredients to mix well with each other.
2. Place Instant Vortex over the kitchen platform. Arrange to drip pan in the lower position.
3. Press —Air Fry,‖ set the timer to 35 minutes, and set the temperature to 375°F.
4. In the rotisserie basket, add chickpea mixture.
5. When the air fryer is pre-heated, it will display —Add Food‖ on its screen. Open the door and lock the basket. Press the red lever and arrange the basket

   on the left side; now, just simply rest the basket rod over the right side.
6. Close door and press —Rotate‖; cooking will start. Cook until evenly toasted and golden brown. Cook for 5-10 minutes more if needed. Open the door after the cooking cycle is over; serve warm

NUTRITION: Calories 132 Fat 13g Carbs 11g Protein 2.4g

Supreme French Fries

Basic Recipe

Preparation Time: 10 minutes **Cooking Time:** 10 minutes **Servings:** 2

INGREDIENTS:

- ½ teaspoon onion powder
- ½ teaspoon garlic powder
- 1-pound potatoes, peeled and cut into strips
- 3 tablespoons olive oil
- 1 teaspoon paprika
- Salt to taste (optional)

DIRECTIONS:

7. In a mixing bowl, add potato strips and water. Soak for an hour; Dry out and dry pieces completely over paper towels.
8. In a mixing bowl, add a strip and other ingredients. Combine the ingredients to mix well with each other.
9. Place Instant Vortex over the kitchen platform. Arrange to drip pan in the lower position.
10. Press —Air Fry,‖ set the timer to 30 minutes, and set the temperature to 375°F. Instant Vortex will start pre-heating.
11. In the rotisserie basket, add potato mix.
12. When Instant Vortex is pre-heated, it will display —Add Food‖ on its screen. Open the door and lock the basket. Press the red lever and arrange the basket on the left side; now, just simply rest the basket rod over the right side.
13. Close door and press —Rotate‖; cooking will start.
14. Open the door after the cooking cycle is over; serve warm.

NUTRITION: Calories 176 Fat 11g Carbs 17g Protein 3g

Butter Cashews

Basic Recipe
Preparation Time: 5 minutes **Cooking Time:** 5 minutes **Servings**: 5-6
INGREDIENTS:

- 1 teaspoon butter, melted
- 1 ½ cups raw cashew nut
- Salt and black pepper to taste

DIRECTIONS:

15. In a mixing bowl, add cashews and other ingredients. Combine the ingredients to mix well with each other.
16. Grease a baking tray with some cooking spray. Place cashews over the tray.
17. Place Instant Vortex over the kitchen platform. Arrange to drip pan in the lower position.
18. Press —Air Fry,‖ set timer to 5 minutes, and set the temperature to 355°F.
19. When the air fryer is pre-heated, it will display —Add Food‖ on its screen. Open the door, and take out the middle roasting tray.
20. Place the baking tray over the roasting tray and push it back; close door and cooking will start. Midway it will display —Turn Food‖ on its screen; shake baking tray and close door.
21. Open the door after the cooking cycle is over; serve warm.

NUTRITION: Calories 233 Fat 15g Carbs 12g Protein 6g

Cinnamon Banana Chips

Basic Recipe
Preparation Time: 10 minutes **Cooking Time**: 6 minutes **Servings:** 4
INGREDIENTS:

- ¼ teaspoon cocoa powder
- A pinch of cinnamon powder
- 5 large firm bananas, peeled

DIRECTIONS:

22. Slice bananas thinly in a horizontal manner and combine with cocoa and cinnamon in a bowl.
23. Place Instant Vortex over the kitchen platform. Arrange to drip pan in the lower position.
24. Press —Air Fry,‖ set timer to 7 minutes, and set the temperature to 380°F.
25. When the air fryer is pre-heated, it will display —Add Food‖ on its screen. Open the door, and take out the middle roasting tray.
26. Place slices (cook in batches if needed) over the tray and push it back; close door and cooking will start. Midway, it will display —Turn Food‖ on its screen; ignore it, and it will continue to cook after 10 seconds. Cook until the slices crisps.
27. Open the door after the cooking cycle is over; serve warm.

NUTRITION: Calories 173 Fat 0.5g Carbs 34g Protein 2.5g

Perfect Cinnamon Toast

Basic Recipe
Preparation Time: 10 minutes **Cooking Time:** 5 minutes **Servings**: 6
INGREDIENTS:

- 2 tsp. pepper
- 1 ½ tsp. vanilla extract
- 1 ½ tsp. cinnamon
- ½ C. sweetener of choice
- 1 C. coconut oil
- 12 slices whole wheat bread

DIRECTIONS:

28. Melt coconut oil and mix with sweetener until dissolved. Mix in remaining ingredients minus bread till incorporated.
29. Spread mixture onto bread, covering all area.
30. Pour the coated pieces of bread into the Oven rack/basket. Place the Rack on the middle-shelf of the Air fryer oven. Set temperature to 400°F, and set time to 5 minutes
31. Remove and cut diagonally. Enjoy!

NUTRITION: Calories 124 Fat 2g Carbs 12g Protein 0g

Easy Baked Chocolate Mug Cake

Basic Recipe
Preparation Time: 5 minutes **Cooking Time:** 10 minutes **Servings**: 3
INGREDIENTS:

- ½ cup cocoa powder
- ½ cup stevia powder
- 1 cup coconut cream
- 1 package cream cheese, room temperature
- 1 tablespoon vanilla extract
- 1 tablespoons butter

DIRECTIONS:

1. Preheat the air fryer oven for 5 minutes
2. In a mixing bowl, combine all ingredients.
3. Use a hand mixer to mix everything until fluffy.
4. Pour into greased mugs.
5. Place the mugs in the fryer basket.
6. Bake it for 15 minutes at 350°F.
7. Place in the fridge to chill before serving. **NUTRITION:** Calories 744 Fat 69.7g Protein 13.9g Carbs: 4g

Angel Food Cake

Basic Recipe
Preparation Time: 5 minutes **Cooking Time**: 30 minutes **Servings**: 12
INGREDIENTS:

- ¼ cup butter, melted
- 1 cup powdered erythritol
- 1 teaspoon strawberry extract
- 12 egg whites
- 2 teaspoons cream of tartar
- A pinch of salt

DIRECTIONS:

1. Preheat the air fryer oven for 5 minutes
2. Mix the egg whites and cream of tartar.
3. Use a hand mixer and whisk until white and fluffy.
4. Add the rest of the ingredients except for the butter and whisk for another minute.
5. Pour into a baking dish.
6. Place in the air fryer basket and cook for 30 minutes at 400°F or if a toothpick inserted in the middle comes out clean.
7. Drizzle with melted butter once cooled.

NUTRITION: Calories 65 Fat 5g Carbs: 1g Protein 3.1g

Fried Peaches

Intermediate Recipe
Preparation Time: 2 hours 10 minutes
Cooking Time: 15 minutes **Servings:** 4 **INGREDIENTS:**

- 4 ripe peaches (1/2 a peach = 1 serving)
- 1 1/2 cups flour
- Salt
- 2 egg yolks
- 3/4 cups cold water
- 1 1/2 tablespoons olive oil
- 2 tablespoons brandy
- 4 egg whites
- Cinnamon/sugar mix

DIRECTIONS:

1. Mix flour, egg yolks, and salt in a mixing bowl. Slowly mix in water, then add brandy. Set the mixture aside for 2 hours and go do something for 1 hour 45 minutes
2. Boil a large pot of water and cut and X at the bottom of each peach. While the water boils fill another large bowl with water and ice. Boil each peach for about a minute, then plunge it in the ice bath. Now the peels should basically fall off the peach. Beat the egg whites and mix into the batter mix. Dip each peach in the mix to coat.
3. Pour the coated peach into the Oven rack/basket. Place the Rack on the middle-shelf of the Air fryer oven. Set temperature to 360°F, and set time to 10 minutes
4. Prepare a plate with cinnamon/sugar mix, roll peaches in mix and serve.

NUTRITION: Calories 306 Fat 3g Protein 10g Carbs: 2.7g

Apple Dumplings

Basic Recipe

Preparation Time: 10 minutes **Cooking Time:** 25 minutes **Servings:** 4 **INGREDIENTS:**

- 2 tbsp. melted coconut oil
- 2 puff pastry sheets
- 1 tbsp. brown sugar
- 2 tbsp. raisins
- 2 small apples of choice

DIRECTIONS:

5. Ensure your air fryer oven is preheated to 356 degrees. Core and peel apples and mix with raisins and sugar. Place a bit of apple mixture into puff pastry sheets and brush sides with melted coconut oil. Place into the air fryer. Cook 25 minutes, turning halfway through. It will be golden when done.

NUTRITION: Calories 367 Fat 7g Protein 2g Sugar: 5g

Apple Pie in Air Fryer

Basic Recipe

Preparation Time: 5 minutes **Cooking Time**: 35 minutes **Serving**: 4

INGREDIENTS:

- ½ teaspoon vanilla extract
- 1 beaten egg
- 1 large apple, chopped
- 1 Pillsbury Refrigerator pie crust
- 1 tablespoon butter
- 1 tablespoon ground cinnamon
- 1 tablespoon raw sugar
- 2 tablespoon sugar
- 2 teaspoons lemon juice
- Baking spray

DIRECTIONS:

6. Lightly grease baking pan of air fryer oven with cooking spray. Spread pie crust on bottom of pan up to the sides.
7. In a bowl, mix vanilla, sugar, cinnamon, lemon juice, and apples. Pour on top of pie crust. Top the apples with butter slices. Cover apples with the other pie crust. Pierce with knife the tops of pie.
8. Spread beaten egg on top of crust and sprinkle sugar. Cover with foil.
9. For 25 minutes, cook it on 390°F.
10. Remove foil cook for 10 minutes at 330oF until tops are browned. Serve and enjoy.

NUTRITION: Calories 372 Fat 19g Protein 4.2g Sugar: 5g

Raspberry Cream Roll-Ups

Basic Recipe Preparation Time:
Cooking Time:
Serving: 4
INGREDIENTS:

- 1 cup of fresh raspberries, rinsed and patted dry
- ½ cup of cream cheese, softened to room temperature
- ¼ cup of brown sugar
- ¼ cup of sweetened condensed milk
- 1 egg
- 1 teaspoon of corn starch
- 6 spring roll wrappers (any brand will do, we like Blue Dragon or Tasty Joy, both available through Target or Walmart, or any large grocery chain)
- ¼ cup of water

DIRECTIONS:

11. Cover the basket of the air fryer oven with a lining of tin foil, leaving the edges uncovered to allow air to circulate through the basket. Preheat the air fryer oven to 350 degrees.
12. In a mixing bowl, combine the cream cheese, brown sugar, condensed milk, cornstarch, and egg. Beat or whip thoroughly, until all ingredients are completely mixed and fluffy, thick and stiff.
13. Spoon even amounts of the creamy filling into each spring roll wrapper, then top each dollop of filling with several raspberries.
14. Roll up the wraps around the creamy raspberry filling, and seal the seams with a few dabs of water.
15. Place each roll on the foil-lined air fryer basket, seams facing down.
16. Set the air fryer oven timer to 10 minutes during cooking; shake the handle of the fryer basket to ensure a nice even surface crisp.
17. After 10 minutes, when the air fryer oven shuts off, the spring rolls should be golden brown and perfect on the outside, while the raspberries and cream filling will have cooked together in a glorious fusion. Remove with tongs and serve hot or cold.

NUTRITION: Calories 351 Fat 20.1g Protein 4.3g Sugar: 5.6g

Air Fryer Chocolate Cake

Basic Recipe
Preparation Time: 5 minutes **Cooking Time**: 35 minutes **Serving:** 8-10
INGREDIENTS:

- ½ C. hot water
- 1 tsp. vanilla
- ¼ C. olive oil
- ½ C. almond milk
- 1 egg
- ½ tsp. salt
- ¾ tsp. baking soda
- ¾ tsp. baking powder
- ½ C. unsweetened cocoa powder
- 2 C. almond flour
- 1 C. brown sugar

DIRECTIONS:

1. Preheat your air fryer oven to 356 degrees.
2. Stir all dry ingredients together. Then stir in wet ingredients. Add hot water last.
3. The batter will be thin, no worries.
4. Pour cake batter into a pan that fits into the fryer. Cover with foil and poke holes into the foil.
5. Bake 35 minutes
6. Discard foil and then bake another 10 minutes

NUTRITION: Calories 378 Fat 9g Protein 4g Sugar: 5g

Banana-Choco Brownies

Basic Recipe
Preparation Time: 5 minutes **Cooking Time**: 30 minutes **Servings**: 12
INGREDIENTS:

- 2 cups almond flour
- 2 teaspoons baking powder
- ½ teaspoon baking powder
- ½ teaspoon baking soda
- ½ teaspoon salt
- 1 over-ripe banana
- 3 large eggs
- ½ teaspoon stevia powder
- ¼ cup coconut oil
- 1 tablespoon vinegar
- 1/3 cup almond flour
- 1/3 cup cocoa powder

DIRECTIONS:

1. Preheat the air fryer oven for 5 minutes. Combine all ingredients in a food processor and pulse until well-combined.
2. Pour into a baking dish that will fit in the air fryer.
3. Place in the air fryer basket and cook for 30 minutes at 350°F or if a toothpick inserted in the middle comes out clean.

NUTRITION: Calories 75 Fat 6.5g Protein 1.7g Sugar: 2g

Chocolate Donuts

Basic Recipe
Preparation Time: 5 minutes **Cooking Time:** 20 minutes **Servings:** 8-10
INGREDIENTS:

- (8-ounce) can jumbo biscuits
- Cooking oil
- Chocolate sauce, such as Hershey's

DIRECTIONS:

4. Separate the biscuit dough into 8 biscuits and place them on a flat work surface. Use a small circle cookie cutter or a biscuit cutter to cut a hole in the center of each biscuit. You can also cut the holes using a knife.
5. Spray the air fryer basket with cooking oil. Place the 4 donuts in the air fryer oven. Do not stack. Spray with cooking oil. Cook for 4 minutes Open the air fryer and flip the donuts. Cook for an additional 4 minutes. Remove the cooked donuts from the air fryer oven, and then repeat for the remaining 4 donuts. Drizzle with chocolate sauce over the donuts and enjoy while warm.

NUTRITION: Calories 181 Fat 98g Protein 3g

Easy Air Fryer Donuts

Basic Recipe
Preparation Time: 5 minutes **Cooking Time:** 10 minutes **Servings:** 8
INGREDIENTS:

- Pinch of allspice
- 4 tbsp. dark brown sugar
- ½ - 1 tsp. cinnamon
- 1/3 C. granulated sweetener
- 3 tbsp. melted coconut oil
- 1 can of biscuits

DIRECTIONS:

6. Mix allspice, sugar, sweetener, and cinnamon together.
7. Take out biscuits from can and with a circle cookie cutter, cut holes from centers and place into air fryer.
8. Cook 5 minutes at 350 degrees. As batches are cooked, use a brush to coat with melted coconut oil and dip each into sugar mixture.
9. Serve warm!

NUTRITION: Calories 209 Fat 4g Carbs: 3g Protein 0g

Chocolate Soufflé for Two

Basic Recipe

Preparation Time: 5 minutes **Cooking Time**: 14 minutes **Servings:** 4 **INGREDIENTS:**

- 2 tbsp. almond flour
- ½ tsp. vanilla
- 3 tbsp. sweetener
- 2 separated eggs
- ¼ C. melted coconut oil
- 3 ounces of semi-sweet chocolate, chopped

DIRECTIONS:

1. Brush coconut oil and sweetener onto ramekins.
2. Melt coconut oil and chocolate together.
3. Beat egg yolks well, adding vanilla and sweetener. Stir in flour and ensure there are no lumps.
4. Preheat the air fryer oven to 330 degrees.
5. Whisk egg whites till they reach peak state and fold them into chocolate mixture.
6. Pour batter into ramekins and place into the air fryer oven.
7. Cook 14 minutes
8. Serve with powdered sugar dusted on top.

NUTRITION: Calories 238; Fat 6g Carbs: 4g Protein 1g

Fried Bananas with Chocolate Sauce

Basic Recipe
Preparation Time: 10 minutes **Cooking Time:** 10 minutes **Servings:** 4
Ingredients:

- 1 large egg
- ¼ cup cornstarch
- ¼ cup plain bread crumbs
- 3 bananas, halved crosswise
- Cooking oil
- Chocolate sauce

DIRECTIONS:

1. In a small bowl, beat the egg. In another bowl, place the cornstarch. Place the bread crumbs in a third bowl. Dip the bananas in the cornstarch, then the egg, and then the bread crumbs.
2. Spray the air fryer basket with cooking oil. Place the bananas in the basket and spray them with cooking oil.
3. Cook for 5 minutes Open the air fryer and flip the bananas. Cook for an additional 2 minutes Transfer the bananas to plates.
4. Drizzle with the chocolate sauce over the bananas, and serve.
5. You can make your own chocolate sauce using 2 tablespoons milk and ¼ cup chocolate chips. Heat a saucepan over medium-high heat. Add the milk and stir for 1 to 2 minutes Add the chocolate chips. Stir it for 2 minutes, or until the chocolate has melted.

NUTRITION: Calories 203 Fat 6g Carbs: 3g Protein 3g

Apple Hand Pies

Basic Recipe
Preparation Time: 5 minutes **Cooking Time:** 10 minutes **Servings:** 6
INGREDIENTS:

- 15-ounces no-sugar-added apple pie filling
- 1 store-bought crust

DIRECTIONS:

6. Lay out pie crust and slice into equal-sized squares. Place the 2 tbsp. filling into each square and seal crust with a fork.Pour into the Oven rack/basket. Place the Rack on the middle-shelf of the Air fryer oven. Set temperature to 390°F, and set time to 8 minutes until golden in color.

NUTRITION: Calories 278 Fat 10g Carbs: 4g Protein 5g

Chocolaty Banana Muffins

Basic Recipe
Preparation Time: 5 minutes **Cooking Time:** 25 minutes **Servings**: 12
INGREDIENTS:

- ¾ cup whole wheat flour
- ¾ cup plain flour
- ¼ cup cocoa powder
- ¼ teaspoon baking powder
- 1 teaspoon baking soda
- ¼ teaspoon salt
- 2 large bananas, peeled and mashed
- 1 cup sugar
- 1/3 cup canola oil
- 1 egg
- ½ teaspoon vanilla essence
- 1 cup mini chocolate chips

DIRECTIONS:

7. In a large bowl, mix together flour, cocoa powder, baking powder, baking soda and salt.
8. In another bowl, add bananas, sugar, oil, egg and vanilla extract and beat till well combined.
9. Slowly, add flour mixture in egg mixture and mix till just combined.
10. Fold in chocolate chips.
11. Preheat the air fryer oven to 345 degrees F. Grease 12 muffin molds.
12. Transfer the mixture into prepared muffin molds and cook for about 20-25 minutes or till a toothpick inserted in the center comes out clean.
13. Remove the muffin molds from Air fryer and keep on wire rack to cool for about 10 minutes. Carefully turn on a wire rack to cool completely before serving.

NUTRITION: Calories 189 Fat 8.3g Carbs 12.2g Protein 3.4g

Blueberry Lemon Muffins

Basic Recipe
Preparation Time: 5 minutes **Cooking Time:** 10 minutes **Servings:** 12
INGREDIENTS:

- 1 tsp. vanilla
- Juice and zest of 1 lemon
- 2 eggs
- 1 C. blueberries
- ½ C. cream
- ¼ C. avocado oil
- ½ C. monk fruit
- 2 ½ C. almond flour s

DIRECTIONS:

14. Mix monk fruit and flour together.
15. In another bowl, mix vanilla, egg, lemon juice, and cream together. Add mixtures together and blend well.
16. Spoon batter into cupcake holders
17. Place in air fryer oven. Bake 10 minutes at 320 degrees, checking at 6 minutes to ensure you don't over bake them.

NUTRITION: Calories 317 Fat 11g Carbs: 5g Protein 3g

Cheese-Filled Bread Bowl

Basic Recipe
Preparation Time: 10 minutes **Cooking Time**: 30 minutes **Servings:** 4
INGREDIENTS:

- 1 (6-inch) round loaf bread, unsliced
- 2 tablespoons olive oil
- 6 ounces cream cheese, at room temperature
- ½ cup mayonnaise
- ¼ cup whole milk
- 1 cup shredded Havarti cheese
- 1 cup shredded provolone cheese
- ¼ cup grated Parmesan cheese
- 2 scallions, sliced
- 1 teaspoon Worcestershire sauce

DIRECTIONS:

18. Cut the top 1 inch of the bread off. Use a serrated bread knife to cut around the inside of the loaf, leaving about a 1-inch shell. Be careful not to cut through the bottom. Cut the pieces of bread and the top of the loaf into 1-inch cubes and Drizzle with the olive oil.

19. Set or preheat the air fryer to 375°F. Put the bread cubes in the air fryer basket and Bake it for 5 to 8 minutes, shaking halfway through cooking time, until toasted. Place in a serving bowl. Keep the air fryer set to 375°F.

20. Meanwhile, beat the cream cheese with the mayonnaise and milk until smooth. Stir in the Havarti, provolone, and Parmesan cheeses, scallions, and Worcestershire sauce.

21. Spoon the cheese mixture into the center of the bread shell. Put the filled bread in the air fryer

   basket and place the basket in the air fryer. Bake at 375°F for 15 to 20 minutes, stirring the mixture halfway through cooking time, until the cheese is melted and starts to brown on top. Serve with the toasted bread and bread sticks, if desired.

NUTRITION: Calories 514 Protein 17g Fat 42g Carbs 17g

Apricots in Blankets

Basic Recipe
Preparation Time: 20 minutes **Cooking Time:** 24 minutes **Servings**: 6
INGREDIENTS:

- 6 dried apricots, halved lengthwise
- 4 tablespoons (2 ounces) cream cheese
- ½ sheet frozen puff pastry, thawed
- 4 tablespoons honey mustard
- 2 tablespoons butter, melted

DIRECTIONS:

22. Stuff each apricot half with a teaspoon of cream cheese and set aside.
23. Roll out the puff pastry until it is 6 by 12 inches. Cut in half lengthwise for two 3-by-12-inch rectangles. Cut each rectangle into six 3-inch strips for a total of 12 puff pastry strips.
24. Spread 1 teaspoon of honey mustard onto each strip. Place a filled apricot on each strip and roll up the pastry, pinching the seam closed but leaving the ends open.
25. Place 6 filled pastries in the air fryer basket. Brush the top of each with some of the melted butter.
26. Set or preheat the air fryer to 375°F. Put the basket in the air fryer. Bake it for 8 to 12 minutes or until the pastry is golden brown. Repeat with the other six pastries, then serve.

NUTRITION: Calories 137 Protein 2g Fat 9g Carbs 12g

Fried Ravioli with Blue Cheese Dipping Sauce

Basic Recipe
Preparation Time: 15 minutes **Cooking Time:** 15 minutes **Servings:** 4
INGREDIENTS:

- ⅔ cup sour cream
- ⅓ cup crumbled blue cheese
- 3 tablespoons whole milk
- 1 large egg, beaten
- 1 tablespoon water
- 1 teaspoon dried Italian seasoning
- 1 cup dried bread crumbs
- ⅓ cup grated Parmesan cheese
- ½ (25-ounce) bag frozen cheese ravioli
- Olive oil spray

DIRECTION:

27. In a small serving bowl, combine the sour cream, blue cheese, and milk and stir to combine. Cover and refrigerate while you prepare the ravioli.
28. In a shallow bowl, whisk together the egg, water, and Italian seasoning until combined. On a plate, combine the bread crumbs and Parmesan cheese and mix.
29. Dip the frozen ravioli, two at a time, into the egg, then into the bread crumb mixture pressing gently to adhere the coating. Put the coated ravioli in the air fryer basket as you work. Spray every layer with some olive oil.
30. When all of the ravioli is coated, in the basket, and sprayed with oil, set or preheat the air fryer to 400°F. Fry for 10 to 13 minutes, shaking the basket halfway through, until the ravioli is hot and crisp on the outside.
31. Serve the ravioli with the dipping sauce.

NUTRITION: Calories 456 Protein 20g Fat 21g Carbs 46g

Roasted Baby Veggies with Dip

Basic Recipe

Preparation Time: 15 minutes **Cooking Time:** 21 minutes **Servings**: 6 **INGREDIENTS:**

- 2 cups baby potatoes
- 1½ cups baby carrots
- 1½ cups baby beets, peeled
- 12 garlic cloves, peeled
- 2 tablespoons olive oil, divided
- 1 teaspoon sea salt
- ⅛ teaspoon freshly ground black pepper
- ½ cup sour cream
- 3 tablespoons crumbled blue or feta cheese
- 1½ teaspoons dried thyme, divided
- 1 teaspoon dried marjoram

DIRECTIONS:

1. Put the potatoes, carrots, beets, and garlic cloves in the air fryer basket. Drizzle with 1 tablespoon of olive oil and sprinkle with the salt and pepper. Toss to coat.
2. Set or preheat the air fryer to 400°F. Put the basket in the air fryer. Roast for 8 minutes
3. Meanwhile, in a small bowl, combine the sour cream, cheese, and ½ teaspoon of thyme; mix and set aside.
4. Remove the basket and toss the vegetables. Put the basket back into the air fryer and continue roasting for another 8 minutes until the vegetables are almost tender. Drizzle with the remaining 1 tablespoon of oil and sprinkle with the marjoram and remaining 1 teaspoon of thyme; toss gently to coat.
5. Roast for 3 to 5 minutes more, or until the vegetables are tender. Serve with the dipping sauce.

NUTRITION: Calories 161 Protein 3g Fat 10g Carbs 16g

Crispy Buffalo Cauliflower Bites

Basic Recipe
Preparation Time: 10 minutes
Cooking Time: 20 minutes

Servings: 4
INGREDIENTS:

- 1 large head cauliflower, broken into florets
- 3 tablespoons hot sauce
- 2 tablespoons butter, melted
- 1 tablespoon honey
- ½ cup dried bread crumbs
- Cooking oil spray

DIRECTIONS:

6. In a large bowl, combine the cauliflower, hot sauce, butter, and honey and toss to coat the florets.
7. Sprinkle the cauliflower with the bread crumbs and toss to coat.
8. Working in two or three batches, place the florets in a single layer in the air fryer basket. Spritz with some cooking oil spray.
9. Set or preheat the air fryer to 375°F and roast 12 to 15 minutes, shaking the basket once during cooking time, until the cauliflower is crisp. Remove the cauliflower from the basket and put on a baking sheet in a 250°F oven to keep warm. Repeat with remaining cauliflower.
10. Serve warm with more hot sauce, blue cheese salad dressing, and celery sticks, if desired.

NUTRITION: Calories 116 Protein 4g Fat 5g Carbs 17g

Tandoori-Style Chickpeas

Basic Recipe
Preparation Time: 5 minutes **Cooking Time:** 15 minutes **Servings**: 6
INGREDIENTS:

- 1 (15-ounce) can chickpeas, dry outed and rinsed
- Cooking oil spray
- 2 teaspoons curry powder
- 1 teaspoon smoked paprika
- 1 teaspoon ground cumin
- ½ teaspoon cayenne pepper

DIRECTIONS:

11. Pat the chickpeas dry with paper towels and put in the air fryer basket.
12. Set or preheat the air fryer to 400°F. Place the basket in the air fryer and roast the chickpeas for 5 minutes
13. Remove the basket and spray the chickpeas with some cooking oil; toss.
14. Return the basket to the air fryer and roast for 8 minutes more, shaking the basket once during cooking time.
15. Meanwhile, in a small bowl combine the curry powder, paprika, cumin, and cayenne pepper.
16. Remove the basket from the air fryer and sprinkle with the spice mixture; toss to coat. Continue roasting for 2 minutes or until the chickpeas are fragrant.
17. Let the chickpeas cool for about 10 minutes, and then serve.

NUTRITION: Calories 72 Protein 4g Fat 1g Carbs 12g

Roasted Garlic and Onion Dip

Basic Recipe
Preparation Time: 10 minutes **Cooking Time**: 30 minutes **Servings**: 6
INGREDIENTS:

- 2 heads garlic
- 1 tablespoon olive oil
- 1 (8-ounce) package cream cheese, at room temperature
- ½ cup mayonnaise
- 2 tablespoons heavy (whipping) cream
- ¼ teaspoon sea salt
- 3 scallions, sliced
- 1 tablespoon minced fresh chives

DIRECTIONS:

1. Using a very sharp knife, cut off and discard the top
   1 inch of the garlic heads, exposing the cloves. Drizzle with each head with the olive oil.
2. Loosely wrap the garlic heads in aluminum foil and place in the air fryer basket.
3. Set or preheat the air fryer to 400°F. Put the basket in the air fryer and roast the garlic for 20 to 30 minutes, opening one foil packet after 20 minutes to see if the garlic cloves are soft. Continue roasting if needed.
4. Remove the foil packets from the air fryer, unwrap the garlic heads, and let cool on a wire rack for 20 minutes
5. Separate the garlic cloves from the head and remove the papery skins; place the cloves in a medium bowl. Mash together until smooth.
6. Beat the cream cheese with the mayonnaise, heavy cream, and salt until smooth. Beat in the roasted garlic paste until well mixed, and then stir in the scallions and chives. Serve.

NUTRITION: Calories 299 Protein 3g Fat 31g Carbs 3g

Parmesan Avocado Fries with Guacamole

Basic Recipe
Preparation Time: 15 minutes **Cooking Time:** 20 minutes **Servings**: 6
INGREDIENTS:

- 4 ripe avocados, divided
- 2 tablespoons freshly squeezed lemon juice
- ⅓ cup sour cream
- ½ teaspoon sea salt
- ⅛ teaspoon freshly ground black pepper
- ⅓ cup all-purpose flour
- 1 large egg
- 2 tablespoons whole milk
- ⅓ cup panko bread crumbs
- 3 tablespoons grated Parmesan cheese

DIRECTIONS:

1. Remove the flesh from 2 avocados (see Tip); place in a bowl and sprinkle with the lemon juice.
2. Mash the avocados and stir in the sour cream, salt, and pepper. Cover with plastic wrap, gently pressing the plastic over the surface of the guacamole. This will keep it from browning. Refrigerate.
3. Halve the remaining 2 avocados and gently twist to separate the halves. Remove the pits by striking them with a chef's knife; twist to remove the pit. Cut each half lengthwise into 4 slices, removing the peel.
4. Put the flour on a plate. Put the egg and milk into a shallow bowl and beat to combine. Put the bread crumbs and Parmesan cheese on a plate and combine.
5. Dip the avocado slices into the flour. Shake off any excess flour, then dip each slice into the egg mixture. Place in the bread crumbs, then flip to coat both sides. Shake off any excess crumbs.
6. Set or preheat the air fryer to 400°F. Working in batches if needed, put the coated avocado slices in a single layer in the air fryer basket. Put the basket in the air fryer and fry for 6 minutes, turning the slices over halfway through cooking time, until the fries are crisp.
7. Serve the fries with the guacamole.

NUTRITION: Calories 463 Protein 12g Fat 35g Carbs 31g

Southwest Egg Rolls

Basic Recipe

Preparation Time: 20 minutes **Cooking Time**: 30 minutes **Servings**: 10

INGREDIENTS:

- 1 cup frozen corn kernels, thawed
- 1 (15-ounce) can pinto beans, Dry outed and rinsed
- ½ cup chopped plum tomatoes, Dry outed
- 2 scallions, chopped
- 1 jalapeño pepper, minced
- 1½ cups shredded pepper Jack cheese
- 2 teaspoons chili powder
- ½ teaspoon dried oregano
- ¼ teaspoon garlic powder
- 1 (20-count) package egg roll wrappers
- Cooking oil spray

DIRECTIONS:

1. In a large bowl, combine the corn, pinto beans, tomatoes, scallions, and jalapeño pepper until well mixed.
2. Add the cheese, chili powder, oregano, and garlic powder and mix well.
3. Place an egg roll wrapper on a work surface. Brush the edges with a bit of water, then place a heaping 2 tablespoons of the corn mixture in the middle. Fold one edge of the egg roll wrapper over the filling, fold in the sides, and roll up. Press the seam to secure. Repeat with the remaining filling and egg roll wrappers.
4. Set or preheat the air fryer to 375°F. Work in batches, put the egg rolls in the basket in a single layer, making sure they don't touch each other. Spray with cooking oil.
5. Place the basket in the air fryer and fry for 10 minutes remove the basket and turn the egg rolls over; spray them once more with oil. Return the basket and fry for another 5 minutes or until crisp. Repeat with remaining egg rolls. Let cool for 10 minutes, and then serve.

NUTRITION: Calories 376 Protein 17g Fat 6g Carbs 68g

Jalapeño Poppers

Basic Recipe
Preparation Time: 15 minutes **Cooking Time:** 20 minutes **Servings**: 6 **INGREDIENTS:**

- 12 jalapeño peppers
- 4 ounces cream cheese, at room temperature
- 2 tablespoons mayonnaise
- 1 cup shredded Cheddar cheese
- ¼ cup grated Parmesan cheese
- All-purpose flour, for dusting
- 1 sheet frozen puff pastry, thawed

DIRECTIONS:

1. Halve the jalapeño peppers lengthwise, cut off the stem, and remove the membranes and seeds. Set aside.
2. In a medium bowl, combine the cream cheese and mayonnaise and beat until smooth. Mix in the Cheddar and Parmesan cheeses. Fill 12 of the jalapeño pepper halves with equal parts of this mixture, then top them with the other pepper half to make 12 poppers.
3. Dust a clean work surface with some flour. Roll out the puff pastry into a 12-inch square. Cut the square in half, then cut each half into twelve 1-by-6-inch rectangular strips.
4. Wind a puff pastry strip around a filled jalapeño half in a spiral shape. Repeat for all the puff pastry strips and stuffed jalapeños.
5. Work in batches, put the filled and wrapped jalapeño peppers in the air fryer basket in a single layer; don't let them touch each other.
6. Set or preheat the air fryer to 400°F. Put the basket in the air fryer and fry for 10 to 12 minutes or until the pastry is golden brown. Repeat with remaining poppers.

NUTRITION: Calories 238 Protein 9g Fat 20g Carbs 6g

Sweet Potato Tots

Basic Recipe
Preparation Time: 15 minutes **Cooking Time**: 40 minutes **Servings:** 8 **INGREDIENTS:**

- 1 (15-ounce) can sweet potatoes, Dry outed
- ½ cup grated Parmesan cheese
- 1 large egg white
- ½ teaspoon sea salt
- ⅛ teaspoon nutmeg
- 1 cup crushed cracker crumbs, such as Ritz or club crackers
- Cooking oil spray

DIRECTIONS:

1. Put the sweet potatoes in a medium bowl and mash them. Stir in the Parmesan cheese, egg white, salt, and nutmeg until well mixed.
2. Create the tots by forming 1 tablespoon of the sweet potato mixture into rounded rectangles.
3. Put the cracker crumbs on a plate. Roll each of the tots in the crumbs to coat.
4. Work in batches, put the tots in a single layer in the air fryer basket and spray with the cooking oil.
5. Set or preheat the air fryer to 400°F. Put the basket in the air fryer and fry for 14 to 17 minutes, turning once, until the tots are crisp and golden brown. Repeat with the remaining sweet potato mixture; serve hot.

NUTRITION: Calories 109 Protein 4g Fat 4g Carbs 16g

Radish Chips

Basic Recipe
Preparation Time: 20 minutes **Cooking Time**: 18 minutes **Servings:** 8
INGREDIENTS:

- 8 large radishes
- 1 tablespoon olive oil
- ½ teaspoon sea salt
- 1 teaspoon curry powder

DIRECTIONS:

1. Scrub the radishes and trim off the stem and root ends.
2. Using a sharp knife, slice the radishes into thin rounds, about ⅛ inch thick. Pat the radish slices dry with a paper towel.
3. Put the radishes into the air fryer basket and Drizzle with the oil; toss to coat. Sprinkle with the salt and toss again.
4. Set or preheat the air fryer to 400°F. Place the basket in the air fryer and fry for 14 to 18 minutes, tossing once during cooking time, until the radish chips are crisp and light golden brown. Remove the basket; sprinkle the chips with the curry powder and toss.
5. Serve immediately or let cool and store in an airtight container at room temperature for up to 3 days.

NUTRITION: Calories 17 Protein 0g Fat 2g Carbs 1g

Spinach-Cranberry Turnovers

Basic Recipe
Preparation Time: 20 minutes **Cooking Time**: 30 minutes **Servings**: 6
INGREDIENTS:

- 4 ounces cream cheese, at room temperature
    - 2 tablespoons sour cream
    - 1 cup frozen chopped spinach, thawed and Dry outed
    - ⅓ cup dried cranberries, chopped
    - 3 (9-by-14-inch) sheets frozen phyllo dough, thawed
    - 3 tablespoons butter, melted

DIRECTIONS:

1. In a medium bowl, beat the cream cheese and sour cream until blended. Stir in the spinach and cranberries until well mixed. Set aside.
2. Place the phyllo dough on the work surface and cover with a damp towel. Remove one sheet of phyllo and cut it into four 3½-by-9-inch rectangles.
3. Place a tablespoon of the filling at the bottom of one of the rectangles, with the short side facing you. Fold the phyllo into triangles (like you would fold a flag), then brush with butter to seal the edges. Repeat with remaining phyllo, filling, and butter.
4. Set or preheat the air fryer to 375°F. Put 4 to 6 triangles in the air fryer basket in a single layer. Put the basket in the air fryer and Bake it for 11 to 12 minutes or until the triangles are golden brown, turning over halfway through cooking time. Repeat with the remaining turnovers. Serve.

NUTRITION: Calories 189 Protein 3g Fat 14g Carbs: 15g

Mushroom Toast with Ginger and Sesame

Intermediate Recipe Preparation Time: 20 minutes **Cooking Time**: 30 minutes
Servings: 6 **INGREDIENTS:**

- 2 teaspoons olive oil
- 2 (4-ounce) cans sliced mushrooms, Dry outed
- 3 scallions, sliced
- 1 tablespoon grated fresh ginger
- 1 tablespoon soy sauce
- 3 slices whole-wheat bread
- 2 tablespoons sesame seeds

DIRECTIONS:

1. Heat the olive oil in a medium saucepan over medium heat. Add the mushrooms and cook, stirring often, for 3 to 4 minutes or until the mushrooms are dry.
2. Add the scallions, ginger, and soy sauce and cook for another 3 minutes or until the mushrooms have absorbed the soy sauce.
3. Transfer the mixture to a blender or food processor and process until it forms a paste.
4. Cut the bread slices into fourths, making triangles. Spread the mushroom mixture onto the bread triangles, dividing evenly, then sprinkle with the sesame seeds.
5. Set or preheat the air fryer to 375°F. Work in batches, place the triangles in the air fryer basket in a single layer. Fry for 7 to 8 minutes or until the toast is crisp. Repeat with the remaining triangles. Serve.

NUTRITION: Calories 80 Protein 4g Fat 4g Carbs 9g

Grape Focaccia Bites

Basic Recipe
Preparation Time: 15 minutes **Cooking Time**: 30 minutes **Servings:** 4
INGREDIENTS:

- 1 cup all-purpose flour
- ½ teaspoon sea salt
- 1½ teaspoons baking powder
- ⅓ cup whole milk
- 4 tablespoons olive oil, divided
- ⅔ cup halved red grapes
- 2 teaspoons fresh thyme

DIRECTIONS:

1. In a medium bowl, combine the flour, salt, and baking powder and mix well.
2. Add the milk and 3 tablespoons of the olive oil and stir just until a dough form. Divide the dough into two balls. Cut two pieces of parchment paper to fit in your air fryer basket. Press the dough onto each piece of paper, spreading the dough so it almost fills the paper.
3. Press down with your fingers to dimple the dough. Drizzle with both with the remaining 1 tablespoon olive oil.
4. Put the grapes on the dough, cut-side down, and press down gently. Sprinkle with the thyme. Place one of the parchment pieces with dough in the air fryer basket. Set or preheat the air fryer to 350°F. Put the basket in the air fryer and Bake it for 11 to
14 minutes or until the bread is golden brown. Remove the focaccia and repeat with the remaining dough.
5. Cut into squares and serve.

NUTRITION: Calories 259 Protein 4g Fat 15g Carbs 28g

LUNCH

Duck and Tea Sauce

Basic Recipe
Preparation Time: 10 minutes **Cooking Time:** 20 minutes **Servings:** 4
INGREDIENTS:

- 2 duck breast halves, boneless

  - 2 and ¼ cup chicken stock
  - ¾ cup shallot, chopped
  - 1 and ½ cup orange juice
  - Salt and black pepper to the taste
  - 3 teaspoons earl gray tea leaves
  - 3 tablespoons butter, melted
  - 1 tablespoon honey

DIRECTIONS:

1. Season duck breast halves with salt and pepper, put in preheated air fryer and cook at 360 degrees F for 10 minutes Meanwhile, heat up a pan with the butter over medium heat, add shallot, stir and cook for 2-3 minutes Add stock, stir and cook for another minute. Add orange juice, tea leaves and honey, stir, cook for 2-3 minutes more and strain into a bowl. Divide duck on plates, Drizzle with tea sauce all over and serve. Enjoy!

NUTRITION: Calories 228 Fat 11 Carbs 20 Protein 12

Marinated Duck Breasts

Intermediate Recipe Preparation Time: 1 day **Cooking Time:** 20 minutes
Servings: 2 **INGREDIENTS:**

- 2 duck breasts
- 1 cup white wine
- ¼ cup soy sauce
- 2 garlic cloves, minced
- 6 tarragon springs
- Salt and black pepper to the taste
- 1 tablespoon butter
- ¼ cup sherry wine

DIRECTIONS:

1. In a bowl, mix duck breasts with white wine, soy sauce, garlic, tarragon, salt and pepper, toss well and keep in the fridge for 1 day. Transfer duck breasts to your preheated air fryer at 350 degrees F and cook for 10 minutes, flipping halfway.
2. Meanwhile, pour the marinade in a pan, heat up over medium heat, add butter and sherry, stir, bring to a simmer, cook for 5 minutes and take off heat. Divide duck breasts on plates, Drizzle with sauce all over and serve. Enjoy!

NUTRITION: Calories 475 Fat 12 Carbs 10 Protein 48

Chicken and Radish Mix

Basic Recipe
Preparation Time: 10 minutes **Cooking Time:** 30 minutes **Servings:** 4
INGREDIENTS:

- 4 chicken things, bone-in
- Salt and black pepper to the taste
- 1 tablespoon olive oil
- 1 cup chicken stock
- 6 radishes, halved
- 1 teaspoon sugar
- 3 carrots cut into thin sticks
- 2 tablespoon chives, chopped

DIRECTIONS:

1. Heat up a pan that fits your air fryer over medium heat, add stock, carrots, sugar and radishes, stir gently, reduce heat to medium, cover pot partly and simmer for 20 minutes Rub chicken with olive oil, season with salt and pepper, put in your air fryer and cook at 350 degrees F for 4 minutes.
2. Add chicken to radish mix, toss, introduce everything in your air fryer, cook for 4 minutes more, divide among plates and serve. Enjoy!

NUTRITION: Calories 237 Fat 10 Carbs 19 Protein 29

Chicken Breasts and BBQ Chili Sauce

Basic Recipe
Preparation Time: 10 minutes **Cooking Time:** 20 minutes **Servings:** 6
INGREDIENTS:

- 2 cups chili sauce
- 2 cups ketchup
- 1 cup pear jelly
- ¼ cup honey
- ½ teaspoon liquid smoke
- 1 teaspoon chili powder
- 1 teaspoon mustard powder
- 1 teaspoon sweet paprika
- Salt and black pepper to the taste
- 1 teaspoon garlic powder
- 6 chicken breasts, skinless and boneless

DIRECTIONS:

1. Season chicken breasts with salt and pepper, put in preheated air fryer and cook at 350 degrees F for 10 minutes Meanwhile, heat up a pan with the chili sauce over medium heat, add ketchup, pear jelly, honey, liquid smoke, chili powder, mustard powder, sweet paprika, salt, pepper and the garlic powder, stir, bring to a simmer and cook for 10 minutes Add air fried chicken breasts, toss well, divide among plates and serve. Enjoy!

NUTRITION: Calories 473 Fat 13 Carbs 39 Protein 33

Duck Breasts and Mango Mix

Intermediate Recipe Preparation Time: 1 hour **Cooking Time:** 20 minutes
Servings: 4 **INGREDIENTS:**

- 4 duck breasts
- 1 and ½ tablespoons lemongrass, chopped
- 3 tablespoons lemon juice
- 2 tablespoons olive oil
- Salt and black pepper to the taste
- 3 garlic cloves, minced
- For the mango mix:

- 1 mango, peeled and chopped
- 1 tablespoon coriander, chopped
- 1 red onion, chopped
- 1 tablespoon sweet chili sauce
- 1 and ½ tablespoon lemon juice
- 1 teaspoon ginger, grated
- ¾ teaspoon sugar

DIRECTIONS:

1. In a bowl, mix duck breasts with salt, pepper, lemongrass, 3 tablespoons lemon juice, olive oil and garlic, toss well, keep in the fridge for 1 hour, transfer to your air fryer and cook at 360 degrees F for 10 minutes, flipping once. Meanwhile, in a bowl, mix mango with coriander, onion, chili sauce, lemon juice, ginger and sugar and toss well. Divide duck on plates, add mango mix on the side and serve. Enjoy!

NUTRITION: Calories 465 Fat 11 Carbs 29 Protein 38

Quick Creamy Chicken Casserole

Basic Recipe

Preparation Time: 10 minutes **Cooking Time:** 15 minutes **Servings:** 4 **INGREDIENTS:**

- 10 ounces spinach, chopped
- 4 tablespoons butter
- 3 tablespoons flour
- 1 and ½ cups milk
- ½ cup parmesan, grated
- ½ cup heavy cream
- Salt and black pepper to the taste
- 2 cup chicken breasts, skinless, boneless and cubed
- 1 cup bread crumbs

DIRECTIONS:

1. Heat up a pan with the butter over medium heat, add flour and stir well. Add milk, heavy cream and parmesan, stir well, cook for 1-2 minutes more and take off heat. In a pan that fits your air fryer, spread chicken and spinach. Add salt and pepper and toss. Add cream mix and spread, sprinkle bread crumbs on top, introduce in your air fryer and cook at 350 for 12 minutes Divide chicken and spinach mix on plates and serve. Enjoy!

NUTRITION: Calories 321 Fat 9 Carbs 22 Protein 17

Chicken and Peaches

Basic Recipe

Preparation Time: 10 minutes **Cooking Time:** 30 minutes **Servings:** 6 **INGREDIENTS:**

- 1 whole chicken, cut into medium pieces
- ¾ cup water
- 1/3 cup honey
- Salt and black pepper to the taste
- ¼ cup olive oil
- 4 peaches, halved

DIRECTIONS:

1. Put the water in a pot, bring to a simmer over medium heat, add honey, whisk really well and leave aside. Rub chicken pieces with the oil, season with salt and pepper, place in your air fryer's basket and cook at 350 degrees F for 10 minutes Brush chicken with some of the honey mix, cook for 6 minutes more, flip again, brush one more time with the honey mix and cook for 7 minutes more. Divide chicken pieces on plates and keep warm. Brush peaches with what's left of the honey marinade, place them in your air fryer and cook them for 3 minutes Divide among plates next to chicken pieces and serve. Enjoy!

NUTRITION: Calories 430 Fat 14 Carbs 15 Protein 20

Tea Glazed Chicken

Basic Recipe

Preparation Time: 10 minutes **Cooking Time:** 30 minutes **Servings:** 6

INGREDIENTS:

- ½ cup apricot preserves
- ½ cup pineapple preserves
- 6 chicken legs
- 1 cup hot water
- 6 black tea bags
- 1 tablespoon soy sauce
- 1 onion, chopped
- ¼ teaspoon red pepper flakes
- 1 tablespoon olive oil
- Salt and black pepper to the taste
- 6 chicken legs

DIRECTIONS:

1. Put the hot water in a bowl, add tea bags, leave aside covered for 10 minutes, discard bags at the end and transfer tea to another bowl. Add soy sauce, pepper flakes, apricot and pineapple preserves, whisk really well and take off heat.
2. Season chicken with salt and pepper, rub with oil, put in your air fryer and cook at 350 degrees F for 5 minutes Spread onion on the bottom of a baking dish that fits your air fryer, add chicken pieces, Drizzle with the tea glaze on top, introduce in your air fryer and cook at 320 degrees F for 25 minutes Divide everything on plates and serve. Enjoy!

NUTRITION: Calories 298 Fat 14 Carbs 14 Protein 30

Ratatouille

Basic Recipe
Preparation Time: 10 minutes **Cooking Time:** 20 minutes **Servings:** 4
INGREDIENTS:

- 4 Roma tomatoes, seeded and chopped
- 3 garlic cloves, sliced
- 1 baby eggplant, peeled and chopped
  - 1 red bell pepper, chopped
  - 1 yellow bell pepper, chopped
  - 1 small onion, chopped
  - 1 teaspoon Italian seasoning
  - 1 teaspoon olive oil

DIRECTIONS:

1. In a medium metal bowl, gently combine the tomatoes, garlic, eggplant, red and yellow bell peppers, onion, Italian seasoning, and olive oil. Place the bowl in the air fryer. Roast for 12 to 16 minutes, stirring once, until the vegetables are tender. Serve warm or cold.

NUTRITION: Calories 69 Fat 2g Protein 2g Carbs 11g

Vegetable Egg Rolls

Basic Recipe
Preparation Time: 15 minutes **Cooking Time:** 10 minutes **Servings:** 4
INGREDIENTS:

- ½ cup chopped yellow summer squash
- ⅓ cup grated carrot
- ½ cup chopped red bell pepper
- 2 scallions, white and green parts, chopped
- 1 teaspoon low-sodium soy sauce
- 4 egg roll wrappers (see Tip)
- 1 tablespoon cornstarch
- 1 egg, beaten

DIRECTIONS:

1. In a medium bowl, mix the yellow squash, carrot, red bell pepper, scallions, and soy sauce.
2. Place the egg roll wrappers on a work surface. Top each with about 3 tablespoons of the vegetable mixture.
3. In a small bowl, thoroughly mix the cornstarch and egg. Brush some egg mixture on the edges of each wrapper. Roll up the wrappers, folding over the sides so the filling is contained. Brush the egg mixture on the outside of each egg roll.
4. Air-fry it for 7 to 10 minutes or until brown and crunchy then serve immediately.

NUTRITION: Calories 130 Fat 2g Protein 6g Carbs 23g

Grilled Cheese and Greens Sandwiches

Basic Recipe

Preparation Time: 15 minutes **Cooking Time:** 10 minutes **Servings:** 4

INGREDIENTS:

- 1½ cups chopped mixed greens (kale, chard, collards; see Tip)
- 2 garlic cloves, thinly sliced
- 2 teaspoons olive oil
- 2 slices low-sodium low-fat Swiss cheese
- 4 slices low-sodium whole-wheat bread
- Olive oil spray, for coating the sandwiches

DIRECTIONS:

1. In a 6-by-2-inch pan, mix the greens, garlic, and olive oil. Cook in the air fryer for 4 to 5 minutes, stirring once, until the vegetables are tender. Dry out, if necessary.
2. Make 2 sandwiches, dividing half of the greens and 1 slice of Swiss cheese between 2 slices of bread. Lightly spray the outsides of the sandwiches with olive oil spray.
3. Grill the sandwiches in the air fryer for 6 to 8 minutes, turning with tongs halfway through, until the bread is toasted and the cheese melts.
4. Cut each sandwich in half to serve.

NUTRITION: Calories 176 Fat 6g Protein 10g Carbs 24g

Veggie Tuna Melts

Basic Recipe
Preparation Time: 15 minutes **Cooking Time:** 10 minutes **Servings:** 4
INGREDIENTS:

- 2 low-sodium whole-wheat English muffins split
- 1 (6-ounce) can chunk light low-sodium tuna, Dry outed
- 1 cup shredded carrot
- ⅓ cup chopped mushrooms
- 2 scallions, white and green parts, sliced
- ⅓ cup nonfat Greek yogurt
- 2 tablespoons low-sodium stone-ground mustard
- 2 slices low-sodium low-fat Swiss cheese, halved

DIRECTIONS:

1. Place the English muffin halves in the air fryer basket. Grill for 3 to 4 minutes, or until crisp. Remove from the basket and set aside.
2. In a medium bowl, thoroughly mix the tuna, carrot, mushrooms, scallions, yogurt, and mustard. Top each half of the muffins with one-fourth of the tuna mixture and a half slice of Swiss cheese.
3. Grill in the air fryer for 4 to 7 minutes, or until the tuna mixture is hot and the cheese melts and starts to brown. Serve immediately.

NUTRITION: Calories 191 Fat 4g Protein 23g Carbs 16g

California Melts

Basic Recipe
Preparation Time: 10 minutes **Cooking Time:** 5 minutes **Servings:** 4
INGREDIENTS:

- 2 low-sodium whole-wheat English muffins split
- 2 tablespoons nonfat Greek yogurt
- 8 fresh baby spinach leaves
- 1 ripe tomato, cut into 4 slices
- ½ ripe avocados, peeled, pitted, and sliced lengthwise (see Tip)
- 8 fresh basil leaves
- 4 tablespoons crumbled fat-free low-sodium feta cheese, divided

DIRECTIONS:

1. Put the English muffin halves into the air fryer. Toast for 2 minutes, or until light golden brown. Transfer to a work surface.
2. Spread each muffin half with 1½ teaspoons of yogurt.
3. Top each muffin half with 2 spinach leaves, 1 tomato slice, one-fourth of the avocado, and 2 basil leaves. Sprinkle each with 1 tablespoon of feta cheese. Toast the sandwiches in the air fryer for 3 to 4 minutes, or until the cheese softens and the sandwich is hot. Serve immediately.

NUTRITION: Calories 110 Fat 3g Protein 8g Carbs 13g

Vegetable Pita Sandwiches

Basic Recipe

Preparation Time: 10 minutes **Cooking Time:** 20 minutes **Servings:** 4 **INGREDIENTS:**

- 1 baby eggplant peeled and chopped (see Tip)
- 1 red bell pepper, sliced
- ½ cup diced red onion
- ½ cup shredded carrot
- 1 teaspoon olive oil
- ⅓ cup low-fat Greek yogurt
- ½ teaspoon dried tarragon
- 2 low-sodium whole-wheat pita breads, halved crosswise

DIRECTIONS:

4. In a 6-by-2-inch pan, stir together the eggplant, red bell pepper, red onion, carrot, and olive oil. Put the vegetable mixture into the air fryer basket and roast for 7 to 9 minutes, stirring once, until the vegetables are tender. Dry out if necessary.
5. In a small bowl, thoroughly mix the yogurt and tarragon until well combined.
6. Stir the yogurt mixture into the vegetables. Stuff one-fourth of this mixture into each pita pocket.
7. Place the sandwiches in the air fryer and cook for 2 to 3 minutes, or until the bread is toasted. Serve immediately.

NUTRITION: Calories 176 Fat 4g Protein 7g Carbs 27g

Falafel

Basic Recipe

Preparation Time: 10 minutes **Cooking Time:** 20 minutes **Servings:** 4 **INGREDIENTS:**

- 1 (16-ounce) can no-salt-added chickpeas rinsed and Dry outed
- ⅓ cup whole-wheat pastry flour
- ⅓ cup minced red onion
- 2 garlic cloves, minced
- 2 tablespoons minced fresh cilantro
- 1 tablespoon olive oil
- ½ teaspoon ground cumin
- ¼ teaspoon cayenne pepper

DIRECTIONS:

8. In a medium bowl, mash the chickpeas with a potato masher until mostly smooth.
9. Stir in the pastry flour, red onion, garlic, cilantro, olive oil, cumin, and cayenne until well mixed. Firm the chickpea mixture into 12 balls. Air-fry the falafel balls, in batches, for 11 to 13 minutes, or until the falafel are firm and light golden brown. Serve.

NUTRITION: Calories 172 Fat 5g Protein 7g Carbs 25g

Stuffed Tomatoes

Basic Recipe
Preparation Time: 5 minutes **Cooking Time:** 20 minutes **Servings:** 4
INGREDIENTS:

- 4 medium beefsteak tomatoes, rinsed and patted dry
- 1 medium onion, chopped
- ½ cup grated carrot
- 1 garlic clove, minced
- 2 teaspoons olive oil
- 2 cups fresh baby spinach
- ¼ cup crumbled low-sodium feta cheese
- ½ teaspoon dried basil

DIRECTIONS:

10. Cut about ½ inch off the top of each tomato. Gently hollow them out (see Tip), leaving a wall about ½ inch thick. Dry out the tomatoes, upside down, on paper towels while you prepare the filling.
11. In a 6-by-2-inch pan, mix the onion, carrot, garlic, and olive oil. Bake it for 4 to 6 minutes, or until the vegetables are crisp-tender.
12. Stir in the spinach, feta cheese, and basil.
13. Fill each tomato with one-fourth of the vegetable mixture. Bake the tomatoes in the air fryer basket for 12 to 14 minutes, or until hot and tender.
14. Serve immediately.

NUTRITION: Calories 79 Fat 3g Protein 3g Carbs 9g

Loaded Mini Potatoes

Basic Recipe
Preparation Time: 5 minutes **Cooking Time:** 25 minutes **Servings:** 2
INGREDIENTS:

- 24 small new potatoes, or creamer potatoes, rinsed, scrubbed, and patted dry
- 1 teaspoon olive oil
- ½ cup low-fat Greek yogurt
- 1 tablespoon low-sodium stone-ground mustard (see Tip)
- ½ teaspoon dried basil
- 3 Roma tomatoes, seeded and chopped
- 2 scallions, white and green parts, chopped
- 2 tablespoons chopped fresh chives

DIRECTIONS:

1. In a large bowl, toss the potatoes with the olive oil. Transfer to the air fryer basket. Roast for 20 to 25
   minutes, shaking the basket once, until the potatoes are crisp on the outside and tender within. Meanwhile, in a small bowl, stir together the yogurt, mustard, and basil.
2. Place the potatoes on a serving platter and carefully smash each one slightly with the bottom of a drinking glass. Top the potatoes with the yogurt mixture. Sprinkle with the tomatoes, scallions, and chives. Serve immediately.

NUTRITION: Calories 100 Fat 2g Protein 5g Carbs 19g

Crustless Veggie Quiche

Basic Recipe
Preparation Time: 5 minutes **Cooking Time:** 20 minutes **Servings:** 3
INGREDIENTS:

- 4 egg whites
- 1 egg
- 1 cup frozen chopped spinach, thawed and Dry outed
- 1 red bell pepper, chopped
- ½ cup chopped mushrooms
- ⅓ cup minced red onion
- 1 tablespoon low-sodium mustard
- 1 slice low-sodium low-fat Swiss cheese, torn into small pieces
- Nonstick cooking spray with flour, for greasing the pan

DIRECTIONS:

1. In a medium bowl, beat the egg whites and egg until blended.
2. Stir in the spinach, red bell pepper, mushrooms, onion, and mustard.
3. Mix in the Swiss cheese.
4. Spray a 6-by-2-inch pan with nonstick cooking spray.
5. Pour the egg mixture into the prepared pan.
6. Bake it for 18 to 22 minutes, or until the egg mixture is puffed, light golden brown, and set. Cool for 5 minutes before serving.

NUTRITION: Calories 76 Fat 3g Protein 8g Carbs 4g

Scrambled Eggs with Broccoli and Spinach

Basic Recipe
Preparation Time: 15 minutes **Cooking Time:** 20 minutes **Servings:** 4
INGREDIENTS:

- 2 teaspoons unsalted butter
- 1 medium onion, chopped
- 1 red bell pepper, chopped
- 1 cup small broccoli florets
- ½ teaspoon dried marjoram
- 6 egg whites
- 2 eggs
- 1 cup fresh baby spinach

DIRECTIONS:

7. In a 6-by-2-inch pan in the air fryer, heat the butter for 1 minute, or until it melts.
8. Add the onion, red bell pepper, broccoli, marjoram, and 1 tablespoon of water. Air-fry for 3 to 5 minutes, or until the vegetables are crisp-tender. Dry out, if necessary.
9. Meanwhile, in a medium bowl, beat the egg whites and eggs until frothy.
10. Add the spinach and eggs to the vegetables in the pan. Air-fry for 8 to 12 minutes, stirring three times during cooking, until the eggs are set and fluffy and reach 160°F on a meat thermometer. Serve immediately.

NUTRITION: Calories 86 Fat 3g Protein 8g Carbs 5g

Beans and Greens Pizza

Basic Recipe
Preparation Time: 10 minutes **Cooking Time:** 20 minutes **Servings:** 4
INGREDIENTS:

- ¾ cup whole-wheat pastry flour
- ½ teaspoon low-sodium baking powder
- 1 tablespoon olive oil, divided
- 1 cup chopped kale
- 2 cups chopped fresh baby spinach
- 1 cup canned no-salt-added cannellini beans, rinsed and Dry outed (see Tip)
- ½ teaspoon dried thyme
- 1 piece low-sodium string cheese, torn into pieces

DIRECTIONS:

11. In a small bowl, mix the pastry flour and baking powder until well combined.
12. Add ¼ cup of water and 2 teaspoons of olive oil. Mix until a dough form.
13. On a floured surface, press or roll the dough into a 7-inch round. Set aside while you cook the greens.In a 6-by-2-inch pan, mix the kale, spinach, and remaining teaspoon of the olive oil. Air-fry it for 3 to 5 minutes until the greens are wilted. Dry out well.
14. Put the pizza dough into the air fryer basket. Top with the greens, cannellini beans, thyme, and string cheese. Air-fry for 11 to 14 minutes or until the crust is golden brown and the cheese is melted. Cut into quarters to serve.

NUTRITION: Calories 175 Fat 5g Protein 9g Carbs 24g

Grilled Chicken Mini Pizzas

Basic Recipe
Preparation Time: 15 minutes **Cooking Time:** 10 minutes **Servings:** 4
INGREDIENTS:

- 2 low-sodium whole-wheat pita breads, split (see Tip)
- ½ cup no-salt-added tomato sauce
- 1 garlic clove, minced
- ½ teaspoon dried oregano
- 1 cooked shredded chicken breast
- 1 cup chopped button mushrooms
- ½ cup chopped red bell pepper
- ½ cup shredded part skim low-sodium mozzarella cheese

DIRECTIONS:

1. Place the pita breads, insides up, on a work surface.
2. In a small bowl, stir together the tomato sauce, garlic, and oregano. Spread about 2 tablespoons of the sauce over each pita half.
3. Top each with ¼ cup of shredded chicken, ¼ cup of mushrooms, and 2 tablespoons of red bell pepper. Sprinkle with the mozzarella cheese.
4. Bake the pizzas for 3 to 6 minutes, or until the cheese melts and starts to brown and the pita bread is crisp. Serve immediately.

NUTRITION: Calories 249 Fat 7g Protein 23g Carbs 25g

Chicken Croquettes

Basic Recipe

Preparation Time: 15 minutes **Cooking Time:** 10 minutes **Servings:** 4 **INGREDIENTS:**

- 2 (5-ounce) cooked chicken breasts, finely chopped (see Tip)
- ⅓ cup low-fat Greek yogurt
- 3 tablespoons minced red onion
- 2 celery stalks, minced
- 1 garlic clove, minced
- ½ teaspoon dried basil
- 2 egg whites, divided
- 2 slices low-sodium whole-wheat bread, crumbled

DIRECTIONS:

1. In a medium bowl, thoroughly mix the chicken, yogurt, red onion, celery, garlic, basil, and 1 egg white. Form the mixture into 8 ovals and gently press into shape.
2. In a shallow bowl, beat the remaining egg white until foamy.
3. Put the bread crumbs on a plate.
4. Dip the chicken croquettes into the egg white and then into the bread crumbs to coat.
5. Air-fry the croquettes, in batches, for 7 to 10 minutes, or until the croquettes reach an internal temperature of 160°F on a meat thermometer and their color is golden brown. Serve immediately.

NUTRITION: Calories 207 Fat 4g Protein 32g Carbs 8g,

Pork Chops and Yogurt Sauce

Basic Recipe

Preparation Time: 10 minutes **Cooking Time:** 30 minutes **Servings:** 4 **INGREDIENTS:**

- 2 tablespoons avocado oil
- 2 pounds pork chops

- 1 cup yogurt
- 2 garlic cloves, minced
- 1 teaspoon turmeric powder
- Salt and black pepper to the taste
- 2 tablespoon oregano, chopped

DIRECTIONS:

1. In the air fryer's pan, mix the pork chops with the yogurt and the other ingredients, toss and cook at 400 degrees F for 30 minutes
2. Divide the mix between plates and serve.

NUTRITION: Calories 301 Fat 7 Carbs 19 Protein 22

Lamb and Macadamia Nuts Mix

Basic Recipe
Preparation Time: 10 minutes **Cooking Time:** 20 minutes **Servings:** 4
INGREDIENTS:

- 2 pounds lamb stew meat, cubed
- 2 tablespoons macadamia nuts, peeled
- 1 cup baby spinach
- ½ cup beef stock
- 2 garlic cloves, minced
- Salt and black pepper to the taste
- 1 tablespoon oregano, chopped

DIRECTIONS:

3. In the air fryer's pan, mix the lamb with the nuts and the other ingredients,
4. Cook at 380 degrees F for 20 minutes,
5. Divide between plates and serve.

NUTRITION: Calories 280 Fat 12 Carbs 20 Protein 19

Beef, Cucumber and Eggplants

Basic Recipe
Preparation Time: 10 minutes **Cooking Time:** 20 minutes **Servings:** 4
INGREDIENTS:

- 1pound beef stew meat, cut into strips
- 2eggplants, cubed
- 2cucumbers, sliced
- 2garlic cloves, minced
- 1cup heavy cream
- 2tablespoons olive oil
- Salt and black pepper to the taste

DIRECTIONS:

6. In a baking dish that fits your air fryer, mix the beef with the eggplants and the other ingredients, toss, introduce the pan in the fryer and cook at 400 degrees F for 20 minutes
7. Divide everything into bowls and serve.

NUTRITION: Calories 283 Fat 11 Carbs 22 Protein 14

Rosemary Pork and Artichokes

Basic Recipe

Preparation Time: 10 minutes **Cooking Time:** 25 minutes **Servings:** 4

INGREDIENTS:

- 1pound pork stew meat, cubed
- 1cup canned artichoke hearts, Dry outed and halved
- 2tablespoons olive oil
- 2tablespoons rosemary, chopped
- ½ teaspoon cumin, ground
- ½ teaspoon nutmeg, ground
- ½ cup sour cream
- Salt and black pepper to the taste

DIRECTIONS:

8. In a pan that fits your air fryer, mix the pork with the artichokes and the other ingredients, introduce in the fryer and cook at 400 degrees F for 25 minutes
9. Divide everything into bowls and serve.

NUTRITION: Calories 280 Fat 13 Carbs 22 Protein 18

Mustard Lamb Loin Chops

Basic Recipe

Preparation Time: 15 minutes **Cooking Time:** 30 minutes **Servings:** 4

INGREDIENTS:

- 4-ounceslamb loin chops
- 2 tablespoons Dijon mustard
- 1 tablespoon fresh lemon juice
- ½ teaspoon olive oil
- 1 teaspoon dried tarragon
- Salt and black pepper, to taste

DIRECTIONS:

10. Preheat the Air fryer to 390-degree F and grease an Air fryer basket.
11. Mix the mustard, lemon juice, oil, tarragon, salt, and black pepper in a large bowl.
12. Coat the chops generously with the mustard mixture and arrange in the Air fryer basket.
13. Cook for about 15 minutes, flipping once in between and dish out to serve hot.

NUTRITION: Calories 433, Fat 17.6g, Carbs 0.6g, Protein 64.1g,

Herbed Lamb Chops

Basic Recipe
Preparation Time: 10 minutes **Cooking Time:** 10 minutes **Servings:** 2
INGREDIENTS:

- 4: 4-ounceslamb chops
- 1 tablespoon fresh lemon juice
- 1 tablespoon olive oil
- 1 teaspoon dried rosemary
- 1 teaspoon dried thyme
- 1 teaspoon dried oregano
- ½ teaspoon ground cumin
- ½ teaspoon ground coriander
- Salt and black pepper, to taste

DIRECTIONS:

14. Preheat the Air fryer to 390-degree F and grease an Air fryer basket.
15. Mix the lemon juice, oil, herbs, and spices in a large bowl.
16. Coat the chops generously with the herb mixture and refrigerate to marinate for about 1 hour.
17. Arrange the chops in the Air fryer basket and cook for about 7 minutes, flipping once in between.
18. Dish out the lamb chops in a platter and serve hot.

NUTRITION: Calories 491 Fat 24g Carbs 1.6g Protein 64g

Za'atar Lamb Loin Chops

Basic Recipe

Preparation Time: 10 minutes **Cooking Time:** 30 minutes **Servings:** 4

INGREDIENTS:

- 8: 3½-ouncesbone-in lamb loin chops, trimmed
- 3 garlic cloves, crushed
- 1 tablespoon fresh lemon juice
- 1 teaspoon olive oil
- 1 tablespoon Za'ataro
- Salt and black pepper, to taste

DIRECTIONS:

19. Preheat the Air fryer to 400-degree F and grease an Air fryer basket.
20. Mix the garlic, lemon juice, oil, Za'atar, salt, and black pepper in a large bowl
21. Coat the chops generously with the herb mixture and arrange the chops in the Air fryer basket.
22. Cook for about 15 minutes, flipping twice in between and dish out the lamb chops to serve hot.

NUTRITION: Calories 433 Fat 17.6g Carbs 0.6g Protein 64.1g

Pesto Coated Rack of Lamb

Basic Recipe

Preparation Time: 15 minutes **Cooking Time:** 15 minutes **Servings:** 4

INGREDIENTS:

- ½ bunch fresh mint
- 1: 1½-poundsrack of lamb
- 1 garlic clove
- ¼ cup extra-virgin olive oil
- ½ tablespoon honey
- Salt and black pepper, to taste

DIRECTIONS:

23. Preheat the Air fryer to 200-degree F and grease an Air fryer basket.
24. Put the mint, garlic, oil, honey, salt, and black pepper in a blender and pulse until smooth to make pesto.
25. Coat the rack of lamb with this pesto on both sides and arrange in the Air fryer basket.
26. Cook for about 15 minutes and cut the rack into individual chops to serve.

NUTRITION: Calories 406 Fat 27.7g Carbs 2.9g Protein 34.9g

Spiced Lamb Steaks

Basic Recipe

Preparation Time: 15 minutes **Cooking Time:** 14 minutes **Servings:** 3 **INGREDIENTS:**

- ½ onion, roughly chopped
- 1½ pounds boneless lamb sirloin steaks
- 5 garlic cloves, peeled
- 1 tablespoon fresh ginger, peeled
- 1 teaspoon garam masala
- 1 teaspoon ground fennel
- ½ teaspoon ground cumin
- ½ teaspoon ground cinnamon
- ½ teaspoon cayenne pepper
- Salt and black pepper, to taste

DIRECTIONS:

27. Preheat the Air fryer to 330-degree F and grease an Air fryer basket.
28. Put the onion, garlic, ginger, and spices in a blender and pulse until smooth.
29. Coat the lamb steaks with this mixture on both sides and refrigerate to marinate for about 24 hours.
30. Arrange the lamb steaks in the Air fryer basket and cook for about 15 minutes, flipping once in between.
31. Dish out the steaks in a platter and serve warm. **NUTRITION:**Calories 252 Fat 16.7g Carbs 4.2g Protein 21.7g

Leg of Lamb with Brussels Sprout

Intermediate Recipe Preparation Time: 20 minutes **Cooking Time:** 1 hour 30 minutes
Servings: 4

INGREDIENTS:

- 2¼ pounds leg of lamb
- 1 tablespoon fresh rosemary, minced
- 1 tablespoon fresh lemon thyme
- 1½ pounds Brussels sprouts, trimmed
- 3 tablespoons olive oil, divided
- 1 garlic clove, minced
- Salt and ground black pepper, as required
- 2 tablespoons honey

DIRECTIONS:

32. Preheat the Air fryer to 300-degree F and grease an Air fryer basket.
33. Make slits in the leg of lamb with a sharp knife.
34. Mix 2 tablespoons of oil, herbs, garlic, salt, and black pepper in a bowl.
35. Coat the leg of lamb with oil mixture generously and arrange in the Air fryer basket.
36. Cook for about 75 minutes and set the Air fryer to 390-degree F.
37. Coat the Brussels sprout evenly with the remaining oil and honey and arrange them in the Air fryer basket with leg of lamb.
38. Cook for about 15 minutes and dish out to serve warm.

NUTRITION: Calories 449 Fats 19.9g Carbs 16.6g Protein 51.7g

Honey Mustard Cheesy Meatballs

Basic Recipe
Preparation Time: 15 minutes **Cooking Time:** 15 minutes **Servings:** 8
INGREDIENTS:

- 2 onions, chopped
- 1-pound ground beef
- 4 tablespoons fresh basil, chopped
- 2 tablespoons cheddar cheese, grated
- 2 teaspoons garlic paste
- 2 teaspoons honey
- Salt and black pepper, to taste
- 2 teaspoons mustard

DIRECTIONS:

39. Preheat the Air fryer to 3850F and grease an Air fryer basket.
40. Mix all the ingredients in a bowl until well combined.
41. Shape the mixture into equal-sized balls gently and arrange the meatballs in the Air fryer basket.
42. Cook for about 15 minutes and dish out to serve warm.

NUTRITION: Calories 134 Fat 4.4g Carbs 4.6g Protein 18.2g

Spicy Lamb Kebabs

Basic Recipe
Preparation Time: 20 minutes **Cooking Time:** 10 minutes **Servings:** 6
INGREDIENTS:

- 4 eggs, beaten
- 1 cup pistachios, chopped
- 1-pound ground lamb
- 4 tablespoons plain flour
- 4 tablespoons flat-leaf parsley, chopped
- 2 teaspoons chili flakes
- 4 garlic cloves, minced
- 2 tablespoons fresh lemon juice
- 2 teaspoons cumin seeds
- 1 teaspoon fennel seeds
- 2 teaspoons dried mint
- 2 teaspoons salt
- Olive oil
- 1 teaspoon coriander seeds
- 1 teaspoon freshly ground black pepper

DIRECTIONS:

43. Preheat the Air fryer to 355-degree F and grease an Air fryer basket.
44. Mix lamb, pistachios, eggs, lemon juice, chili flakes, flour, cumin seeds, fennel seeds, coriander seeds, mint, parsley, salt and black pepper in a large bowl.
45. Thread the lamb mixture onto metal skewers to form sausages and coat with olive oil.
46. Place the skewers in the Air fryer basket and cook for about 8 minutes
47. Dish out in a platter and serve hot.

NUTRITION: Calories 284 Fat 15.8g Carbs 8.4g Protein 27.9g

Simple Beef Burgers

Basic Recipe
Preparation Time: 20 minutes **Cooking Time:** 10 minutes **Servings:** 6
INGREDIENTS:

- 2 pounds ground beef
- 12 cheddar cheese slices
- 12 dinner rolls
- 6 tablespoons tomato ketchup
- Salt and black pepper, to taste

DIRECTIONS:

48. Preheat the Air fryer to 390-degree F and grease an Air fryer basket.
49. Mix the beef, salt and black pepper in a bowl.
50. Make small equal-sized patties from the beef mixture and arrange half of patties in the Air fryer basket.
51. Cook for about 12 minutes and top each patty with 1 cheese slice.
52. Arrange the patties between rolls and Drizzle with ketchup.
53. Repeat with the remaining batch and dish out to serve hot.

NUTRITION: Calories 537 Fat 28.3g Carbs 7.6g Protein 60.6g

Lamb with Potatoes

Basic Recipe
Preparation Time: 20 minutes **Cooking Time:** 20 minutes **Servings:** 2
INGREDIENTS:

- ½ pound lamb meat
- 2 small potatoes, peeled and halved
- ½ small onion, peeled and halved
- ¼ cup frozen sweet potato fries
- 1 garlic clove, crushed
- ½ tablespoon dried rosemary, crushed
- 1 teaspoon olive oil

DIRECTIONS:

54. Preheat the Air fryer to 355-degree F and arrange a divider in the Air fryer. Rub the lamb evenly with garlic and rosemary and place on one side of Air fryer divider.

55. Cook for about 20 minutes and meanwhile, microwave the potatoes for about 4 minutes. Dish out the potatoes in a large bowl and stir in the olive oil and onions.

56. Transfer into the Air fryer divider and change the side of lamb ramp.

57. Cook for about 15 minutes, flipping once in between and dish out in a bowl.

NUTRITION: Calories 399 Fat 18.5g Carbs 32.3g Protein 24.5g

Nutmeg Beef Mix

Basic Recipe
Preparation Time: 10 minutes **Cooking Time:** 30 minutes **Servings:** 4
INGREDIENTS:

- 2 pounds beef stew meat, cubed
- 1 teaspoon nutmeg, ground
- 2 tablespoons avocado oil
- ½ teaspoon chili powder
- ¼ cup beef stock
- 2 tablespoons chives, chopped
- Salt and black pepper to the taste

DIRECTIONS:

58. In a pan that fits your air fryer, mix the beef with the nutmeg and the other ingredients, toss, introduce the pan in the fryer and cook at 400 degrees F for 30 minutes
59. Divide the mix into bowls and serve.

NUTRITION: Calories 280 Fat 12 Carbs 17 Protein 14

Oregano Daikon

Basic Recipe
Preparation Time: 10 minutes **Cooking Time:** 10 minutes **Servings**: 5
INGREDIENTS:

- 1-pound daikon
- ½ teaspoon sage
- 1 teaspoon salt
- 1 tablespoon olive oil
- 1 teaspoon dried oregano

DIRECTIONS:

1. Peel the daikon and cut it into cubes.
2. Sprinkle the daikon cubes with sage, salt, and dried oregano.
3. Mix well
4. Preheat the air fryer to 360 F.
5. Place the daikon cubes in the air fryer rack and Drizzle with olive oil.
6. Cook the daikon for 6 minutes
7. Turn the daikon and cook for 4 minutes more or until soft and golden brown.

NUTRITION: Calories 43 Fat 2.8 Carbs 3.9 Protein 1.9

Creamy Spinach

Basic Recipe
Preparation Time: 10 minutes

Cooking Time: 12 minutes **Servings:** 4 **INGREDIENTS:**

- 2 oz chive stems
- 2 cup spinach
- 1 cup chicken stock
- 1 cup heavy cream
- 1 teaspoon salt
- 1 teaspoon paprika
- ½ teaspoon chili flakes
- 1 teaspoon ground black pepper
- ½ teaspoon minced garlic
- 3 oz. Parmesan, shredded

DIRECTIONS:

1. Preheat the air fryer to 390 F.
2. Chop the spinach roughly.
3. Place the spinach in the air fryer basket bowl.
4. Add the chicken stock and heavy cream.
5. Add salt, paprika, chili flakes, and ground black pepper.
6. Add the chives and minced garlic.
7. Mix gently and cook it for 10 minutes
8. Blend using a hand blender. You should get the creamy texture of a soup.
9. Sprinkle with the shredded cheese and cook it for 2 minutes at 400 F.
10. Serve hot.

NUTRITION: Calories 187 Fat 16 Carbs 4.4 Protein 8.4

Eggplant with Grated Cheddar

Basic Recipe

Preparation Time: 15 minutes **Cooking Time:** 10 minutes **Servings:** 10 **INGREDIENTS:**

- 2 eggplants
- 1 teaspoon minced garlic
- 1 teaspoon olive oil
- 5 oz. Cheddar cheese, grated
- ½ teaspoon ground black pepper

DIRECTIONS:

1. Wash the eggplants carefully and slice them.
2. Rub the slices with minced garlic, salt, and ground black pepper.
3. Leave the slices for 5 minutes to marinade.
4. Preheat the air fryer to 400 F.
5. Place the eggplant circles in the air fryer rack and cook them for 6 minutes
6. Then turn them over cook for 5 minutes more.
7. Sprinkle the eggplants with the grated cheese and cook for 30 seconds.
8. Serve hot.

NUTRITION: Calories 97 Fat 6.2 Carbs 7.7 Protein 5.2

Coriander Garlic Bulbs

Basic Recipe
Preparation Time: 10 minutes
Cooking Time: 10 minutes

Servings: 18
INGREDIENTS:

- 1-pound garlic heads
- 2 tablespoons olive oil
- 1 teaspoon dried oregano
- 1 teaspoon dried basil
- 1 teaspoon ground coriander
- ¼ teaspoon ground ginger

DIRECTIONS:

1. Cut the ends of the garlic bulbs.
2. Place each bulb on foil.
3. Coat them with olive oil, dried oregano, dried basil, ground coriander, and ground ginger.
4. Preheat the air fryer to 400 F.
5. Wrap the garlic in foil and place in the air fryer.
6. Cook for 10 minutes until soft.
7. Let them cool for at least 10 minutes before serving.

NUTRITION: Calories 57 Fat 1.4 Carbs 8.2 Protein 1.3

Parmesan Sticks

Basic Recipe
Preparation Time: 10 minutes **Cooking Time:** 10 minutes **Servings:** 3
INGREDIENTS:

- 8 oz. Parmesan
- 1 egg
- ½ cup heavy cream
- 4 tablespoons almond flour
- ¼ teaspoon ground black pepper

DIRECTIONS:

1. Crack the egg in a bowl and whisk.
2. Add the heavy cream and almond flour.
3. Sprinkle the mixture with ground black pepper.
4. Whisk carefully or use a hand mixer.
5. Cut the cheese into thick short sticks
6. Dip the sticks in the heavy cream mixture.
7. Place the cheese sticks in freezer bags and freeze them.
8. Preheat the air fryer to 400 F.
9. Place the cheese sticks in the air fryer rack.
10. Cook for 8 minutes

NUTRITION: Calories 389 Fat 29.5 Carbs 5.5 Protein 28.6

Creamy Snow Peas

Basic Recipe
Preparation Time: 10 minutes **Cooking Time:** 5 minutes **Servings**: 5
INGREDIENTS:

- ½ cup heavy cream
- 1 teaspoon butter
- 1 teaspoon salt
- 1 teaspoon paprika
- 1-pound snow peas
- ¼ teaspoon nutmeg

DIRECTIONS:

1. Preheat the air fryer to 400 F.
2. Wash the snow peas carefully and place them in the air fryer basket tray.
3. Then sprinkle the snow peas with the butter, salt, paprika, nutmeg, and heavy cream.
4. Cook the snow peas for 5 minutes
5. When the time is over – shake the snow peas gently and transfer them to the serving plates.
6. Enjoy!

NUTRITION: Calories 98 Fat 5.9 Carbs 6.9 Protein 3.5

Sesame Okra

Basic Recipe

Preparation Time: 10 minutes **Cooking Time:** 4 minutes **Servings:** 4

INGREDIENTS:

- 1 tablespoon sesame oil
- 1 teaspoon sesame seed
- 11 oz. okra
- ½ teaspoon salt
- 1 egg

DIRECTIONS:

1. Wash the okra and chop it roughly.
2. Crack the egg into a bowl and whisk it.
3. Add the chopped okra to the whisked egg.
4. Sprinkle with the sesame seeds and salt.
5. Preheat the air fryer to 400 F.
6. Mix the okra mixture carefully.
7. Place the mixture in the air fryer basket.
8. Drizzle with olive oil.
9. Cook the okra for 4 minutes
10. Stir and serve.

NUTRITION: Calories 81 Fat 5 Carbs 6.1 Protein 3

Fennel Oregano Wedges

Basic Recipe
Preparation Time: 15 minutes **Cooking Time:** 6 minutes **Servings:** 4
INGREDIENTS:

- 1 teaspoon stevia extract
- ½ teaspoon fresh thyme
- ½ teaspoon salt
- 1 teaspoon olive oil
- 14 oz. fennel
- 1 teaspoon butter
- 1 teaspoon dried oregano
- ½ teaspoon chili flakes

DIRECTIONS:

1. Slice the fennel into wedges. Melt the butter. Combine the butter, olive oil, dried oregano, and chili flakes in a bowl.
2. Combine well.
3. Add salt, fresh thyme, and stevia extract. Whisk gently.
4. Brush the fennel wedges with the mixture. Preheat the air fryer to 370 F.
5. Place the fennel wedges in the air fryer rack.
6. Cook the fennel wedges for 3 minutes on each side.

NUTRITION: Calories 41 Fat 1.9 Carbs 6.1 Protein 1

Parsley Kohlrabi Fritters

Basic Recipe
Preparation Time: 10 minutes **Cooking Time:** 7 minutes **Servings:** 4
INGREDIENTS:

- 8 oz. kohlrabi
- 1 egg
- 1 tablespoon almond flour
- ½ teaspoon salt
- 1 teaspoon olive oil
- 1 teaspoon ground black pepper
- 1 tablespoon dried parsley
- ¼ teaspoon chili pepper

DIRECTIONS:

1. Peel the kohlrabi and grate it. Combine the grated kohlrabi with salt, ground black pepper, dried parsley, and chili pepper.
2. Crack the egg into the mixture and whisk it. Make medium fritters from the mixture.
3. Preheat the air fryer to 380 F. Grease the air fryer basket tray with olive oil and place the fritters inside. Cook the fritters for 4 minutes Turn the fritters and cook for 3 minutes more. Allow to cool slightly before serving.

NUTRITION: Calories 66 Fat 4.7 Carbs 4.4 Protein 3.2

Chives Bamboo Shoots

Basic Recipe
Preparation Time: 10 minutes **Cooking Time:** 4 minutes **Servings:** 2
INGREDIENTS:

- 8 oz. bamboo shoots
- 2 garlic cloves, sliced
- 1 tablespoon olive oil
- ½ teaspoon chili flakes
- 2 tablespoon chives
- ½ teaspoon salt
- 3 tablespoons fish stock

DIRECTIONS:

4. Preheat the air fryer to 400 F. Cut the bamboo shoots into strips.
5. Combine the sliced garlic cloves, olive oil, chili flakes, salt, and fish stock in the air fryer basket tray. Cook for 1 minute.
6. Stir the mixture gently. Add the bamboo strips and chives.
7. Stir the dish carefully and cook for 3 minutes more.
8. Stir again before serving.

NUTRITION: Calories 100 Fat 7.6 Carbs 7 Protein 3.7

Summer Eggplant & Zucchini

Basic Recipe
Preparation Time: 15 minutes
Cooking Time: 15 minutes **Servings:** 8 **INGREDIENTS:**

- 1 eggplant
- 1 tomato
- 1 zucchini
- 3 oz chive stems
- 2 green peppers
- 1 teaspoon paprika
- 1 tablespoon olive oil
- ½ teaspoon ground nutmeg
- ½ teaspoon ground thyme
- 1 teaspoon salt

DIRECTIONS:

1. Preheat the air fryer to 390 F.
2. Wash the eggplant, tomato, and zucchini carefully.
3. Chop all the vegetables roughly.
4. Place the chopped vegetables in the air fryer basket tray.
5. Coat the vegetables with the paprika, olive oil, ground nutmeg, ground thyme, and salt.
6. Stir the vegetables using two spatulas.
7. Cut the green peppers into squares.
8. Add the squares into the vegetable mixture. Stir gently.
9. Cook for 15 minutes, stirring after 10 minutes then serve.

NUTRITION: Calories 48 Fat 2.1 Fiber 3.3 Carbs 7.4

Protein 1.4

Zucchini Hassel back

Basic Recipe
Preparation Time: 15 minutes **Cooking Time:** 12 minutes **Servings:** 2 **INGREDIENTS:**

- 1 zucchini
- 4 oz. Cheddar, sliced
- ½ teaspoon salt
- ½ teaspoon dried oregano
- ½ teaspoon ground coriander
- ½ teaspoon paprika
- 3 tablespoons heavy cream
- 1 teaspoon olive oil
- ¼ teaspoon minced garlic

DIRECTIONS:

1. Cut the zucchini into a Hassel back shape.
2. Then fill the zucchini with the sliced cheese.
3. Coat the zucchini Hassel back with salt, dried oregano, ground coriander, paprika, minced garlic, olive oil, and heavy cream.
4. Preheat the air fryer to 400 F.
5. Wrap the zucchini Hassel back in foil and place in the preheated air fryer.
6. Cook for 12 minutes
7. When the zucchini is cooked, remove it from the foil and cut into 2 pieces.

NUTRITION: Calories 215 Fat 14.9 Carbs 5.7 Protein 15.6

Butternut Squash Hash

Basic Recipe
Preparation Time: 10 minutes **Cooking Time:** 14 minutes **Servings:** 4
INGREDIENTS:

- 1 cup chicken stock
- 10 oz. butternut squash
- 1 teaspoon salt
- 1 tablespoon butter
- 1 teaspoon dried dill
- ¼ teaspoon paprika

DIRECTIONS:

1. Peel the butternut squash and chop it.
2. Preheat the air fryer to 370 F.
3. Pour the chicken stock into the air fryer basket tray.
4. Add salt, chopped butternut squash, butter, dried dill, and paprika.
5. Stir gently.
6. Cook for 14 minutes
7. Transfer to a bowl.
8. Use a fork to mash.
9. Serve immediately.

NUTRITION: Calories 61 Fat 3.3 Carbs 6.2 Protein 0.9

Butter Mushrooms with Chives

Basic Recipe
Preparation Time: 10 minutes **Cooking Time:** 10 minutes **Servings:** 2
INGREDIENTS:

- 1 cup white mushrooms
- 4 oz chive stems
- 1 tablespoon butter
- 1 teaspoon olive oil
- 1 teaspoon dried rosemary
- 1/3 teaspoon salt
- ¼ teaspoon ground nutmeg

DIRECTIONS:

1. Preheat the air fryer to 400 F.
2. Pour the olive oil and butter in the air fryer basket tray.
3. Add dried rosemary, salt, and ground nutmeg.
4. Stir gently.
5. Dice the chives.
6. Add the diced chives in the air fryer basket tray.
7. Cook for 5 minutes
8. Meanwhile, chop the white mushrooms.
9. Add the mushrooms.
10. Stir the mixture and cook it for a further 5 minutes at the same temperature.
11. Stir then serve.

NUTRITION: Calories 104 Fat 8.4 Carbs 6.8 Protein 1.8

Fennel & Spinach Quiche

Basic Recipe
Preparation Time: 15 minutes
Cooking Time: 10 minutes

Servings: 5
INGREDIENTS:

- 10 oz. fennel, chopped
- 1 cup spinach
- 5 eggs
- ½ cup almond flour
- 1 teaspoon olive oil
- 1 tablespoon butter
- 1 teaspoon salt
- ¼ cup heavy cream
- 1 teaspoon ground black pepper

DIRECTIONS:

1. Chop the spinach and combine it with the chopped fennel in a large bowl.
2. Crack the egg in a separate bowl and whisk.
3. Combine the whisked eggs with the almond flour, butter, salt, heavy cream, and ground black pepper.
4. Whisk together to mix
5. Preheat the air fryer to 360 F.
6. Grease the air fryer basket tray with the olive oil.
7. Add both mixtures.
8. Cook the quiche for 18 minutes
9. Let the quiche cool.
10. Remove it from the air fryer and slice into servings.

NUTRITION: Calories 209 Fat 16.1 Carbs 7.4 Protein 8.3

Lemony Baby Potatoes

Basic Recipe
Preparation Time: 10 minutes **Cooking Time:** 25 minutes **Servings:** 6
INGREDIENTS:

- 2 tablespoons olive oil
- 2 springs rosemary, chopped
- 2 tablespoons parsley, chopped
- 2 tablespoons oregano, chopped
- Salt and black pepper to the taste
- 1 tablespoon lemon rind, grated
- 3 garlic cloves, minced
- 2 tablespoons lemon juice
- 2 pounds baby potatoes

DIRECTIONS:

1. In a bowl, mix baby potatoes with oil, rosemary, parsley, oregano, salt, pepper, lemon rind, garlic and lemon juice, toss, transfer potatoes to your air fryer's basket and cook at 356 degrees F for 25 minutes
2. Divide potatoes between plates and serve as a side dish.
3. Enjoy!

NUTRITION: Calories 204 Fat 4 Carbs 17 Protein 6

White Mushrooms with Snow Peas

Basic Recipe
Preparation Time: 10 minutes **Cooking Time:** 15 minutes **Servings:** 2
INGREDIENTS:

- Salt and black pepper to the taste
- 7 ounces snow peas
- 8 ounces white mushrooms, halved
- 1 yellow onion, cut into rings
- 2 tablespoons coconut aminos
- 1 teaspoon olive oil

DIRECTIONS:

1. In a bowl, snow peas with mushrooms, onion, aminos, oil, salt and pepper, toss well, transfer to a pan that fits your air fryer, introduce in the fryer and cook at 350 degrees F for 15 minutes. Divide between plates and serve as a side dish. Enjoy!

NUTRITION: Calories 175 Fat 4 Carbs 12 Protein 7

Gold Potatoes and Bell Pepper Mix

Basic Recipe

Preparation Time: 10 minutes **Cooking Time:** 25 minutes **Servings:** 4

INGREDIENTS:

- 4 gold potatoes, cubed
- 1 yellow onion, chopped
- 2 teaspoons olive oil
- 1 green bell pepper, chopped
- Salt and black pepper to the taste
- ½ teaspoon thyme, dried

DIRECTIONS:

2. Heat up your air fryer at 350 degrees F, add oil, heat it up, add onion, bell pepper, salt and pepper, stir and cook for 5 minutes
3. Add potatoes and thyme, stir, cover and cook at 360 degrees F for 20 minutes
4. Divide between plates and serve as a side dish.
5. Enjoy!

NUTRITION: Calories 201 Fat 4 Carbs 12 Protein 7

Potato with Bell Peppers

Basic Recipe

Preparation Time: 10 minutes **Cooking Time:** 25 minutes **Servings:** 6

INGREDIENTS:

- 6 ounces jarred roasted red bell peppers, chopped
- 3 garlic cloves, minced
- 2 tablespoons parsley, chopped
- Salt and black pepper to the taste
- 2 tablespoons chives, chopped
- 4 potatoes, peeled and cut into wedges
- Cooking spray

DIRECTIONS:

1. In a pan that fits your air fryer, combine roasted bell peppers with garlic, parsley, salt, pepper, chives, potato wedges and the oil, toss, transfer to your air fryer and cook at 350 degrees F for 25 minutes
2. Divide between plates and serve as a side dish.
3. Enjoy!

NUTRITION: Calories 212 Fat 6 Carbs 11 Protein 5

Chinese Long Beans Mix

Basic Recipe

Preparation Time: 10 minutes **Cooking Time:** 10 minutes **Servings:** 4 **INGREDIENTS:**

- ½ teaspoon coconut aminos
- 1 tablespoon olive oil
- A pinch of salt and black pepper
- 4 garlic cloves, minced
- 4 long beans, trimmed and sliced

DIRECTIONS:

4. In a pan that fits your air fryer, combine long beans with oil, aminos, salt, pepper and garlic, toss, introduce in your air fryer and cook at 350 degrees F for 10 minutes
5. Divide between plates and serve as a side dish.
6. Enjoy!

NUTRITION: Calories 170 Fat 3 Carbs 7 Protein 3

Portobello Mushrooms with Spinach

Basic Recipe
Preparation Time: 10 minutes **Cooking Time:** 12 minutes **Servings:** 4 **INGREDIENTS:**

- 4 big Portobello mushroom caps
- 1 tablespoon olive oil
- 1 cup spinach, torn
- 1/3 cup vegan breadcrumbs
- ¼ teaspoon rosemary, chopped

DIRECTIONS:

1. Rub mushrooms caps with the oil, place them in your air fryer's basket and cook them at 350 degrees F for 2 minutes
2. Meanwhile, in a bowl, mix spinach, rosemary and breadcrumbs and stir well.
3. Stuff mushrooms with this mix, place them in your air fryer's basket again and cook at 350 degrees F for 10 minutes
4. Divide them between plates and serve as a side dish.
5. Enjoy!

NUTRITION: Calories 152 Fat 4 Carbs 9 Protein 5

Summer Squash Mix

Basic Recipe

Preparation Time: 10 minutes **Cooking Time:** 10 minutes **Servings:** 4 **INGREDIENTS:**

- 3 ounces coconut cream
- ½ teaspoon oregano, dried
- Salt and black pepper
- 1 big yellow summer squash, peeled and cubed
- 1/3 cup carrot, cubed
- 2 tablespoons olive oil

DIRECTIONS:

1. In a pan that fits your air fryer, combine squash with carrot, oil, oregano, salt, pepper and coconut cream, toss, transfer to your air fryer and cook at 400 degrees F for 10 minutes
2. Divide between plates and serve as a side dish.
3. Enjoy!

NUTRITION: Calories 170 Fat 4 Carbs 8 Protein 6

Corn with Tomatoes Salad

Basic Recipe
Preparation Time: 10 minutes **Cooking Time:** 10 minutes **Servings:** 4
INGREDIENTS:

- 3 cups corn
- A Drizzle with of olive oil
- Salt and black pepper to the taste
- 1 teaspoon sweet paprika
- 1 tablespoon stevia
- ½ teaspoon garlic powder
- ½ iceberg lettuce head, cut into medium strips
- ½ romaine lettuce head, cut into medium strips
- 1 cup canned black beans, Dry outed
- 3 tablespoons cilantro, chopped
- 4 green onions, chopped
- 12 cherry tomatoes, sliced

DIRECTIONS:

1. Put the corn in a pan that fits your air fryer, Drizzle with the oil, add salt, pepper, paprika, stevia and garlic powder, introduce in your air fryer and cook at 350 degrees F for 10 minutes
2. Transfer corn to a salad bowl, add lettuce, black beans, tomatoes, green onions and cilantro, toss, divide between plates and serve as a side salad.
3. Enjoy!

NUTRITION: Calories 162 Fat 6 Carbs 7 Protein 6

Colored Veggie Mix

Basic Recipe
Preparation Time: 10 minutes **Cooking Time:** 12 minutes **Servings:** 6
INGREDIENTS:

- 1 zucchini, sliced in half and roughly chopped
- 1 orange bell pepper, roughly chopped
- 1 green bell pepper, roughly chopped
- 1 red onion, roughly chopped
- 4 ounces brown mushrooms, halved
- Salt and black pepper to the taste
- 1 teaspoon Italian seasoning
- 1 cup cherry tomatoes, halved
- ½ cup kalamata olives, pitted and halved
- ¼ cup olive oil
- 3 tablespoons balsamic vinegar
- 2 tablespoons basil, chopped

DIRECTIONS:

1. In a bowl, mix zucchini with mushrooms, orange bell pepper, green bell pepper, red onion, salt, pepper, Italian seasoning and oil, toss well, transfer to preheated air fryer at 380 degrees F and cook them for 12 minutes
2. In a large bowl, combine mixed veggies with tomatoes, olives, vinegar and basil, toss, divide between plates and serve cold as a side dish.
3. Enjoy!

NUTRITION: Calories 180 Fat 5 Carbs 10 Protein 6

Minty Leeks Medley

Basic Recipe

Preparation Time: 10 minutes **Cooking Time:** 12 minutes **Servings:** 4

INGREDIENTS:

- 6 leeks, roughly chopped
- 1 tablespoon cumin, ground
- 1 tablespoon mint, chopped
- 1 tablespoon parsley, chopped
- 1 teaspoon garlic, minced
- A Drizzle with of olive oil
- Salt and black pepper to the taste

DIRECTIONS:

1. In a pan that fits your air fryer, combine leeks with cumin, mint, parsley, garlic, salt, pepper and the oil, toss, introduce in your air fryer and cook at 350 degrees F for 12 minutes
2. Divide Minty Leeks Medley between plates and serve as a side dish.
3. Enjoy!

NUTRITION: Calories 131 Fat 7 Carbs 10 Protein 6

Corn and Tomatoes

Basic Recipe

Preparation Time: 10 minutes **Cooking Time:** 13 minutes **Servings:** 4

INGREDIENTS:

- 2 cups corn
- 4 tomatoes, roughly chopped
- 1 tablespoon olive oil
- Salt and black pepper to the taste
- 1 tablespoon oregano, chopped
- 1 tablespoon parsley, chopped
- 2 tablespoons soft tofu, pressed and crumbled

DIRECTIONS:

1. In a pan that fits your air fryer, combine corn with tomatoes, oil, salt, pepper, oregano and parsley, toss, introduce the pan in your air fryer and cook at 320 degrees F for 10 minutes
2. Add tofu, toss, introduce in the fryer for 3 minutes more, divide between plates and serve as a side dish.
3. Enjoy!

NUTRITION: Calories 171 Fat 7 Carbs 9 Protein 6

Soft Tofu with Veggies

Basic Recipe
Preparation Time: 10 minutes **Cooking Time:** 14 minutes **Servings:** 2
INGREDIENTS:

- 1 broccoli head, florets separated and steamed
- 1 tomato, chopped
- 3 carrots, chopped and steamed
- 2 ounces soft tofu, crumbled
- 1 teaspoon parsley, chopped
- 1 teaspoon thyme, chopped
- Salt and black pepper to the taste

DIRECTIONS:

4. In a pan that fits your air fryer, combine broccoli with tomato, carrots, thyme, parsley, salt and pepper, toss, introduce the fryer and cook at 350 degrees F for 10 minutes
5. Add tofu, toss, introduce in the fryer for 4 minutes more, divide between plates and serve as a side dish.
6. Enjoy!

NUTRITION: Calories 174 Fat 4 Carbs 12 Protein 3

Oregano Bell Peppers

Basic Recipe
Preparation Time: 10 minutes **Cooking Time:** 15 minutes **Servings:** 4
INGREDIENTS:

- 1 tablespoon olive oil
- 1 sweet onion, chopped
- 1 red bell pepper, chopped
- 1 orange bell pepper, chopped
- 1 green bell pepper, chopped
- Salt and black pepper to the taste
- ½ cup cashew cheese, shredded
- 1 tablespoon oregano, chopped

DIRECTIONS:

7. In a pan that fits your air fryer, combine onion with red bell pepper, green bell pepper, orange bell pepper, salt, pepper, oregano and oil, toss, introduce in the fryer and cook at 320 degrees F for 10 minutes
8. Add cashew cheese, toss, introduce in the fryer for 4 minutes more, divide between plates and serve as a side dish.
9. Enjoy!

NUTRITION: Calories 172 Fat 4 Carbs 8 Protein 7

Yellow Lentils Herbed Mix

Basic Recipe

Preparation Time: 10 minutes **Cooking Time:** 20 minutes **Servings:** 4

INGREDIENTS:

- 1 cup yellow lentils soaked in water for 1 hour and dry outed
- 1 hot chili pepper, chopped
- 1-inch ginger piece, grated
- ½ teaspoon turmeric powder
- 1 teaspoon garam masala
- Salt and black pepper to the taste
- 2 teaspoons olive oil
- ½ cup cilantro, chopped
- 1 and ½ cup spinach, chopped
- 4 garlic cloves, minced
- ¾ cup red onion, chopped

DIRECTIONS:

1. In a pan that fits your air fryer, mix lentils with chili pepper, ginger, turmeric, garam masala, salt, pepper, olive oil, cilantro, spinach, onion and garlic, toss, introduce in your air fryer and cook at 400 degrees F for 15 minutes
2. Divide lentils mix between plates and serve as a side dish.
3. Enjoy!

NUTRITION: Calories 202 Fat 2 Carbs 12 Protein 4

Creamy Zucchini and Sweet Potatoes

Basic Recipe

Preparation Time: 10 minutes **Cooking Time:** 16 minutes **Servings:** 8 **INGREDIENTS:**

- 1 cup veggie stock
- 2 tablespoons olive oil
- 2 sweet potatoes, peeled and cut into medium wedges
- 8 zucchinis, cut into medium wedges
- 2 yellow onions, chopped
- 1 cup coconut milk
- Salt and black pepper to the taste
- 1 tablespoon coconut aminos
- ¼ teaspoon thyme, dried
- ¼ teaspoon rosemary, dried
- 4 tablespoons dill, chopped
- ½ teaspoon basil, chopped

DIRECTIONS:

1. Heat up a pan that fits your air fryer with the oil over medium heat, add onion, stir and cook for 2 minutes
2. Add zucchinis, thyme, rosemary, basil, potato, salt, pepper, stock, milk, aminos and dill, stir, introduce in your air fryer, cook at 360 degrees F for 14 minutes, divide between plates and serve as a side dish.
3. Enjoy!

NUTRITION: Calories 133 Fat 3 Carbs 10 Protein 5

Meaty Egg Rolls

Basic Recipe

Preparation Time: 5 minutes **Cooking Time:** 20 minutes **Servings:** 4

INGREDIENTS:

- ½ Cup almond flour
- 1 teaspoon sea salt, fine
- ¼ cup water
- 7 ounces ground beef
- 1 egg
- 1 teaspoon paprika
- 1 teaspoon black pepper
- 1 tablespoon olive oil

DIRECTIONS:

1. Preheat your water until it boils, and then get out your almond flour and sea salt. Mix it in a bowl.
2. Add in your boiling water, and mix well. Knead into a soft dough, and then set it to the side.
3. Combine your ground beef, black pepper and paprika, mixing well.
4. Roast your meat for five minutes on medium heat, stirring frequently using a saucepan. Beat your egg in.
5. Cook your ground beef for four minutes, and then roll the dough out. Cut it into six squares.
6. Put your ground beef in each square, and then roll them into sticks.
7. Sprinkle with olive oil, and preheat your air fryer to 350.
8. Cook for eight minutes

NUTRITION: Calories 150 Protein 13g Fat 9.6g Carbs 1.3g

Ham Hash

Basic Recipe
Preparation Time: 5 minutes **Cooking Time:** 20 minutes **Servings:** 4
INGREDIENTS:

- 5 ounces parmesan
- 10 ounces ham
- 1 teaspoon black pepper
- 1 teaspoon paprika
- 1 egg
- ½ onions
- 1 tablespoon butter

DIRECTIONS:

1. Start by shredding your parmesan, and then slice your ham into strips.
2. Peel your onion before dicing it, and then crack your egg open in a bowl. Whisk well, and then add in your butter, diced onions, and ham strips.
3. Sprinkle this mixture with paprika and black pepper.
4. Mix well, and heat your air fryer to 350.
5. Transfer this mixture into three separate ramekins, sprinkling with parmesan.
6. Make sure to preheat your air fryer, and cook for ten minutes Serve warm.

NUTRITION: Calories 372 Protein 33.2g Fat 23.7g Carbs 5.9g

Pork Fried Rice

Basic Recipe
Preparation Time: 5 minutes **Cooking Time:** 20 minutes **Servings:** 3
INGREDIENTS:

- 2 eggs
- 2 cloves garlic, chopped
- ½ cauliflower head, medium
- 3 green capsicums, mini
- 2 cups pork belly
- 2 onions
- 1 teaspoon black sesame seeds
- 1 teaspoon picked ginger
- 1 tablespoon soy sauce

DIRECTIONS:

1. Start by chopping your cauliflower to make small florets.
2. Get out a food processor, placing your cauliflower inside, and pulse until you get cauliflower rice.
3. Preheat your air fryer to 400, and then grease down your basket.
4. Beat your eggs, and then swirl them into your air fryer. Allow them to cook for five minutes, turning it down to 350.
5. Add in your cauliflower rice and pork next before tossing in your soy sauce and onion. Cook for another ten minutes at 375.
6. Garnish with picked ginger and sesame seeds.

NUTRITION: Calories 376 Protein 34 g Fat 33 g Carbs
9.6 g

Ketogenic Mac & Cheese

Basic Recipe
Preparation Time: 5 minutes **Cooking Time:** 20 minutes **Servings:** 4
INGREDIENTS:

- 3 tablespoons avocado oil
- Sea salt & black pepper to taste
- 1 cauliflower, medium
- ¼ cup heavy cream
- ¼ cup almond milk, unsweetened
- 1 cup cheddar cheese, shredded

DIRECTIONS:

1. Start by preheating your air fryer to 400, and then make sure to grease your air fryer basket.
2. Chop your cauliflower into florets, and then Drizzle with oil over them. Toss until they're well coated, and then season with salt and pepper to taste.
3. Heat your cheddar, heavy cream, milk and avocado oil in a pot, pouring the mixture over your cauliflower.
4. Cook for fourteen minutes, and then serve warm. **NUTRITION:** Calories 135.5 Protein 27 g Fat 10.2 g Carbs 1.4 g

Salmon Pie

Intermediate Recipe Preparation Time: 5 minutes **Cooking Time:** 45 minutes
Servings: 8 **INGREDIENTS:**

- 1 teaspoon paprika
- ½ cup cream
- ½ teaspoons baking soda
- 1 ½ cups almond flour
- 1 onion, diced
- 1 tablespoon apple cider vinegar
- 1 lb. Salmon
- 1 tablespoon chives
- 1 teaspoon dill
- 1 teaspoon oregano
- 1 teaspoon butter
- 1 teaspoon parsley
- 1 egg

DIRECTIONS:

5. Start by beating your eggs in a bowl, making sure they're whisked well. Add in your cream, whisking for another two minutes
6. Add in your apple cider vinegar and baking soda, stirring well.
7. Add in your almond flour, combining until it makes a non-stick, smooth dough.
8. Chop your salmon into pieces, and then sprinkle your seasoning over it.
9. Mix well, and then cut your dough into two parts.
10. Place parchment paper over your air fryer basket tray, placing the first part of your dough in the tray to form a crust. Add in your salmon filling.
11. Roll out the second part, covering your salmon filling. Secure the edges, and then heat your air fryer to 360.
12. Cook for fifteen minutes, and then reduce the heat to 355, cooking for another fifteen minutes
13. Slice and serve warm.

NUTRITION: Calories 134 Protein 13.2 g Fat 8.1 g Carbs
2.2 g

Garlic Chicken Stir

Basic Recipe

Preparation Time: 5 minutes **Cooking Time:** 20 minutes **Servings:** 4

INGREDIENTS:

- ½ Cup coconut milk
- ½ cup chicken stock
- 2 tablespoons curry paste
- 1 tablespoon lemongrass
- 1 tablespoon apple cider vinegar
- 2 teaspoons garlic, minced
- 1 onion
- 1 lb. Chicken breast, skinless & boneless
- 1 teaspoon olive oil

DIRECTIONS:

1. Start by cubing your chicken, and then peel your onion before dicing it.
2. Combine your onion and chicken together in your air fryer basket, and then preheat it to 365. Cook for five minutes
3. Add in your garlic, apple cider vinegar, coconut milk, lemongrass, curry paste and chicken stock. Mix well, and cook for ten minutes more.
4. Stir well before serving.

NUTRITION: Calories 275 Protein 25.6 g Fat 15.7 g

Carbs 5.9 g

Chicken Stew

Basic Recipe

Preparation Time: 5 minutes **Cooking Time:** 25 minutes **Servings:** 4 **INGREDIENTS:**

- 1 teaspoon cilantro
- 8 ounces chicken breast, boneless & skinless
- 1 onion
- ½ cup spinach
- 2 cups chicken stock
- 5 ounces cabbage
- 6 ounces cauliflower
- 1 teaspoon salt
- 1 green bell pepper
- 1/3 cup heavy cream
- 1 teaspoon paprika
- 1 teaspoon butter
- 1 teaspoon cayenne pepper

DIRECTIONS:

1. Start by cubing your chicken breast, and then sprinkling your cilantro, cayenne, salt and paprika over it.
2. Heat your air fryer to 365, and then melt your butter in your air fryer basket.
3. Add your chicken cubes in, cooking it for four minutes
4. Chop your spinach, and then dice your onion.
5. Shred your cabbage and cut your cauliflower into florets. Chop your green pepper next, and then add them into your air fryer.
6. Pour your chicken stock and heavy cream in, and then reduce your air fryer to 360. Cook for eight minutes, and stir before serving.

NUTRITION: Calories 102 Protein 9.8 g Fat 4.5 g Carbs 4.1 g

Goulash

Basic Recipe

Preparation Time: 5 minutes **Cooking Time:** 11 minutes **Serving**: 6 **INGREDIENTS:**

- 1 white onion
- 2 green peppers, chopped
- 1 teaspoon olive oil
- 14 ounces ground chicken
- 2 tomatoes
- ½ cup chicken stock
- 1 teaspoon sea salt, fine
- 2 cloves garlic, sliced
- 1 teaspoon black pepper
- 1 teaspoon mustard

DIRECTIONS:

1. Peel your onion before chopping it roughly.
2. Spray your air fryer down with olive oil before preheating it to 365.
3. Add in your chopped green pepper, cooking for five minutes
4. Add your ground chicken and cubed tomato next. Mix well, and cook for six minutes
5. Add in the chicken stock, salt, pepper, mustard and garlic. Mix well, and cook for six minutes more. Serve warm.

NUTRITION: Calories 161 Protein 20.3 g Fat 6.1 g Carbs 4.3 g

Beef & broccoli

Basic recipe
Preparation time: 5 minutes **Cooking time:** 20 minutes **Servings:** 4
INGREDIENTS:

- 1 teaspoon paprika
- 1 onion
- 1/3 cup water
- 6 ounces broccoli
- 10 ounces beef brisket
- 1 teaspoon canola oil
- 1 teaspoon butter
- ½ teaspoon chili flakes
- 1 tablespoon flax seeds

DIRECTIONS:

1. Start by chopping your beef brisket, and then sprinkle it with chili flakes and paprika. Mix your meat well, and then preheat your air fryer to 360.
2. Spray your air fryer down with canola oil, placing your beef in the basket tray. Cook for seven minutes, and make sure to stir once while cooking.
3. Chop your broccoli into florets, and then add them into your air fryer basket next.
4. Add in your butter and flax seeds before mixing in your water. Slice your onion, adding it into to, and stir well.
5. Cook at 265 for six minutes
6. Serve warm.

NUTRITION: Calories 187 Protein 23.4 g Fat 7.3 g Carbs
3.8 g

Ground Beef Mash

Basic Recipe

Preparation Time: 5 minutes **Cooking Time:** 20 minutes **Servings:** 4

INGREDIENTS:

- 1 lb. Ground beef
- 1 onion
- 1 teaspoon garlic, sliced
- ¼ cup cream
- 1 teaspoon white pepper
- 1 teaspoon olive oil
- 1 teaspoon dill
- 2 teaspoons chicken stock
- 2 green peppers
- 1 teaspoon cayenne pepper

DIRECTIONS:

1. Start by peeling your onion before grating it. Combine it with your sliced garlic, and then sprinkle your ground beef down with it. Add in your white pepper, and then add your cayenne and dill.
2. Coat your air fryer basket down with olive oil, heating it up to 365.
3. Place the spiced beef in the basket, cooking for three minutes before stirring. Add in the rest of your grated onion mixture and chicken stock, and then cook for two minutes more.
4. Chop your green peppers into small pieces, and then add them in.
5. Add in your cream, and stir well.
6. Allow it to cook for ten minutes more.
7. Mash your mixture to make sure it's scrambled before serving warm.

NUTRITION: Calories 258   Protein 35.5 G Fat 9.3 G
Carbs 4.9 G

Chicken Casserole

Basic Recipe

Preparation Time: 5 minutes **Cooking Time:** 30 minutes **Servings:** 4

INGREDIENTS:

- 1 tablespoon butter
- 9 ounces round chicken
- ½ onion
- 5 ounces bacon
- Sea salt & black pepper to taste
- 1 teaspoon turmeric
- 1 teaspoon paprika
- 6 ounces cheddar cheese, shredded
- 1 egg
- ½ cup cream
- 1 tablespoon almond flour

DIRECTIONS:

1. Spread your butter into your air fryer tray, and then add in your ground chicken. Season it with salt and pepper, and then add in your turmeric and paprika. Stir well, and then add in your cheddar cheese.
2. Beat your egg into your ground chicken, and mix well. Whisk your cream and almond flour together.
3. Peel and dice your onion, and ten add it into your air fryer too.
4. Layer your cheese and bacon, and then heat your air fryer to 380. Cook for eighteen minutes, and then allow it to cool slightly before serving.

NUTRITION: Calories 396 Protein 30.4 g Fat 28.6 g
Carbs 2.8 g

Chicken Hash

Basic Recipe
Preparation Time: 5 minutes **Cooking Time:** 20 minutes **Servings:** 3
INGREDIENTS:

- 1 Tablespoon Water
- 1 Green Pepper
- ½ Onion
- 6 Ounces Cauliflower
- Chicken Fillet, 7 Ounces
- 1 Tablespoon cream
- 3 Tablespoon Butter
- Black Pepper to taste

DIRECTIONS:

5. Start by roughly chopping your cauliflower before placing it in a blender. Blend until you get a cauliflower rice.
6. Chop your chicken into small pieces, and then get out your chicken fillets. Sprinkle with black pepper.
7. Heat your air fryer to 380, and then put your chicken in the air fryer basket. Add in your water and cream, cooking for six minutes
8. Reduce the heat to 360, and then dice your green pepper and onion.
9. Add this to your cauliflower rice, and then add in your butter. Mix well, and then add it to your chicken. Cook for eight minutes
10. Serve warm.

NUTRITION: Calories 261 Protein 21 g Fat 16.8 g Carbs 4.4 g

Air Fried Section and Tomato

Intermediate Recipe Preparation Time: 10 minutes **Cooking Time:** 10 minutes
Serving: 2
INGREDIENTS:

- 1 aubergine, sliced thickly into 4 disks
- 1 tomato, sliced into 2 thick disks
- 2 tsp. feta cheese, reduced Fat
- 2 fresh basil leaves, minced
- 2 balls, small buffalo mozzarella, reduced fat, roughly torn
- Pinch of salt
- Pinch of black pepper

DIRECTIONS:

1. Preheat Air Fryer to 330 degrees F.
2. Spray small amount of oil into the Air fryer basket. Fry aubergine slices for 5 minutes or until golden brown on both sides. Transfer to a plate.
3. Fry tomato slices in batches for 5 minutes or until seared on both sides.
4. To serve, stack salad starting with an aubergine base, buffalo mozzarella, basil leaves, tomato slice, and ½-teaspoon feta cheese.
5. Top of with another slice of aubergine and ½ tsp. feta cheese. Serve.

NUTRITION: Calorie: 140.3 Carbs 26.6 Fat 3.4g Protein 4.2g Fiber 7.3g

Quick Fry Chicken with Cauliflower and Water Chestnuts

Intermediate Recipe Preparation Time: 15 minutes **Cooking Time:** 10 minutes **Serving**: 3

INGREDIENTS:

- 1½ pounds chicken thigh fillets, diced
- 1-piece, small red bell pepper, julienned
- 1 piece, thumb-sized ginger, grated
- 2 Tbsp. olive oil
- 1 clove, large garlic, minced
- 2 stalks, large leeks, minced
- 1 can, 5 oz. water chestnuts, quartered
- 1 head, small cauliflower, cut into bite-sized florets
- ¾ cups chicken stock, low sodium
- Seasonings
- 1 tsp. stevia
- 1 Tbsp. fish sauce
- ½ Tbsp. cornstarch, dissolved in
- 4 Tbsp. water
- Pinch of salt
- Pinch of black pepper, to taste
- Garnish:
- Leeks, minced
- 1-piece, large lime, cut into 6 wedges

DIRECTIONS:

1. Preheat Air Fryer to 330 degrees F.
2. Pour olive oil in a pan. Swirl pan to coat. Sauté the garlic, ginger, and leeks for 2 minutes then set aside. Add in water chestnuts, cauliflower, red bell pepper, and chicken broth. Stir well. Cook for 15 minutes.
3. Meanwhile, put the chicken in the Air fryer basket. Fry until seared and golden brown.
4. Add in seasoning into the pan. Stir and cook until the juice thickens.
5. Ladle 1 portion of quick fry veggies and chicken, Garnish with leeks and lemon wedges on the side. Serve.

NUTRITION: Calorie: 220 Carbs 13.6g   Fat 9 Protein 30.5g Fiber 3.8g

Cheesy Salmon Fillets

Intermediate Recipe Preparation Time: 15 minutes **Cooking Time:** 10 minutes **Serving**: 3

INGREDIENTS:

- 2 pieces, 4 oz. each salmon fillets, choose even cuts
- ½ cup sour cream, reduced fat
- ¼ cup cottage cheese, reduced Fat
- ¼ cup Parmigiano-Reggiano cheese, freshly grated
- Garnish:
- Spanish paprika
- ½ piece lemon, cut into wedges

DIRECTIONS:

1. Preheat Air Fryer to 330 degrees F.
2. To make the salmon fillets, mix sour cream, cottage cheese, and Parmigiano-Reggiano cheese in a bowl.
3. Layer the salmon fillets in the Air fryer basket. Fry for 20 minutes or until cheese turns golden brown.
4. To assemble, place a salmon fillet and sprinkle paprika. Garnish with lemon wedges and squeeze lemon juice on top. Serve.

NUTRITION: Calorie: 274 Carbs 1g Fat 19g Protein 24g Fiber 0.5g

Tuna Steaks

Intermediate Recipe Preparation Time: 5 minutes **Cooking Time:** 20 minutes
Serving: 1 **INGREDIENTS:**

- 2 pieces bone-in tuna steaks
- Pinch of salt
- 1 Tbsp. olive oil
- Garnish:
- 1 Tbsp. homemade garlic and parsley butter, divided
- 2 Tbsp. toasted garlic flakes, divided
- ½ small lemons cut into wedges

DIRECTIONS:

1. Preheat Air Fryer to 330 degrees F.
2. Season the tuna steaks with salt.
3. Layer the tuna inside the Air Fryer basket. Fry for 2 minutes on each side. Transfer on a plate.
4. To assemble, place steaks in each plate. Spread parsley and garlic butter. Serve with lemon wedges.

NUTRITION: Calorie: 120 Carbs 0g Fat 1g Protein 27g Fiber 0g

Air-Fried Lean Pork Tenderloin

Intermediate Recipe Preparation Time: 7 minutes **Cooking Time:** 20 minutes
Serving: 1 **INGREDIENTS:**

- 2 pork tenderloin lean, sliced into matchsticks
- ½ red bell pepper, julienned
- ½ green bell pepper, julienned
- 1 white onion, sliced thinly
- 1 Tbsp. almond flour, finely milled
- 1 tsp. sea salt

    - 1 tsp. ground black pepper
    - ½ tsp. dried pepper flakes

DIRECTIONS:

1. Preheat Air Fryer to 330 degrees F.
2. Season the pork tenderloin with salt, pepper, pepper flakes, and almond flour. Set aside.
3. Layer the pork tenderloin in the Air fryer basket. Cook for 5 minutes or until golden brown.
4. Meanwhile, heat oil in a pan and stir fry onions and bell peppers for 1 minute. To assemble, add cooked pork in a plate and put vegetables on the side. Serve.

NUTRITION: Calorie: 221 Carbs 8g Fat 10g Protein 22g Fiber 0g

Air Fried Artichoke Hearts

Intermediate Recipe Preparation Time: 7 minutes **Cooking Time:** 20 minutes
Serving: 3 **INGREDIENTS:**

- 1-pound frozen artichoke hearts, thawed, quartered
- 1-cup plain yogurt, low Fat
- 2 eggs, whisked
- 1 cup almond flour, finely milled
- 1 cup almond flour, coarsely milled
- 1 small lime, sliced into wedges, pips removed
- ½ cup sour cream, reduced Fat
- Pinch of sea salt

DIRECTIONS:

5. Preheat Air Fryer to 330 degrees F.
6. In a bowl, combine yogurt and salt. Soak artichoke hearts for at 15 minutes. Dry out. Discard yogurt. Dredge artichokes in almond flour first, then into eggs, and into coarse-milled almond flour.
7. Layer the artichoke hearts into the Air Fryer basket. Fry for 5 minutes or until golden brown on all sides. Dry out on paper towels. Squeeze lime juice. Serve with lime wedges and sour cream on the side.

NUTRITION: Calorie: 67 Carbs 7g Fat 3g Protein 2g Fiber 1g

Air-Fryer Onion Strings

Intermediate Recipe Preparation Time: 10 minutes **Cooking Time:** 20 minutes
Serving: 4

INGREDIENTS:

- 2 cups buttermilk
- 1-piece, whole white onion, halved, julienned
- 2 cups almond flour, finely milled
- ½ tsp. cayenne pepper
- Pinch of sea salt
- Pinch of black pepper to taste

DIRECTIONS:

1. Preheat Air Fryer to 330 degrees F.
2. Soak onion strings in buttermilk for 1 hour before frying. Dry out.
3. Meanwhile, mix almond flour, cayenne pepper, salt and pepper in a bowl. Coat onion strings with flour mixture.
4. Layer the onions in Air fryer basket. Fry until golden brown and crisp. Dry out on paper towels. Season it with salt. Serve.

NUTRITION: Calorie: 150 Carbs 13g Fat 17g Protein 2g Fiber 1g

Air Fried Spinach

Basic Recipe
Preparation Time: 5 minutes **Cooking Time:** 10 minutes **Serving:** 3
INGREDIENTS:

- 2½ pounds fresh spinach leaves and tender stems only
- Pinch of sea salt, to taste

DIRECTIONS:

8. Preheat Air Fryer to 330 degrees F. Put spinach in the Air fryer basket. Fry for 20 seconds. Dry out on paper towels. Repeat step with the rest of the spinach. Season it with salt. Serve.

NUTRITION: Calorie: 81.6 Carbs 4.5 Fat 6.9g Protein 1.3g Fiber 1.1g

Air Fried Zucchini Blooms

Basic Recipe
Preparation Time: 5 minutes **Cooking Time:** 10 minutes **Serving:** 3
INGREDIENTS:

- 2½ pounds zucchini flowers, rinsed
- 1 cup almond flour, finely milled
- Pinch of sea salt, to taste
- Balsamic vinegar, for garnish

DIRECTIONS:

1. Preheat Air Fryer to 330 degrees F.
2. Half-fill deep fryer with oil. Set this at medium heat. Lightly season zucchini flowers with salt, and then dredge in almond flour.
3. Layer breaded flowers into the Air Fryer basket Fry until golden brown. Dry out on paper towels. Transfer to a plate. Pour balsamic vinegar if using. Serve.

NUTRITION: Calorie: 117 Carbs 8g Fat 8g Protein 1g Fiber 0g

Air Fried Salmon Belly

Intermediate Recipe Preparation Time: 10 minutes **Cooking Time:** 20 minutes
Serving: 2
INGREDIENTS:

- 1-pound salmon belly, skin on, trimmed, sliced into ¾-inch thick sliver
- 2 Tbsp. almond flour, finely milled
- Pinch of sea salt
- Dip
- ¼ tsp. fresh garlic, minced
- ½ cup coconut or palm vinegar
- ¼ cup white onion, minced
- ¼ tsp. fish sauce
- 1-piece bird's eye chili, deseeded, minced
- Black pepper to taste

DIRECTIONS:

1. Preheat Air Fryer to 330 degrees F.
2. Combine palm vinegar, fish sauce, white onion, bird's eye chili, garlic, and pepper in a small bowl. Set aside. Season salmon belly with the mixture. Roll in almond flour.
3. Layer the fillet in the Air Fryer's basket. Fry for 5 minutes or until golden brown. Dry out on paper towels.
4. Serve with dip or on bed of rice.

NUTRITION: Calorie: 129 Carbs 5.35g Fat 0.8 Protein 11.99g Fiber 0.3g

Stuffed Portabella Mushrooms

Intermediate Recipe Preparation Time: 10 minutes **Cooking Time:** 20 minutes **Serving:** 2

INGREDIENTS:

- 2 dozen fresh portabella mushrooms, minced
- 2 tsp. olive oil, add more for drizzling/greasing
- Filling
- 1 tbsp. olive oil
- 1 onion, minced
- 2 garlic cloves, grated
- 3 tbsp. butter, unsalted
- ¼ cup apple cider vinegar
- 2 tbsp. fresh parsley, minced
- ¼ cup roasted cashew nuts, crushed
- ¼-cup cheddar cheese, reduced fat, grated
- ¼ cup parmesan cheese, grated
- pinch of sea salt
- pinch of black pepper to taste

DIRECTIONS:

1. Preheat Air Fryer to 330 degrees F.
2. Meanwhile, in a pan heat the oil. Sauté the onion and garlic for 2 minutes or until translucent and fragrant
3. Stir in butter, almonds, mushrooms stems, salt, and pepper. Cook for 3 minutes or until mushrooms turn brown in color.
4. Pour vinegar. Cook until the liquid is reduced. Stir in nuts and Parmesan cheese. Allow mixture to cool.
5. Spoon the mixture into mushroom caps. Layer mushrooms in the prepared baking dish. Place inside the Air fryer basket. Cook for 20 minutes. Serve.

NUTRITION: Calorie: 129 Carbs 5.35g Fat 0.8g Protein 11.99g Fiber 0.3g

Breaded Lean Pork Chops on Spinach Salad

Intermediate Recipe Preparation Time: 40 Minutes **Cooking Time**: 30 minutes
Serving: 2
INGREDIENTS:

- 2 pieces lean pork chops, pounded ¼-inch thick using a meat mallet
- Breading and seasonings
- 1 egg, whisked
- ½ tsp. Dijon mustard
- ¼ tsp. dried oregano
- ½ cup almond flour, finely milled
- ¼-cup Parmesan cheese
- Pinch of sea salt
- Pinch of black pepper to taste
- Salad
- 6 cups baby spinach leaves, rinsed, spun-dried
- 2 Tbsp. apple cider vinegar
- 1 Tbsp. extra virgin olive oil
- Pinch of sea salt, to taste

DIRECTIONS:

1. Preheat Air Fryer to 330 degrees F.
2. In a bowl, mix egg, oregano, and mustard. Season it with salt and pepper. Marinate pork chops for 30 minutes. Put inside the refrigerator before frying. In another bowl, mix almond flour and Parmesan cheese. Roll pork chops into breading. Layer pork chops in the Air Fryer basket for 5 minutes or until golden brown. Dry out on paper towels. Put salad ingredients in a salad bowl. Put pork chop slivers. Mix well to combine. Serve.

NUTRITION: Calorie: 165 Carbs 7.15g Fat 9.9g Protein 11.08g Fiber 0.5g

Peppery Butter Swordfish Steaks

Intermediate Recipe Preparation Time: 30 minutes **Cooking Time:** 35 minutes
Serving: 4
INGREDIENTS:

- Swordfish steaks and seasoning
- 4 pieces swordfish steaks make shallow incisions through skin
- 1/16 tsp. salt
- 1 tsp. olive oil, for greasing
- Peppery Butter
- 2 tsp. butter, unsalted
- ½ tsp. toasted garlic, store-bought
- 1 tsp. fresh parsley, minced
- ½ tsp. mixed dried ground peppercorns
- ½ lime, sliced into 4 equal wedges, for garnish

DIRECTIONS:

1. Preheat the Air Fryer to 400 degrees F.
2. Using a pastry brush, lightly grease four sheets of aluminum foil with olive oil. This will prevent steak from sticking to the foil, while preserving most of its juices.
3. Season the swordfish steaks with salt. Wrap each piece individually in prepared sheets of aluminum foil.
4. Place two steaks into Air Fryer basket. Place double layer rack into the basket. Layer the remaining fish on top.
5. Fry for 10 minutes. Shake contents of basket once midway through.
6. Remove steaks from machine. Place on a plate. Rest the meat for 10 minutes before removing aluminum foil sheets. Place swordfish steaks directly into plates, and Drizzle with in cooking juices.
7. Combine ingredients in a small microwave oven- safe bowl. Microwave for 3 seconds on highest heat until butter softens. Stir well.
8. Top each steak off with equal portions of peppery butter.
9. Squeeze lime juice over fish before eating. **NUTRITION:** Calorie : 140   Carbs 0g Fat 0 Protein 23g Fiber 0g

Lean Pork Belly Crisp

Intermediate Recipe Preparation Time: 15 minutes **Cooking Time:** 25 minutes
Serving: 2
INGREDIENTS:

- 2½ pounds lean pork belly, whole
- 2 dried bay leaves
- 2 tablespoons olive oil
- 2 Tbsp. fish sauce
- 2 cups vinegar
- 2 cups water
- 2 Tbsp. black peppercorns, lightly cracked

DIRECTIONS:

1. Preheat the Air Fryer to 330 degrees F.
2. Heat the oil in the saucepan. Add pork belly, vinegar, water, fish sauce, bay leaves, and black peppercorns. Bring mixture to a boil.
3. Turn down heat to low. Allow to simmer for 10 minutes. Remove from heat. Dry out pork in a colander.
4. Layer the pork bell in the Air Fryer basket. Fry for 5 minutes or until golden brown. Serve with vegetable salad.

NUTRITION: Calorie: 145 Carbs 0g Fat 15g Protein 2g Fiber 0g

Easy Beef Curry with Carrots and Cauliflower

Intermediate Recipe Preparation Time: 15 minutes **Cooking Time:** 35 minutes
Serving: 4

INGREDIENTS:

- Beef curry and sauce
- 1 can thick coconut cream
- ¼ lean beef, sliced into sukiyaki strips
- ½ tsp. curry powder
- ½ tsp. garam masala
- ¼ tsp. ghee
- ⅛ Tsp. fresh ginger, grated
- 1/16 tsp. fish sauce
- 1/16 tsp. salt
- 1/16 tsp. red pepper flakes
- 1/16 tsp. white pepper
- ¼ cup cauliflower, sliced into bite-sized florets
- ¼-cup shallots, peeled, diced
- 1 banana chili, stemmed, halved lengthwise, for garnish
- 1-cup fresh straw mushrooms, bases trimmed, halved lengthwise, rinsed, and Dry out
- ¼ cup frozen baby peas, thawed, dry out well

DIRECTIONS:

10. Preheat the Air Fryer to 355 degrees F. Season the beef with salt and pepper.
11. Combine remaining ingredients in a separate bowl.
12. Sprinkle veggies and mushrooms on top. Drape beef sukiyaki slices on top of veggies so these are partially covered. Leave some veggies exposed.
13. Pour in beef curry sauce. Seal lid. Place filled tiffin box into Air Fryer basket. Cook dish for 5 minutes. Turn down heat to 285 degrees F. Continue cooking for another 20 minutes. Turn off machine immediately. Leave tiffin box in the basket for 5 minutes to rest.
14. Remove tiffin box. Carefully take off lid. Garnish with banana chili. Serve right out of tiffin box.

NUTRITION: Calorie: 20 Carbs 11g Fat 13g Protein 29g Fiber 2.9g

Mackerel Steaks

Intermediate Recipe Preparation Time: 10 minutes **Cooking Time:** 35 minutes
Serving: 2

INGREDIENTS:

- 2 pieces, 6 oz. each Spanish mackerel steak
- 2 Tbsp. butter, unsalted, divided
- ¼ cup garlic, grated
- 2 Tbsp. olive oil
- Pinch of sea salt to taste

DIRECTIONS:

15. Preheat the Air Fryer to 330 degrees F.
16. Season the mackerel steaks with salt.
17. Meanwhile, in a skillet, heat the oil. Sauté the garlic for 3 minutes or until limp and aromatic then set aside.
18. Layer the mackerel steaks in the Air Fryer basket. Fry got 4 minutes. Do not overcook. Transfer steaks to a plate. Drizzle with in cooking liquid. Sprinkle garlic on top. Serve.

NUTRITION: Calorie: 220 Carbs 0g Fat 9.2g   Protein 34.4g

Classic Ribs with Bell Peppers

Intermediate Recipe Preparation Time: 20 minutes **Cooking Time:** 35 minutes **Serving:** 4

INGREDIENTS:

- 1-pound St. Louis-style pork spareribs individually cut
- 1 teaspoon seasoned salt
- 1/2 teaspoon ground black pepper
- 1 tablespoon sweet paprika
- 1/2 teaspoon mustard powder
- 2 tablespoons sesame oil
- 4 bell pepper, seeded

DIRECTIONS

19. Toss and rub the spice all over the pork ribs; Drizzle with 1 tablespoon of sesame oil.
20. Cook the pork ribs at 360 degrees F for 15 minutes; flip the ribs and cook an additional 20 minutes or until they are tender inside and crisp on the outside.
21. Toss the peppers with the remaining 1 tablespoon of oil; season to taste and cook in the preheated Air Fryer at 390 degrees F for 15 minutes.
22. Serve the warm spareribs with the roasted peppers on the side. Enjoy!

NUTRITION: 406 Calories 25.4g Fat 10g Carbs 49g Protein

Spicy Pork Curry

Intermediate Recipe Preparation Time: 5 minutes **Cooking Time:** 30 minutes **Serving:** 4

INGREDIENTS:

- 2 cardamom pods, only the seeds, crushed
- 1 teaspoon fennel seeds
- 1 teaspoon cumin seeds
- 1 teaspoon coriander seeds
- 2 teaspoons peanut oil
- 2 scallions, chopped
- 2 garlic cloves, smashed
- 2 jalapeno peppers, minced
- 1/2 teaspoon ginger, freshly grated
- 1-pound pork loin, cut into bite-sized cubes
- 1 cup coconut milk
- 1 cup chicken broth
- 1 teaspoon turmeric powder
- 1 tablespoon tamarind paste
- 1 tablespoon fresh lime juice

DIRECTIONS

23. Place the cardamom, fennel, cumin, and coriander seeds in a nonstick skillet over medium-high heat. Stir for 6 minutes until the spices become aromatic

    and start to brown. Stir frequently to prevent the spices from burning. Set aside.
24. Preheat your Air Fryer to 370 degrees F. Then, in a baking pan, heat the peanut oil for 2 minutes. Once hot, sauté the scallions for 2 to 3 minutes until tender.
25. Stir in the garlic, peppers, and ginger; cook an additional minute, stirring frequently. Next, cook the pork for 3 to 4 minutes.
26. Pour in the coconut milk and broth. Add the reserved seeds, turmeric, and tamarind paste. Let it cook for 15 minutes in the preheated Air Fryer.
27. Divide between individual bowls; Drizzle with fresh lime juice over the top and serve immediately.

NUTRITION: 396 Calories 20.1g Fat 4.9g Carbs 44.2g Protein

Nana"s Pork Chops with Cilantro

Intermediate Recipe Preparation Time: 5 minutes **Cooking Time:** 20 minutes
Serving: 6 **INGREDIENTS:**

- 1/3 cup pork rinds
- Roughly chopped fresh cilantro, to taste
- 2 teaspoons Cajun seasonings
- Nonstick cooking spray
- 2 eggs, beaten
- 3 tablespoons almond meal
- 1 teaspoon seasoned salt
- Garlic & onion spice blend, to taste
- 6 pork chops
- 1/3 teaspoon freshly cracked black pepper

DIRECTIONS:

28. Coat the pork chops with Cajun seasonings, salt, pepper, and the spice blend on all sides.
29. Then, add the almond meal to a plate. In a shallow dish, whisk the egg until pale and smooth. Place the pork rinds in the third bowl.
30. Dredge each pork piece in the almond meal; then, coat them with the egg finally, coat them with the pork rinds. Sprits them with cooking spray on both sides.
31. Now, air-fry pork chops for about 18 minutes at 345 degrees F; make sure to taste for doneness after first 12 minutes of cooking. Lastly, garnish with fresh cilantro. Bon appétit!

NUTRITION: 390 Calories 21.3g Fat 1g Carbs 42g Protein

Paprika Burgers with Blue Cheese

Intermediate Recipe Preparation Time: 5 minutes **Cooking Time:** 40Minutes

Serving: 6 **INGREDIENTS:**

- 1 cup blue cheese, sliced
- 2 teaspoons dried basil
- 1 teaspoon smoked paprika
    - 2 tablespoons tomato puree
    - 2 small-sized onions, peeled and chopped
    - 1/2 teaspoon ground black pepper
    - 3 garlic cloves, minced
    - 1 teaspoon fine sea salt

DIRECTIONS:

32. Start by preheating your Air Fryer to 385 degrees F.
33. In a mixing dish, combine the pork, onion, garlic, tomato puree, and seasonings; mix to combine well.
34. Form the pork mixture into six patties; cook the burgers for 23 minutes. Pause the machine, turn the temperature to 365 degrees F and cook for 18 more minutes.
35. Place the prepared burgers on a serving platter; top with blue cheese and serve warm.

NUTRITION: 493 Calories 38.6g Fat 4.1g Carbs 30.1g Protein

Tangy Pork Chops with Vermouth

Intermediate Recipe Preparation Time: 5 minutes **Cooking Time:** 30 minutes
Serving: 5 **INGREDIENTS:**

- 5 pork chops
- 1/3 cup vermouth
- 1/2 teaspoon paprika
- 2 sprigs thyme, only leaves, crushed
- 1/2 teaspoon dried oregano
- Fresh parsley, to serve
- 1 teaspoon garlic salt
- ½ lemon, cut into wedges
- 1 teaspoon freshly cracked black pepper
- 3 tablespoons lemon juice
- 3 cloves garlic, minced
- 2 tablespoons canola oil

DIRECTIONS

36. Firstly, heat the canola oil in a sauté pan over a moderate heat. Now, sweat the garlic until just fragrant.
37. Remove the pan from the heat and pour in the lemon juice and vermouth. Now, throw in the seasonings. Dump the sauce into a baking dish, along with the pork chops.
38. Tuck the lemon wedges among the pork chops and air-fry for 27 minutes at 345 degrees F. Bon appétit!

NUTRITION: 400 Calories 23g Fat 4.1g Carbs 40.5g
Protein

French-Style Pork and Pepper Meatloaf

Intermediate Recipe Preparation Time: 5 minutes **Cooking Time:** 30 minutes
Serving: 4 **INGREDIENTS:**

- 1-pound pork, ground

- 1/2 cup parmesan cheese, grated
- 1 ½ tablespoons green garlic, minced
- 1½ tablespoon fresh cilantro, minced
- 1/2 tablespoon fish sauce
- 1/3 teaspoon dried basil
- 1 leek, chopped
- 1 Serrano pepper, chopped
- 2 tablespoons tomato puree
- 1/2 teaspoons dried thyme
- Salt and ground black pepper, to taste

DIRECTIONS

39. Add all ingredients to a large-sized mixing dish and combine everything using your hands.
40. Then, form a meatloaf using a spatula.
41. Bake it for 23 minutes at 365 degrees Fahrenheit. Afterward, allow your meatloaf to rest for 10 minutes before slicing and serving. Bon appétit!

NUTRITION: Calories 417 Fat 27.1g Carbs 7.6g Protein 33.9g

Ham and Kale Egg Cups

Basic Recipe
Preparation Time: 5 minutes **Cooking Time:** 20 minutes **Serving:** 2
INGREDIENTS:

- 2 eggs
- 1/4 teaspoon dried or fresh marjoram
- 2 teaspoons chili powder
- 1/3 teaspoon kosher salt
- ½ cup steamed kale
- 1/4 teaspoon dried or fresh rosemary
- 4 pork ham slices
- 1/3 teaspoon ground black pepper, or more to taste

DIRECTIONS:

42. Divide the kale and ham among 2 ramekins; crack an egg into each ramekin. Sprinkle with seasonings.
43. Cook for 15 minutes at 335 degrees F or until your eggs reach desired texture.
44. Serve warm with spicy tomato ketchup and pickles. Bon appétit!

NUTRITION: Calories 398 Fat 17.8g Carbs3g Protein61g

Spicy Ground Pork Omelet with Cream Cheese

Basic Recipe
Preparation Time: 5 minutes **Cooking Time:** 20 minutes **Serving:** 2
INGREDIENTS:

- 4 garlic cloves, peeled and minced
- 1/2 tablespoon fresh basil, chopped
- 1/3-pound ground pork
- 1/3 teaspoon ground black pepper
- 1/2 small-sized onion, peeled and finely chopped
- 1 1/2 tablespoons olive oil
- 3 medium-sized eggs, beaten

- 1/2 jalapeno pepper, seeded and chopped
- 4 tablespoons cream cheese
- 1/3 teaspoon salt

DIRECTIONS

1. In a nonstick skillet that is preheated over a moderate flame, heat the oil; then, sweat the onion, garlic and ground pork in the hot oil.
2. Spritz an Air Fryer baking dish with a cooking spray.
3. Throw in the sautéed mixture, followed by the remaining ingredients.
4. Bake at 325 degrees F approximately 15 minutes. Serve with the salad of choice. Bon appétit!

NUTRITION: Calories 438 Fat 22.2g Carbs 4.7g Protein 28.2g

Pork Belly with Lime Aromatics

Intermediate Recipe Preparation Time: 15 minutes
Cooking Time: 1 hour and 5 minutes
Serving: 4
INGREDIENTS:

- 1-pound pork belly
- 2 garlic cloves, halved
- 1 teaspoon shallot powder
- 1 teaspoon sea salt
- 1 teaspoon dried basil
- 1 teaspoon dried oregano
- 1 teaspoon dried thyme
- 1 teaspoon dried marjoram
- 1 teaspoon ground black pepper
- 1 lime, juiced

DIRECTIONS

45. Blanch the pork belly in a pot of boiling water for 10 to 13 minutes.
46. Pat it and dry with a kitchen towel. Now, poke holes all over the skin by using a fork.
47. Then, mix the remaining ingredients to make the rub. Massage the rub all over the pork belly. Drizzle with lime juice all over the meat; place the pork belly in the refrigerator for 3 hours.
48. Preheat your Air Fryer to 320 degrees F. Cook the pork belly for 35 minutes.
49. Turn up the temperature to 360 degrees F and continue cooking for 20 minutes longer. Serve warm. Bon appétit!

NUTRITION: 590 Calories 60.1g Fat 0.5g Carbs 10.6g Protein

Mexican Stuffed Peppers with Pork and Cheese

Intermediate Recipe Preparation Time: 5 minutes **Cooking Time:** 30 minutes **Serving:** 3

INGREDIENTS:

- 3 bell peppers, stems and seeds removed
- 1 tablespoon canola oil
- 1/2 cup onions, chopped
- 1 teaspoon fresh garlic, minced
- 1 Mexican chili pepper, finely chopped
- 1-pound lean pork, ground
- 1/2 teaspoon sea salt
- 1/2 teaspoon black pepper
- 1 tablespoon Mexican oregano
- 1 ripe tomato, pureed
- 3 ounces Cotija cheese, grated

DIRECTIONS

50. Cook the peppers in boiling salted water for 4 minutes
51. In a nonstick skillet, heat the canola oil over medium heat. Then, sauté the onions, garlic and Mexican chili pepper until tender and fragrant.
52. Stir in the ground pork and continue sautéing until the pork has browned; Dry out off the excess fat.
53. Add the salt, black pepper, Mexican oregano, and pureed tomato; give it a good stir.
54. Divide the filling among the bell peppers. Arrange the peppers in a baking dish lightly greased with cooking oil.
55. Bake in the preheated Air Fryer at 380 degrees F for 13 minutes. Top with grated Cotija cheese and bake another 6 minutes. Serve warm and enjoy!

NUTRITION: 425 Calories 25.9g Fat 9.5g Carbs 38.3g Protein

Italian Twisted Pork Chops

Basic Recipe
Preparation Time: 5 minutes **Cooking Time:** 20 minutes **Serving:** 4
INGREDIENTS:

- 1/4 cup balsamic vinegar
- 3 center-cut loin pork chops
- 1/4 cup almond meal
- 2 tablespoons golden flaxseed meal
- 1 teaspoon turmeric powder
- 1 egg
- 1 teaspoon mustard
- Kosher salt, to taste
- 1/4 teaspoon freshly ground black pepper
- 1/2 cup pork rinds, crushed
- 1/2 teaspoon garlic powder
- 1 teaspoon shallot powder

DIRECTIONS

56. Drizzle with the balsamic vinegar over pork chops and spread to evenly coat.
57. Place the almond meal, flaxseed meal, and turmeric in a shallow bowl. In another bowl, whisk the eggs, mustard, salt, and black pepper.
58. In the third bowl, mix the pork rinds with the garlic powder and shallot powder.
59. Preheat your Air Fryer to 390 degrees F. Dredge the pork chops in the almond meal mixture, then in the egg, followed by the pork rind mixture.

60. Cook the pork chops for 7 minutes per side, spraying with cooking oil. Bon appétit!

NUTRITION: Calories 517 Fat 19.3g Carbs 7.3g Protein 62g

Herby Pork with Celery Chips

Intermediate Recipe Preparation Time: 5 minutes
Cooking Time: 1 hour and 10 minutes
Serving: 4
INGREDIENTS:

- 1 tablespoon peanut oil
- 1 ½ pounds pork loin, cut into 4 pieces
- Coarse sea salt and ground black pepper, to taste
- 1/2 teaspoon onion powder
- 1 teaspoon garlic powder
- 1/2 teaspoon cayenne pepper
- 1/2 teaspoon dried rosemary
- 1/2 teaspoon dried basil
- 1/2 teaspoon dried oregano
- 1-pound celery, cut into matchsticks
- 1 tablespoon coconut oil, melted

DIRECTIONS

61. Drizzle with 1 tablespoon of peanut oil all over the pork loin. Season it with salt, black pepper, onion powder, garlic powder, cayenne pepper, rosemary, basil, and oregano.
62. Cook in the preheated Air Fryer at 360 degrees F for 55 minutes; make sure to turn the pork over every 15 minutes to ensure even cooking.
63. Test for doneness with a meat thermometer.
64. Toss the carrots with melted coconut oil; season to taste and cook in the preheated Air Fryer at 380 degrees F for 15 minutes.
65. Serve the warm pork loin with the carrots on the side. Enjoy!

NUTRITION: 442 Calories 25.8g Fat 5.5g Carbs 44g Protein

Favorite Taco Casserole

Intermediate Recipe Preparation Time: 5 minutes **Cooking Time:** 40Minutes
Serving: 4 **INGREDIENTS:**

- 1 tablespoon olive oil
- 1-pound pork, ground
- 1 tablespoon taco seasoning mix
- Sea salt and ground black pepper, to taste
- 1 medium-sized leek, sliced
- 1 teaspoon fresh garlic, minced
- 1/2 cup celery, trimmed and sliced
- 1 (2-ounce) jar pimiento, Dry outed and chopped
- 1 can (10 ¾-ounces) condensed cream of mushroom soup
- 1 cup water
- 1/2 cup Mexican beer

- 1/2 cup cream cheese, grated
- 1 cup Mexican cheese, shredded
- 1 tablespoon fresh cilantro, chopped

DIRECTIONS

1. Start by preheating your Air Fryer to 320 degrees F.
2. Add the olive oil to a baking dish and heat for 1 to 2 minutes. Add the pork, taco seasoning mix, salt, pepper and cook for 6 minutes, crumbling with a fork.
3. Add the leeks and cook for 4 to 5 minutes, stirring occasionally.
4. Add the garlic, celery, pimiento, mushroom soup, water, beer, and cream cheese. Gently stir to combine.
5. Turn the temperature to 370 degrees F.
6. Top with Mexican cheese. Place the baking dish in the cooking basket and cook approximately 30 minutes or until everything is thoroughly cooked.
7. Serve garnished with fresh cilantro. Bon appétit!

NUTRITION: Calories 601 Fat 49g Carbs8.2g Protein32.5g

Chinese-Style Pork Shoulder

Intermediate Recipe Preparation Time: 5 minutes **Cooking Time:** 20 minutes
Serving: 3 **INGREDIENTS:**

- 2 tablespoons coconut aminos
- 2 tablespoons Shaoxing wine
- 2 garlic cloves, minced
- 1 teaspoon fresh ginger, minced
- 1 tablespoon cilantro stems and leaves, finely chopped
- 1-pound boneless pork shoulder
- 2 tablespoons sesame oil

DIRECTIONS

1. In a large-sized ceramic dish, thoroughly combine the coconut aminos, Shaoxing wine, garlic, ginger, and cilantro; add the pork shoulder and allow it to marinate for 2 hours in the refrigerator.
2. Then, grease the cooking basket with sesame oil. Place the pork shoulder in the cooking basket; reserve the marinade.
3. Cook in the preheated Air Fryer at 395 degrees F for 14 to 17 minutes, flipping and basting with the marinade halfway through. Let it rest for 5 to 6 minutes before slicing and serving.
4. While the pork is roasting, cook the marinade in a preheated skillet over medium heat; cook until it has thickened.
5. Brush the pork shoulder with the sauce and enjoy! **NUTRITION:** 353 Calories 19.6g Fat 13.5g Carbs 29.2g Protein

Cheesy Mini Meatloaves

Intermediate Recipe Preparation Time: 5 minutes **Cooking Time:** 50Minutes
Serving: 4

INGREDIENTS:

- 1-pound ground pork
- 1/2-pound ground beef
- 1 package onion soup mix
- 1/2 cup Romano cheese, grated
- 2 eggs
- 1 bell pepper, chopped
- 1 Serrano pepper, minced
- 2 scallions, chopped
- 2 cloves garlic, finely chopped
- Sea salt and black pepper, to your liking
- Glaze:
- 1/2 cup tomato paste
- 1 tablespoon brown mustard
- 1 teaspoon smoked paprika

DIRECTIONS

1. In a large mixing bowl, thoroughly combine all ingredients for meatloaves. Mix with your hands until everything is well incorporated.
2. Then, shape the mixture into four mini loaves. Transfer them to the cooking basket previously generously greased with cooking oil.
3. Cook in the preheated Air Fryer at 385 degrees F approximately 43 minutes.
4. Mix all ingredients for the glaze. Spread the glaze over mini meatloaves and cook for another 6 minutes. Bon appétit!

NUTRITION: 535 Calories 37.4g Fat 4.8g Carbs 42.1gProtein

DINNER

Crispy Indian Wrap

Basic Recipe
Preparation Time: 20 minutes **Cooking Time:** 8 minutes **Servings:** 4 **INGREDIENTS:**

- Cilantro Chutney
- 2¾ cups diced potato, cooked until tender
- 2 teaspoons oil (coconut, sunflower, or safflower)
- 3 large garlic cloves, minced or pressed
- 1½ tablespoons fresh lime juice
- 1½ teaspoons cumin powder
- 1 teaspoon onion granules
- 1 teaspoon coriander powder
- ½ teaspoon sea salt
- ½ teaspoon turmeric
- ¼ teaspoon cayenne powder
- 4 large flour tortillas, preferably whole grain or sprouted
- 1 cup cooked garbanzo beans (canned are fine), rinsed and Dry out
- ½ cup finely chopped cabbage
- ¼ cup minced red onion or scallion
- Cooking oil spray (sunflower, safflower, or refined coconut)

DIRECTIONS:

1. Make the Cilantro Chutney and set aside.
2. In a large bowl, mash the potatoes well, using a potato masher or large fork. Add the oil, garlic, lime, cumin, onion, coriander, salt, turmeric, and cayenne. Stir very well, until thoroughly combined. Set aside.
3. Lay the tortillas out flat on the counter. In the middle of each, evenly distribute the potato filling. Add some of the garbanzo beans, cabbage, and red onion to each, on top of the potatoes.
4. Spray the air fryer basket with oil and set aside. Enclose the Indian wraps by folding the bottom of the tortillas up and over the filling, then folding the

   sides in—and finally rolling the bottom up to form, essentially, an enclosed burrito.
5. Place the wraps in the air fryer basket, seam side down. They can touch each other a little bit, but if they're too crowded, you'll need to cook them in batches. Fry for 5 minutes Spray with oil again, flip over, and cook an additional 2 or 3 minutes, until nicely browned and crisp. Serve topped with the Cilantro Chutney.

NUTRITION: Calories 288 Fat 7g Carbs 50g Protein 9g

Easy Peasy Pizza

Basic Recipe

Preparation Time: 5 minutes **Cooking Time:** 10 minutes **Servings:** 4

INGREDIENTS:

- Cooking oil spray (coconut, sunflower, or safflower)
- 1 flour tortilla, preferably sprouted or whole grain
- ¼ cup vegan pizza or marinara sauce
- ⅓Cup grated vegan mozzarella cheese or Cheesy Sauce
- Toppings of your choice

DIRECTIONS:

1. Spray the air fryer basket with oil. Place the tortilla in the air fryer basket. If the tortilla is a little bigger than the base, no problem! Simply fold the edges up a bit to form a semblance of a —crust.‖

2. Pour the sauce in the center, and evenly distribute it around the tortilla —crust‖ (I like to use the back of a spoon for this purpose).

3. Sprinkle evenly with vegan cheese, and add your toppings. Bake it for 9 minutes, or until nicely browned. Remove carefully, cut into four pieces, and enjoy.

NUTRITION: Calories 210 Fat 6g Carbs 33g Protein 5g

Eggplant Parmigiana

Basic Recipe

Preparation Time: 15 minutes **Cooking Time:** 40 minutes **Servings:** 4

INGREDIENTS:

- 1 medium eggplant (about 1 pound), sliced into ½- inch-thick rounds
- 2 tablespoons tamari or shoyu
- 3 tablespoons nondairy milk, plain and unsweetened
- 1 cup chickpea flour (see Substitution Tip)
- 1 tablespoon dried basil
- 1 tablespoon dried oregano
- 2 teaspoons garlic granules
- 2 teaspoons onion granules
- ½ teaspoon sea salt
- ½ teaspoons freshly ground black pepper
- Cooking oil spray (sunflower, safflower, or refined coconut)
- Vegan marinara sauce (your choice)
    - Shredded vegan cheese (preferably mozzarella; see Ingredient Tip)

DIRECTIONS:

1. Place the eggplant slices in a large bowl, and pour the tamari and milk over the top. Turn the pieces over to coat them as evenly as possible with the liquids. Set aside.
2. Make the coating: In a medium bowl, combine the flour, basil, oregano, garlic, onion, salt, and pepper and stir well. Set aside.
3. Spray the air fryer basket with oil and set aside.
4. Stir the eggplant slices again and transfer them to a plate (stacking is fine). Do not discard the liquid in the bowl.
5. Bread the eggplant by tossing an eggplant round in the flour mixture. Then, dip in the liquid again. Double up on the coating by placing the eggplant again in the flour mixture, making sure that all sides are nicely breaded. Place in the air fryer basket.
6. Repeat with enough eggplant rounds to make a (mostly) single layer in the air fryer basket. (You'll need to cook it in batches, so that you don't have too much overlap and it cooks perfectly.)
7. Spray the tops of the eggplant with enough oil so that you no longer see dry patches in the coating. Fry for 8 minutes. Remove the air fryer basket and spray the tops again. Turn each piece over, again taking care not to overlap the rounds too much. Spray the tops with oil, again making sure that no dry patches remain. Fry for another 8 minutes, or until nicely browned and crisp.
8. Repeat steps 5 to 7 one more time, or until all of the eggplant is crisp and browned.
9. Finally, place half of the eggplant in a 6-inch round, 2-inch deep baking pan and top with marinara sauce and a sprinkle of vegan cheese. Fry for 3 minutes, or until the sauce is hot and cheese is melted (be careful not to overcook, or the eggplant edges will burn). Serve immediately, plain or over pasta. Otherwise, you can store the eggplant in the fridge for several days and then make a fresh batch whenever the mood strikes by repeating this step!

NUTRITION: Calories 217 Fat 9g Carbs 38g Protein 9g

Luscious Lazy Lasagna

Basic Recipe

Preparation Time: 15 minutes **Cooking Time:** 15 minutes **Servings:** 4

INGREDIENTS:

- 8 ounces lasagna noodles, preferably bean-based, but any kind will do
- 1 tablespoon extra-virgin olive oil
- 2 cups crumbled extra-firm tofu, Dry out and water squeezed out
- 2 cups loosely packed fresh spinach
- 2 tablespoons nutritional yeast
- 2 tablespoons fresh lemon juice
- 1 teaspoon onion granules
- 1 teaspoon sea salt
- ⅛ Teaspoon freshly ground black pepper
- 4 large garlic cloves, minced or pressed
- 2 cups vegan pasta sauce, your choice
- ½ cup shredded vegan cheese (preferably mozzarella)

DIRECTIONS:

1. Cook the noodles until a little firmer than al dente (they'll get a little softer after you air-fry them in the lasagna). Dry out and set aside.
2. While the noodles are cooking, make the filling. In a large pan over medium-high heat, add the olive oil, tofu, and spinach. Stir-fry for a minute, then add the nutritional yeast, lemon juice, onion, salt, pepper, and garlic. Stir well and cook just until the spinach is nicely wilted. Remove from heat.
3. To make half a batch (one 6-inch round, 2-inch deep baking pan) of lasagna: Spread a thin layer of pasta sauce in the baking pan. Layer 2 or 3 lasagna noodles on top of the sauce. Top with a little more sauce and some of the tofu mixture. Place another 2 or 3 noodles on top, and add another layer of sauce and then another layer of tofu. Finish with a layer of noodles, and then a final layer of sauce. Sprinkle about half of the vegan cheese on top (omit if you prefer; see the Ingredient Tip from the Eggplant Parmigiana). Place the pan in the air fryer and Bake it for 15 minutes, or until the noodles are browning around the edges and the cheese is melted. Cut and serve.

NUTRITION: Calories 317 Fat 8g Carbs 46g Protein 20g

Pasta with Creamy Cauliflower Sauce

Basic Recipe
Preparation Time: 10 minutes **Cooking Time:** 20 minutes **Servings:** 4
INGREDIENTS:

- 4 cups cauliflower florets
- Cooking oil spray (sunflower,
- Safflower, or refined coconut)
- 1 medium onion, chopped
- 8 ounces pasta, your choice (about 4 cups cooked; use gluten-free pasta if desired)
- Fresh chives or scallion tops, for garnish
- ½ cup raw cashew pieces (see Ingredient Tip)
- 1½ cups water
- 1 tablespoon nutritional yeast
- 2 large garlic cloves, peeled
- 2 tablespoons fresh lemon juice
- 1½ teaspoons sea salt
- ¼ teaspoons freshly ground black pepper

DIRECTIONS:

1. Place the cauliflower in the air fryer basket, sprits the tops with oil spray, and roast for 8 minutes Remove the air fryer basket, stir, and add the onion. Sprits with oil again and roast for another 10

   minutes, or until the cauliflower is browned and the onions are tender.
2. While the vegetables are roasting in the air fryer, cook the pasta according to the package directions and mince the chives or scallions. Set aside.
3. In a blender jar, place the roasted cauliflower and onions along with the cashews, water, nutritional yeast, garlic, lemon, salt, and pepper. Blend well, until very smooth and creamy. Serve a generous portion of the sauce on top of the warm pasta, and top with the minced chives or scallions. The sauce will store, refrigerated in an airtight container, for about a week.

NUTRITION: Calories 341 Fat 9g Carbs 51g Protein 14g

Lemony Lentils with "Fried" Onions

Basic Recipe

Preparation Time: 10 minutes **Cooking Time:** 30 minutes **Servings:** 4 **INGREDIENTS:**

- 1 cup red lentils
- 4 cups water
- Cooking oil spray (coconut, sunflower, or safflower)
- 1 medium-size onion, peeled and cut into ¼-inch- thick rings
- Sea salt
- ½ cup kale, stems removed, thinly sliced
- 3 large garlic cloves, pressed or minced
- 2 tablespoons fresh lemon juice
- 2 teaspoons nutritional yeast
- 1 teaspoon sea salt
- 1 teaspoon lemon zest (see Ingredient Tip)
- ¾ teaspoons freshly ground black pepper

DIRECTIONS:

1. In a medium-large pot, bring the lentils and water to a boil over medium-high heat.
2. Reduce the heat to low and simmer, uncovered, for about 30 minutes (or until the lentils have dissolved completely), making sure to stir every 5 minutes or so as they cook (so that the lentils don't stick to the bottom of the pot).
3. While the lentils are cooking, get the rest of your dish together.
4. Spray the air fryer basket with oil and place the onion rings inside, separating them as much as possible. Spray them with the oil and sprinkle with a little salt. Fry for 5 minutes.
5. Remove the air fryer basket, shake or stir, spray again with oil, and fry for another 5 minutes.
6. (Note: You're aiming for all of the onion slices to be crisp and well browned, so if some of the pieces begin to do that, transfer them from the air fryer basket to a plate.)
7. Remove the air fryer basket, spray the onions again with oil, and fry for a final 5 minutes or until all the pieces are crisp and browned.
8. To finish the lentils: Add the kale to the hot lentils, and stir very well, as the heat from the lentils will steam the thinly sliced greens.
9. Stir in the garlic, lemon juice, nutritional yeast, salt, zest, and pepper.
10. Stir very well and then distribute evenly in bowls. Top with the crisp onion rings and serve.

NUTRITION: Calories 220 Fat 1g Carbs 39g Protein 15g

Our Daily Bean

Basic Recipe
Preparation Time: 5 minutes **Cooking Time:** 10 minutes **Servings:** 4
INGREDIENTS:

- 1 (15-ounce) can pinto beans, Dry out
- ¼ cup tomato sauce
- 2 tablespoons nutritional yeast
- 2 large garlic cloves, pressed or minced
- ½ teaspoon dried oregano
- ½ teaspoon cumin
- ¼ teaspoon sea salt
- ⅛ Teaspoon freshly ground black pepper
- Cooking oil spray (sunflower, safflower, or refined coconut)

DIRECTIONS:

1. In a medium bowl, stir together the beans, tomato sauce, nutritional yeast, garlic, oregano, cumin, salt, and pepper until well combined.
2. Spray the 6-inch round, 2-inch deep baking pan with oil and pour the bean mixture into it. Bake it for 4 minutes Remove, stir well, and Bake it for another 4 minutes, or until the mixture has thickened and is heated through. It will most likely form a little crust on top and be lightly browned in spots. Serve hot. This will keep, refrigerated in an airtight container, for up to a week.

NUTRITION: Calories 284 Fat 4g Carbs 47g Protein 20g

Taco Salad with Creamy Lime Sauce

Basic Recipe
Preparation Time: 10 minutes **Cooking Time:** 10 minutes **Servings:** 4
INGREDIENTS:
For The Sauce

- 1 (12.3-ounce) package of silken-firm tofu
- ¼ cup plus 1 tablespoon fresh lime juice
- Zest of 1 large lime (1 teaspoon)
- 1½ tablespoons coconut sugar
- 3 large garlic cloves, peeled
- 1 teaspoon sea salt
- ½ teaspoon ground chipotle powder For The Salad
- 6 cups romaine lettuce, chopped (1 large head)

  - 1 (15-ounce) can vegan refried beans (or whole pinto or black beans if you prefer)
  - 1 cup chopped red cabbage
  - 2 medium tomatoes, chopped
  - ½ cup chopped cilantro
  - ¼ cup minced scallions
  - Double batch of garlic lime tortilla chips

DIRECTIONS:
1. To Make the Sauce
2. Dry out the tofu (pour off any liquid) and place in a blender.
3. Add the lime juice and zest, coconut sugar, garlic, salt, and chipotle powder. Blend until very smooth. Set aside.
4. To Make the Salad
5. Distribute the lettuce equally into three big bowls.
6. In a small pan over medium heat, warm the beans, stirring often, until hot (this should take less than a minute). Place on top of the lettuce.
7. Top the beans with the cabbage, tomatoes, cilantro, and scallions.
8. Drizzle with generously with the Creamy Lime Sauce and serve with the double batch of air-fried chips. Enjoy immediately.

NUTRITION: Calories 422 Fat 7g Carbs 71g Protein 22g

BBQ Jackfruit Nachos

Basic Recipe
Preparation Time: 30 minutes **Cooking Time:** 20 minutes **Servings:** 4
INGREDIENTS:

- 1 (20-ounce) can jackfruit, dry out
- ⅓ cup prepared vegan bbq sauce
- ¼ cup water
- 2 tablespoons tamari or shoyu
- 1 tablespoon fresh lemon juice
- 4 large garlic cloves, pressed or minced
- 1 teaspoon onion granules
- ⅛ Teaspoon cayenne powder
- ⅛ Teaspoon liquid smoke
- Double batch garlic lime tortilla chips
- 2½ cups prepared cheesy sauce
- 3 medium-size tomatoes, chopped
- ¾ cup guacamole of your choice
- ¾ cup chopped cilantro
- ½ cup minced red onion
- 1 jalapeño, seeds removed and thinly sliced (optional)

DIRECTIONS:

1. In a large skillet over high heat, place the jackfruit, BBQ sauce, water, tamari, lemon juice, garlic, onion granules, cayenne, and liquid smoke. Stir well and break up the jackfruit a bit with a spatula.
2. Once the mixture boils, reduce the heat to low. Continue to cook, stirring often (and breaking up the jackfruit as you stir), for about 20 minutes, or

   until all of the liquid has been absorbed. Remove from the heat and set aside.
3. Assemble the nachos: Distribute the chips onto three plates, and then top evenly with the jackfruit mixture, warmed Cheesy Sauce, tomatoes, guacamole, cilantro, onion, and jalapeño (if using). Enjoy immediately, because soggy chips are tragic.

NUTRITION: Calories 661 Fat 15g Carbs 124g Protein 22g

10-Minute Chimichanga

Basic Recipe
Preparation Time: 5 minutes **Cooking Time:** 10 minutes **Servings:** 4
INGREDIENTS:

- 1 whole-grain tortilla
- ½ cup vegan refried beans
- ¼ cup grated vegan cheese (optional)
- Cooking oil spray (sunflower, safflower, or refined coconut)
- ½ cup fresh salsa (or Green Chili Sauce)
- 2 cups chopped romaine lettuce (about ½ head)
- Guacamole (optional)
- Chopped cilantro (optional)
- Cheesy Sauce (optional)

DIRECTIONS:

4. Lay the tortilla on a flat surface and place the beans in the center. Top with the cheese, if using. Wrap the bottom up over the filling, and then fold in the sides. Then roll it all up so as to enclose the beans inside the tortilla (you're making an enclosed burrito here).
5. Spray the air fryer basket with oil, place the tortilla wrap inside the basket, seam-side down, and spray the top of the chimichanga with oil. Fry for 5 minutes Spray the top (and sides) again with oil, flip over, and spray the other side with oil. Fry for an additional 2 or 3 minutes, until nicely browned and crisp.
6. Transfer to a plate. Top with the salsa, lettuce, guacamole, cilantro, and/or Cheesy Sauce, if using. Serve immediately.

NUTRITION: Calories 317 Fat 6g Carbs 55g Protein 13g

Mexican Stuffed Potatoes

Intermediate Recipe Preparation Time: 15 minutes **Cooking Time:** 40 minutes
Servings: 4 **INGREDIENTS:**

- 4 large potatoes, any variety (I like Yukon Gold or russets for this dish; see Cooking Tip)
- Cooking oil spray (sunflower, safflower, or refined coconut)
- 1½ cups Cheesy Sauce
- 1 cup black or pinto beans (canned beans are fine; be sure to Dry out and rinse)

- 2 medium tomatoes, chopped
- 1 scallion, finely chopped
- ⅓Cup finely chopped cilantro
- 1 jalapeño, finely sliced or minced (optional)
- 1 avocado, diced (optional)

DIRECTIONS:

1. Scrub the potatoes, prick with a fork, and spray the outsides with oil. Place in the air fryer (leaving room in between so the air can circulate) and Bake it for 30 minutes
2. While the potatoes are cooking, prepare the Cheesy Sauce and additional items. Set aside.
3. Check the potatoes at the 30-minute mark by poking a fork into them. If they're very tender, they're done. If not, continue to cook until a fork inserted proves them to be well-done. (As potato sizes vary, so will your cook time— the average cook time is usually about 40 minutes)
4. When the potatoes are getting very close to being tender, warm the Cheesy Sauce and the beans in separate pans.
5. To assemble: Plate the potatoes and cut them across the top. Then, pry them open with a fork— just enough to get all the goodies in there. Top each potato with the Cheesy Sauce, beans, tomatoes, scallions, cilantro, and jalapeño and avocado, if using. Enjoy immediately.

NUTRITION: Calories 420 Fat 5g Carbs 80g Fiber 17g Protein 15g

Kids" Taquitos

Basic Recipe

Preparation Time: 5 minutes **Cooking Time:** 10 minutes **Servings:** 4 **INGREDIENTS:**

- 8 corn tortillas
- Cooking oil spray (coconut, sunflower, or safflower)
- 1 (15-ounce) can vegan refried beans
- 1 cup shredded vegan cheese
- Guacamole (optional)
- Cheesy Sauce (optional)
- Vegan sour cream (optional)
- Fresh salsa (optional)

DIRECTIONS:

7. Warm the tortillas (so they don't break): Run them under water for a second, and then place in an oil- sprayed air fryer basket (stacking them is fine). Fry for 1 minute.
8. Remove to a flat surface, laying them out individually. Place an equal amount of the beans in a line down the center of each tortilla. Top with the vegan cheese.
9. Roll the tortilla sides up over the filling and place seam-side down in the air fryer basket (this will help them seal so the tortillas don't fly open). Add just enough to fill the basket without them touching too

   much (you may need to do another batch, depending on the size of your air fryer basket).
10. Spray the tops with oil. Fry for 7 minutes, or until the tortillas are golden-brown and lightly crisp. Serve immediately with your preferred toppings.

NUTRITION: Calories 286 Fat 9g Carbs 44g Protein 9g

Immune-Boosting Grilled Cheese Sandwich

Basic Recipe
Preparation Time: 5 minutes **Cooking Time:** 15 minutes **Servings:** 4
INGREDIENTS:

- 2 slices sprouted whole-grain bread (or substitute a gluten-free bread)
- 1 teaspoon vegan margarine or neutral-flavored oil (sunflower, safflower, or refined coconut)
- 2 slices vegan cheese (Violife cheddar or Chao creamy original) or Cheesy Sauce
- 1 teaspoon mellow white miso
- 1 medium-large garlic clove, pressed or finely minced
- 2 tablespoons fermented vegetables, kimchi, or sauerkraut
- Romaine or green leaf lettuce

DIRECTIONS:

11. Spread the outsides of the bread with the vegan margarine. Place the sliced cheese inside and close the sandwich back up again (buttered sides facing out). Place the sandwich in the air fryer basket and fry for 6 minutes Flip over and fry for another 6 minutes, or until nicely browned and crisp on the outside.

12. Transfer to a plate. Open the sandwich and evenly spread the miso and garlic clove over the inside of one of the bread slices. Top with the fermented vegetables and lettuce, close the sandwich back up, cut in half, and serve immediately.

NUTRITION: Calories 288 Fat 13g Carbs 34g Protein 8g

Tamale Pie with Cilantro Lime Cornmeal Crust

Basic Recipe
Preparation Time: 25 minutes **Cooking Time:** 20 minutes **Servings:** 4
INGREDIENTS:
For the filling

- 1 medium zucchini, diced (1¼ cups)
- 2 teaspoons   neutral-flavored   oil   (sunflower, safflower, or refined coconut)
- 1 cup cooked pinto beans, Dry out
- 1 cup canned diced tomatoes (unsalted) with juice
- 3 large garlic cloves, minced or pressed
- 1 tablespoon chickpea flour
- 1 teaspoon dried oregano
- 1 teaspoon onion granules

    - ½ teaspoon salt
    - ½ teaspoon crushed red chili flakes
    - Cooking oil spray (sunflower, safflower, or refined coconut)

For the crust

    - ½ cup yellow cornmeal, finely ground
    - 1½ cups water
    - ½ teaspoon salt
    - 1 teaspoon nutritional yeast
    - 1 teaspoon   neutral-flavored   oil   (sunflower, safflower, or refined coconut)
    - 2 tablespoons finely chopped cilantro
    - ½ teaspoon lime zest

DIRECTIONS:
13. To make the filling
14. In a large skillet set to medium-high heat, sauté the zucchini and oil for 3 minutes or until the zucchini begins to brown.
15. Add the beans, tomatoes, garlic, flour, oregano, onion, salt, and chili flakes to the mixture. Cook it over medium heat, stirring often, for 5 minutes, or until the mixture is thickened and no liquid remains. Remove from the heat.
16. Spray a 6-inch round, 2-inch deep baking pan with oil and place the mixture in the bottom. Smooth out the top and set aside.
17. To make the crust
18. In a medium pot over high heat, place the cornmeal, water, and salt. Whisk constantly as you bring the mixture to a boil. Once it boils, reduce the heat to very low. Add the nutritional yeast and oil and continue to cook, stirring very often, for 10 minutes or until the mixture is very thick and hard to whisk. Remove from the heat.
19. Stir the cilantro and lime zest into the cornmeal mixture until thoroughly combined. Using a rubber spatula, gently spread it evenly onto the filling in the baking pan to form a smooth crust topping. Place in the air fryer basket and Bake it for 20 minutes, or until the top is golden-brown. Let it cool for 5 to 10 minutes, then cut and serve.

NUTRITION: Calories 165 Fat 5g Carbs 26g Protein 6g

Herbed Eggplant

Basic Recipe
Preparation Time: 15 minutes **Cooking Time:** 15 minutes **Servings:** 2
INGREDIENTS

- ½ teaspoon dried marjoram, crushed
- ½ teaspoon dried oregano, crushed
- ½ teaspoon dried thyme, crushed
- ½ teaspoon garlic powder
- Salt and ground black pepper, as required
- 1 large eggplant, cubed
- Olive oil cooking spray

DIRECTIONS:

20. Set the temperature of air fryer to 390 degrees F. Grease an air fryer basket.
21. In a small bowl, mix well herbs, garlic powder, salt, and black pepper.
22. Spray the eggplant cubes evenly with cooking spray and then, rub with the herbs mixture.
23. Arrange eggplant cubes into the prepared air fryer basket in a single layer.
24. Air fry for about 6 minutes
25. Flip and spray the eggplant cubes with cooking spray.
26. Air fry for another 6 minutes
27. Flip and again, spray the eggplant cubes with cooking spray.
28. Air fry for 2-3 more minutes
29. Remove from air fryer and transfer the eggplant cubes onto serving plates.
30. Serve hot.

NUTRITION: Calories 62 Carbs 14.5g Protein 2.4g Fat 0.5g

Spices Stuffed Eggplants

Basic Recipe
Preparation Time: 15 minutes **Cooking Time:** 12 minutes **Servings:** 4
INGREDIENTS

- 4 teaspoons olive oil, divided
- ¾ tablespoon dry mango powder
- ¾ tablespoon ground coriander
- ½ teaspoon ground cumin
- ½ teaspoon ground turmeric
- ½ teaspoon garlic powder
- Salt, to taste
- 8 baby eggplants

DIRECTIONS:

31. In a small bowl, mix together one teaspoon of oil, and spices.
32. From the bottom of each eggplant, make 2 slits, leaving the stems intact.
33. With a small spoon, fill each slit of eggplants with spice mixture.
34. Now, brush the outer side of each eggplant with remaining oil.
35. Set the temperature of air fryer to 369 degrees F. Grease an air fryer basket.
36. Arrange eggplants into the prepared air fryer basket in a single layer.
37. Air fry for about 8-12 minutes
38. Remove from air fryer and transfer the eggplants onto serving plates.
39. Serve hot.

NUTRITION: Calories 317 Carbs 65g Protein 10.9g Fat 6.7g

Salsa Stuffed Eggplants

Basic Recipe
Preparation Time: 15 minutes
Cooking Time: 25 minutes

Servings: 2
INGREDIENTS

- 1 large eggplant
- 2 teaspoons olive oil, divided
- 2 teaspoons fresh lemon juice, divided
- 8 cherry tomatoes, quartered
- 2 tablespoons tomato salsa
- ½ tablespoon fresh parsley
- Salt and ground black pepper, as required

DIRECTIONS:

1. Set the temperature of air fryer to 390 degrees F. Grease an air fryer basket.
2. Place eggplant into the prepared air fryer basket.
3. Air fry for about 15 minutes
4. Remove from air fryer and cut the eggplant in half lengthwise.
5. Drizzle with the eggplant halves evenly with one teaspoon of oil.
6. Now, set the temperature of air fryer to 355 degrees F. Grease the air fryer basket.
7. Arrange eggplant into the prepared air fryer basket, cut-side up.
8. Air fry for another 10 minutes
9. Remove eggplant from the air fryer and set aside for about 5 minutes
10. Carefully, scoop out the flesh, leaving about ¼-inch away from edges.
11. Drizzle with the eggplant halves with one teaspoon of lemon juice.
12. Transfer the eggplant flesh into a bowl.
13. Add the tomatoes, salsa, parsley, salt, black pepper, remaining oil, and lemon juice and mix well.
14. Stuff the eggplant haves with salsa mixture and serve.

NUTRITION: Calories 192 Carbs 33.8g Protein 6.9g Fat 6.1g

Sesame Seeds Bok Choy

Basic Recipe
Preparation Time: 10 minutes **Cooking Time:** 6 minutes **Servings:** 4
INGREDIENTS

- 4 bunches baby bok choy, bottoms removed and leaves separated
- Olive oil cooking spray
- 1 teaspoon garlic powder
- 1 teaspoon sesame seeds

DIRECTIONS:

40. Set the temperature of air fryer to 325 degrees F.
41. Arrange bok choy leaves into the air fryer basket in a single layer.
42. Spray with the cooking spray and sprinkle with garlic powder.
43. Air fry for about 5-6 minutes, shaking after every 2 minutes
44. Remove from air fryer and transfer the bok choy onto serving plates.
45. Garnish with sesame seeds and serve hot.

NUTRITION: Calories 26 Carbs 4g Protein 2.5g Fat 0.7g

Basil Tomatoes

Basic Recipe
Preparation Time: 10 minutes **Cooking Time:** 10 minutes **Servings:** 2
INGREDIENTS:

- 2 tomatoes, halved
- Olive oil cooking spray
- Salt and ground black pepper, as required
- 1 tablespoon fresh basil, chopped

DIRECTIONS:

46. Set the temperature of air fryer to 320 degrees F. Grease an air fryer basket.
47. Spray the tomato halves evenly with cooking spray and sprinkle with salt, black pepper and basil.
48. Arrange tomato halves into the prepared air fryer basket, cut sides up.
49. Air-fry it for about 10 minutes or until desired doneness.
50. Remove from air fryer and transfer the tomatoes onto serving plates.
51. Serve warm.

NUTRITION: Calories 22 Carbs 4.8g Protein 1.1g Fat 4.8g

Overloaded Tomatoes

Basic Recipe

Preparation Time: 15 minutes **Cooking Time:** 22 minutes **Servings:** 4

INGREDIENTS:

- 4 tomatoes
- 1 teaspoon olive oil
- 1 carrot, peeled and finely chopped
- 1 onion, chopped
- 1 cup frozen peas, thawed
- 1 garlic clove, minced
- 2 cups cold cooked rice
- 1 tablespoon soy sauce

DIRECTIONS:

52. Cut the top of each tomato and scoop out pulp and seeds. In a skillet, heat oil over low heat and sauté the carrot, onion, garlic, and peas for about 2 minutes
53. Stir in the soy sauce and rice and remove from heat. Set the temperature of air fryer to 355 degrees F. Grease an air fryer basket.
54. Stuff each tomato with the rice mixture.
55. Arrange tomatoes into the prepared air fryer basket.
56. Air fry for about 20 minutes
57. Remove from air fryer and transfer the tomatoes onto a serving platter.
58. Set aside to cool slightly.
59. Serve warm.

NUTRITION: Calories 421 Carbs 89.1g Protein 10.5g Fat 2.2g

Sweet & Spicy Cauliflower

Basic Recipe
Preparation Time: 15 minutes **Cooking Time:** 30 minutes **Servings:** 4
INGREDIENTS

- 1 head cauliflower, cut into florets
- ¾ cup onion, thinly sliced
- 5 garlic cloves, finely sliced
- 1½ tablespoons soy sauce
- 1 tablespoon hot sauce
- 1 tablespoon rice vinegar
- 1 teaspoon coconut sugar
- Pinch of red pepper flakes
- Ground black pepper, as required
- 2 scallions, chopped

DIRECTIONS:

1. Set the temperature of air fryer to 350 degrees F. Grease an air fryer pan. Arrange cauliflower florets into the prepared air fryer pan in a single layer.
2. Air fry for about 10 minutes
3. Remove from air fryer and stir in the onions.
4. Air fry for another 10 minutes
5. Remove from air fryer and stir in the garlic.
6. Air fry for 5 more minutes
7. Meanwhile, in a bowl, mix well soy sauce, hot sauce, vinegar, coconut sugar, red pepper flakes, and black pepper.
8. Remove from the air fryer and stir in the sauce mixture.
9. Air fry for about 5 minutes
10. Remove from air fryer and transfer the cauliflower mixture onto serving plates. Garnish with scallions and serve.

NUTRITION: Calories 72 Carbs 13.8g Protein 3.6g Fat 0.2g

Spiced Butternut Squash

Basic Recipe

Preparation Time: 15 minutes **Cooking Time:** 20 minutes **Servings:** 4

INGREDIENTS

- 1 medium butternut squash, peeled, seeded and cut into chunk
- 2 teaspoons cumin seeds
- 1/8 teaspoon garlic powder
- 1/8 teaspoon chili flakes, crushed
- Salt and ground black pepper, as required
- 1 tablespoon olive oil
- 2 tablespoons pine nuts
- 2 tablespoons fresh cilantro, chopped

DIRECTIONS:

1. Set the temperature of air fryer to 375 degrees F. Grease an air fryer basket.
2. In a bowl, mix together the squash, spices, and oil.
3. Arrange butternut squash chunks into the prepared fryer basket.
4. Air fry it for about 20 minutes, flipping occasionally.
5. Remove from air fryer and transfer the squash chunks onto serving plates.
6. Garnish with pine nuts and cilantro.
7. Serve.

NUTRITION: Calories 165 Carbs 27.6g Protein 3.1g Fat 6.9g

Herbed Potatoes

Basic Recipe
Preparation Time: 10 minutes **Cooking Time:** 16 minutes **Servings:** 4
INGREDIENTS

- 6 small potatoes, chopped
- 3 tablespoons olive oil
- 2 teaspoons mixed dried herbs
- Salt and ground black pepper, as required
- 2 tablespoons fresh parsley, chopped

DIRECTIONS:

1. Set the temperature of air fryer to 356 degrees F. Grease an air fryer basket.
2. In a large bowl, add the potatoes, oil, herbs, salt and black pepper and toss to coat well. Arrange the chopped potatoes into the prepared air fryer basket in a single layer.
3. Air fry it for about 16 minutes, tossing once halfway through.
4. Remove from air fryer and transfer the potatoes onto serving plates. Garnish with parsley and serve.

NUTRITION: Calories 268 Carbs 40.4g Protein 4.4g Fat 10.8g

Spicy Potatoes

Basic Recipe

Preparation Time: 10 minutes **Cooking Time:** 20 minutes **Servings:** 6

INGREDIENTS

- 1¾ pounds waxy potatoes, peeled and cubed
- 1 tablespoon olive oil
- ½ teaspoon ground cumin
- ½ teaspoon ground coriander
- ½ teaspoon paprika
- Salt and freshly ground black pepper, as required

DIRECTIONS:

1. In a large bowl of water, add the potatoes and set aside for about 30 minutes
2. Dry out the potatoes completely and dry with paper towels.
3. In a bowl, add the potatoes, oil, and spices and toss to coat well.
4. Set the temperature of air fryer to 355 degrees F. Grease an air fryer basket.
5. Arrange potato pieces into the prepared air fryer basket in a single layer.
6. Air fry for about 20 minutes
7. Remove from air fryer and transfer the potato pieces onto serving plates.
8. Serve hot.

NUTRITION: Calories 113 Fat 2.5g Carbs 21g Protein 2.3g

Crispy Kale Chips

Basic Recipe

Preparation Time: 5 minutes **Cooking Time:** 7 minutes **Servings:** 3 **INGREDIENTS:**

- 3 cups kale leaves, stems removed
- 1 tablespoon olive oil
- Salt and pepper, to taste

DIRECTIONS:

1. In a bowl, combine all of the ingredients. Toss to coat the kale leaves with oil, salt, and pepper.
2. Arrange the kale leaves on the double layer rack and insert inside the air fryer.
3. Close the air fryer and cook for 7 minutes at 3700F.
4. Allow to cool before serving.

NUTRITION: Calories 48 Carbs 1.4g Protein 0.7g Fat 4.8g

Grilled Buffalo Cauliflower

Basic Recipe

Preparation Time: 5 minutes **Cooking Time:** 5 minutes **Servings:** 1 **INGREDIENTS:**

- 1 cup cauliflower florets
- Cooking oil spray
- Salt and pepper, to taste
- ½ cup buffalo sauce

DIRECTIONS

1. Place the cauliflower florets in a bowl and spray with cooking oil. Season it with salt and pepper.
2. Toss to coat.
3. Place the grill pan in the air fryer and add the cauliflower florets.
4. Close the lid and cook for 5 minutes at 3900F.
5. Once cooked, place in a bowl and pour the buffalo sauce over the top. Toss to coat.

NUTRITION: Calories 25 Fat 0.1g Carbs 5.3g Protein 2g

Faux Fried Pickles

Basic Recipe

Preparation Time: 5 minutes **Cooking Time:** 5 minutes **Servings:** 2 **INGREDIENTS:**

- 1 cup pickle slices
- 1 egg, beaten
- ½ cup grated Parmesan cheese
- ½ cup almond flour
- ¼ cup pork rinds, crushed
- Salt and pepper, to taste

DIRECTIONS

6. Place the pickles in a bowl and pour the beaten egg over the top. Allow to soak.
7. In another dish or bowl, combine the Parmesan cheese, almond flour, pork rinds, salt, and pepper.
8. Dredge the pickles in the Parmesan cheese mixture and place on the double layer rack.
9. Place the rack with the pickles inside of the air fryer.
10. Close the lid and cook for 5 minutes at 3900F. **NUTRITION:** Calories 664 Carbs 17.9g Protein 42g Fat 49.9g

Greatest Green Beans

Basic Recipe
Preparation Time: 5 minutes **Cooking Time:** 5 minutes **Servings:** 2
INGREDIENTS:

- 1 cup green beans, trimmed
- ½ teaspoon oil
- Salt and pepper, to taste

DIRECTIONS

11. Place the green beans in a bowl and add in oil, salt, and pepper.
12. Toss to coat the beans.
13. Place the grill pan in the air fryer and add the green beans in a single layer.
14. Close the lid and cook for 5 minutes at 3900F.

NUTRITION Calories 54 Fat 2.5g Carbs 7.7g Protein 2g

Summer Grilled Corn

Basic Recipe

Preparation Time: 5 minutes **Cooking Time:** 10 minutes **Servings:** 2

INGREDIENTS:

- 2 corns on the cob cut into halves widthwise
- ½ teaspoon oil
- Salt and pepper, to taste

DIRECTIONS:

1. Brush the corn cobs with oil and season with salt and pepper.
2. Place the grill pan accessory into the air fryer.
3. Place the corn cobs on the grill pan.
4. Close the lid and cook for 3 minutes at 3900F.
5. Open the air fryer and turn the corn cobs.
6. Cook for another 3 minutes at the same temperature.

NUTRITION: Calories 173 Carbs 29g Protein 4.5 g Fat 4.5g

Cheesy Bean Bake

Basic Recipe

Preparation Time: 5 minutes **Cooking Time:** 55 minutes **Servings:** 6

INGREDIENTS:

- 2 tbsp. extra-virgin olive oil
  - ½ tsp. black pepper
  - 1 1/3 cups mozzarella coarsely grated
  - 1 1/2 tsp. garlic, sliced
  - 3 tbsp. tomato paste
  - 1 1/3 cups dried beans
  - ½ tsp. kosher salt

DIRECTIONS:

7. Pressure Cook beans with 4 cups water on High for 25 minutes. Sauté beans with oil.
8. Add garlic and cook for 1 minute. Add beans, tomato paste, water, a pinch of salt and pepper.
9. Top with cheese.
10. Press Broil for 7 minutes with Air Fryer Lid. Serve with toasted bread or nacho chips

NUTRITION: Calories 761 kcal Fat 28 g Carbs 54 g Protein 45 g

Barbacoa Beef

Basic Recipe

Preparation Time: 15 minutes **Cooking Time:** 1hour and 20 minutes **Servings:** 10

INGREDIENTS:

- 2/3 cup beer
- 4 cloves garlic
- 2 chipotles in adobo sauce
- 1 tsp. black pepper
- 1/4 tsp. ground cloves
- 1 tbsp. olive oil
- 3-pound beef chuck roast, 2-inch chunks
- 3 bay leaves
- 1 onion, chopped
- 4 oz. chopped green chilies
- 1/4 cup lime juice
- 2 tbsp. apple cider vinegar
- 1 tbsp. ground cumin
- 1 tbsp. dried Mexican oregano
- 2 tsp. salt

DIRECTIONS:

11. Puree beer, garlic, chipotles, onion, green chilies, lime juice, vinegar, and seasonings.
12. Sauté roast in oil.
13. Add the bay leaves and pureed sauce.
14. Cook on High Pressure for 60 minutes
15. Discard the leaves.
16. Shred beef and serve with sauce.

NUTRITION: Calories 520 kcal Fat 23g Carbs 56 g Protein 31g

Maple Smoked Brisket

Basic Recipe
Preparation Time: 15 minutes **Cooking Time:** 1hour and 20 minutes **Servings:** 4
INGREDIENTS:

- 1.5 lb. beef brisket
- 2 tbsp. maple sugar

- 2 c. bone broth or stock of choice
- 1 tbsp. liquid smoke
- 3 fresh thyme sprigs
- 2 tsp. smoked sea salt
- 1 tsp. black pepper
- 1 tsp. mustard powder
- 1 tsp. onion powder
- ½ tsp. smoked paprika

DIRECTIONS:

1. Coat the brisket with all spices and sugar.
2. Sauté brisket in oil for 3 minutes
3. Add broth, liquid smoke, and thyme to the Instant Pot and cover.
4. Cook at High Pressure for 50 minutes
5. Remove brisket.
6. Sauté sauce for 10 minutes
7. Serve sliced brisket with any whipped vegetable and sauce.

NUTRITION: Calories 1671 kcal Fat 43g Carbs 98 g Protein 56g

Philly Cheesesteak Sandwiches

Basic Recipe
Preparation Time: 5 minutes **Cooking Time:** 30 minutes **Servings:** 8
INGREDIENTS:

- 3-pound beef top sirloin steak, sliced
- 2 onions, julienned
- 1 can condensed French onion soup, undiluted
- 2 garlic cloves, minced
- 1 package Italian salad dressing mix
- 2 tsp. beef base
- 1/2 tsp. pepper
- 2 large red peppers, julienned
- 1/2 cup pickled pepper rings
- 8 hoagie buns, split
- 8 slices provolone cheese

DIRECTIONS:

1. Combine the first 7 ingredients in the pressure cooker. Adjust to pressure-cook on High for 10 minutes. Add peppers and pepper rings. Pressure- cook on High for 5 minutes
2. Put beef, cheese, and vegetables on bun bottoms. Broil 1-2 minutes and serve.

NUTRITION: Calories 4852 kcal Fat 67g Carbs 360 g Protein 86g

Pot Roast and Potatoes

Basic Recipe
Preparation Time: 15 minutes **Cooking Time:** 1 hour and 15 minutes **Servings:** 8
INGREDIENTS:

- 2 tbsp. all-purpose flour
- 1 tbsp. kosher salt
- 3 lb. chuck roast
- 1 tbsp. black pepper
- 3 c. low-sodium beef broth
- 1/2 c. red wine
- 1 lb. baby potatoes, halved
- 1 tbsp. Worcestershire sauce
- 4 carrots, sliced
- 1 onion, chopped
- 1 tbsp. extra-virgin olive oil
- 3 cloves garlic, minced
- 1 tsp. thyme, chopped
- 2 tsp. rosemary, chopped
- 3 tbsp. tomato paste

DIRECTIONS:

1. Coat chuck roast with pepper and salt.
2. Sauté the beef for 5 minutes on each side then set aside.
3. Cook onion for 5 minutes
4. Add herbs, garlic, and tomato paste and cook for 1 minute.
5. Add four and wine and cook for 2 minutes
6. Add Worcestershire sauce, broth, carrots, potatoes, salt and pepper.
7. Put beef on top of the mixture
8. High-Pressure Cook for an hour and serve. **NUTRITION:** Calories 3274 kcal Fat 42 g Carbs 286 g Protein 78 g

Butter Chicken

Intermediate Recipe Preparation Time: 10 minutes
Cooking Time: 1hour and 10 minutes
Servings: 6
INGREDIENTS:

- 1 tbsp. vegetable oil
- 1 tbsp. butter
- 1 onion, diced
- 2 tsp. grated ginger
- 1 tsp. ground cumin
- 1/2 tsp. turmeric
- 1/ 2 tsp. kosher salt
- ½ tsp. black pepper
- 3/4 c. heavy cream
- 5 cloves garlic, chopped
- 6 oz. tomato paste
- 2 lb. boneless chicken thighs, 1" pieces
- 1 tbsp. garam masala
- 1 tsp. paprika
- 1 tbsp. sugar

DIRECTIONS:

1. Sauté the onion, ginger, and garlic in oil and butter
2. Add tomato paste and cook for 3 minutes
3. Add ½ cup water, chicken, and spices to the Pot.
4. Pressure Cook on High for 5 minutes
5. Add heavy cream.
6. Serve with rice, naan, yogurt, and cilantro. **NUTRITION:** Calories 3841 Fat 100g Carbs 244g Protein 150g

Curried Chicken Meatball Wraps

Basic Recipe
Preparation Time: 5 minutes **Cooking Time:** 15 minutes **Servings:** 12
INGREDIENTS:

- 1 egg, beaten
- 1 onion, chopped
- 1/2 cup Rice Krispies
- 1/4 cup golden raisins
- 1/4 cup minced cilantro
- 2 tsp. curry powder
- 1/2 tsp. salt
- 24 Boston lettuce leaves
- 1 carrot, shredded
- 1/2 cup chopped salted peanuts
- 1-pound lean ground chicken
- 2 tbsp. olive oil
- 1 cup plain yogurt

DIRECTIONS:

1. Mix the first 7 ingredients.
2. Shape mixture into 24 balls.
3. Sauté meatballs on medium with oil
4. Add water to pot.
5. Put meatballs on the trivet in the pressure cooker.
6. Pressure-cook on High for 7 minutes
7. Mix yogurt and cilantro.
8. Place 2 teaspoons sauce and 1 meatball in each lettuce leaf; top with remaining ingredients and serve.

NUTRITION: Calories 2525 Fat 80g Carbs 225g Protein 120g

Fall-Off-The-Bone Chicken

Intermediate Recipe Preparation Time: 10 minutes
Cooking Time: 1hour and 10 minutes
Servings: 4
INGREDIENTS:

- 1 tbsp. packed brown sugar
- 1 tbsp. chili powder
- 1 tbsp. smoked paprika
- 1 tsp. chopped thyme leaves
- ¼ tbsp. kosher salt
- ¼ tbsp. black pepper
- 1 whole small chicken
- 1 tbsp. extra-virgin olive oil
- 2/3 c. low-sodium chicken broth
- 2 tbsp. chopped parsley

DIRECTIONS:

1. Coat chicken with brown sugar, chili powder, sugar, pepper, paprika, and thyme.
2. Sauté chicken in oil for 3-4 minutes
3. Pour broth in the Pot.
4. Pressure Cook on High for 25 minutes
5. Garnish sliced chicken with parsley and serve.

   NUTRITION: Calories 1212 Fat 10g Carbs 31g Protein 15g

White Chicken Chili

Basic Recipe
Preparation Time: 5 minutes **Cooking Time:** 30 minutes **Servings:** 6
INGREDIENTS:

- 1 tbsp. vegetable oil
- 1 red bell pepper, diced
- 10.5 oz. condensed cream of chicken soup
- 5 tbsp. shredded Cheddar cheese
- 2 green onions, sliced
- 1 cup Kernel corn
- 1 tbsp. chili powder
- 6 oz. (2) boneless, skinless chicken breast
- 15 oz. white cannellini beans
- 1 cup Chunky Salsa

DIRECTIONS:

1. Sauté pepper, corn, and chili powder in oil for 2 minutes
2. Season chicken with salt and pepper.
3. Layer the beans, salsa, water, chicken, and soup over the corn mixture.
4. Pressure Cook on High for 4 minutes
5. Shred chicken and return to pot.
6. Serve topped with cheese and green onions. **NUTRITION:** Calories 1848 Fat 70g Carbs 204g Protein 90g

Coconut Curry Vegetable Rice Bowls

Basic Recipe
Preparation Time: 5 minutes **Cooking Time:** 40minutes **Servings:** 6
INGREDIENTS:

- 2/3 cup uncooked brown rice
- 1 tsp. curry powder
- 3/4 tsp. salt divided
- 1 cup chopped green onion
- 1 cup sliced red bell pepper
- 1 tbsp. grated ginger
- 1 1/2 tbsp. sugar
- 1 cup matchstick carrots
- 1 cup chopped red cabbage
- 8 oz. sliced water chestnuts
- 15 oz. no salt added chickpeas
- 13 oz. coconut milk

DIRECTIONS:

1. Add rice, water, curry powder, and 1/4 tsp. of the salt in the Instant Pot. Pressure Cook for 15 minutes. Sauté for 2 minutes and serve.

NUTRITION: Calories 1530 Fat 110g Carbs 250g Protein 80g

Egg Roll in a Bowl

Basic Recipe
Preparation Time: 5 minutes **Cooking Time:** 20 minutes **Servings:** 4
INGREDIENTS:

- 1/3 cup low-sodium soy sauce
- 2 tbsp. sesame oil
- 1 cup matchstick cut carrots
- 1 bunch green onions, sliced
- 2 bags coleslaw mix
- 1 lb. ground chicken
- 2 tbsp. sesame seeds
- 4 cloves garlic, minced
- 8 oz. shiitake mushrooms, sliced
- 1 1/2 cups chicken broth

DIRECTIONS:

1. Add sesame oil, ground chicken, soy sauce, garlic, chicken broth and mushrooms to Instant Pot.
2. Cook for 2 minutes on High Pressure.
3. Add in coleslaw mix and carrots.
4. Let sit for 5 minutes
5. Serve with sesame seeds and green onions. **NUTRITION:** Calories 3451 Fat 130g Carbs 301g Protein 150g

Frittata Provencal

Basic Recipe
Preparation Time: 5 minutes **Cooking Time**: 45 minutes **Servings:** 6
INGREDIENTS:

- 12 eggs
- 1 tsp. minced thyme
- 1 tsp. hot pepper sauce
- 1/2 tsp. salt
- 1/4 tsp. pepper
- 4 oz. goat cheese, divided
- 1/2 cup chopped sun-dried tomatoes
- 1 tbsp. olive oil
- 1 potato, peeled and sliced
- 1 onion, sliced
- 1/2 tsp. smoked paprika

DIRECTIONS:

1. Sauté potato, paprika, and onion in oil for 5-7 minutes
2. Transfer potato mixture to a greased baking dish.
3. Pour the first 6 ingredients over potato mixture.
4. Cover baking dish with foil.
5. Add water and trivet to pot.
6. Use a foil sling to lower the dish onto the trivet.
7. Adjust to pressure-cook on high for 35 minutes and serve.

NUTRITION: Calories 2554 Fat 70g Carbs 190g Protein 80g

Ramekin Eggs

Basic Recipe

Preparation Time: 2 minutes **Cooking Time:** 3minutes **Servings:** 2 **INGREDIENTS:**

- 1 tbsp. ghee, plus more for greasing
- 2 cups mushrooms, chopped
- ¼ tsp. salt
- 1 tbsp. chives, chopped
- 3 eggs
- 3 tbsp. heavy cream

DIRECTIONS:

1. Sauté mushrooms with ghee and salt until tender.
2. Put mushrooms into greased ramekins.
3. Add chives, egg, and cream.
4. Add water, trivet, and ramekins to pot.
5. Pressure Cook on Low for 1-2 minutes
6. Serve with freshly toasted bread.

NUTRITION: Calories 703 Fat 5g Carbs 20g Protein 7g

Easter Ham

Basic Recipe

Preparation Time: 5 minutes **Cooking Time:** 15 minutes **Servings:** 8 **INGREDIENTS:**

- 1/2 c. orange marmalade
- ¼ tsp. black pepper
- 1 (4-6 lb.) fully cooked, spiral, bone-in ham
- 1/4 c. brown sugar
- 1/4 c. orange juice
- 2 tbsp. Dijon mustard

DIRECTIONS:

8. Mix marmalade, brown sugar, orange juice, Dijon, and black pepper.
9. Coat ham with glaze.
10. Cook on Meat for 15 minutes
11. Serve ham with more glaze from the Pot. **NUTRITION:** Calories 3877 Fat 80g Carbs 207g Protein 100g

Korean Lamb Chops

Intermediate Recipe Preparation Time: 10 minutes **Cooking Time:** 50 minutes **Servings:** 6 **INGREDIENTS:**

- 2 lbs. Lamb chops
- 6 1/2 tsp. Red pepper powder
- 2 tbsp. granulated sugar
- 1 tbsp. curry powder
- 8 1/2 tbsp. soy sauce
- 3 tbsp. rice wine
- 2 tbsp. garlic, minced
- 1 tsp. ginger, minced
- 3 bay leaves
- 1 cup carrots, diced
- 2 cups onions, diced
- 1 cup celery, diced
- 2 tbsp. Korean red pepper paste
- 2 tbsp. ketchup
- 6 tbsp. Corn syrup
- 1/2 tbsp. sesame oil
- 1/2 tsp. cinnamon powder
- 1 tsp. sesame seeds
- 1 tsp. black pepper
- 1/3 cup Asian pear ground
- 1/3 cup onion powder
- 1/2 tbsp. Green plum extract
- 1 cup red wine

DIRECTIONS:

12. Put all ingredients except cilantro and green onions into the Instant Pot.
13. Pressure Cook for 20 minutes
14. Sauté until sauce is thickened.
15. Add water and lamb on trivet to pot.
16. Broil at 400°F for 5 minutes
17. Serve with chopped cilantro and green onions. **NUTRITION:** Calories 2728 Fat 220g Carbs 551g Protein 250g

Air Fryer Chicken Kabobs

Basic Recipe
Preparation Time: 15 minutes **Cooking Time:** 15 minutes **Servings:** 2
INGREDIENTS:

- 2 Chicken breasts, chopped
- 6 Mushrooms cut into halves
- ⅓ Cup honey
- ⅓ Cup Soy sauce -
- 1 teaspoon Pepper, crushed
- 1 teaspoon Sesame seeds
- 3 Bell peppers, in different colors
- Cooking oil spray as required

DIRECTIONS:

18. Cut the chicken breasts into small cubes, wash and pat dry. Rub little pepper and salt over the chicken. Sprits some oil on it. In a small bowl, combine honey and soy sauce thoroughly.
19. Add the sesame seeds into the mix. Drive in chicken, bell peppers and mushrooms onto the skewers.
20. Set the air fryer at 170 degrees Celsius and preheat.
21. Drizzle with the kabobs with the honey and soy sauce mixture.
22. Put all the skewed chicken kabobs into the air fryer basket and cook for 20 minutes
23. Rotate the skewer intermittently in between.
24. Serve hot.

NUTRITION: Calories 392 Fat 5g Carbs 65.4g Protein 6.7g

Chicken Fried Rice in Air Fryer

Basic Recipe

Preparation Time: 20 minutes **Cooking Time:** 20 minutes **Servings:** 4

INGREDIENTS:

- 3 cups cooked cold white rice
- 1 cup chicken cooked & diced
- 1 cup carrots and peas, frozen
- 1 tablespoon vegetable oil
- 1 tablespoon soy sauce
- ½ cup onion
- ¼ teaspoon salt

DIRECTIONS:

1. In a large bowl, put the cooked cold rice.
2. Stir in soy sauce and vegetable oil.
3. Now add the frozen carrots and peas, diced chicken, diced onion, salt and combine.
4. Transfer the rice mixture into the mix.
5. Take a non-stick pan which you can comfortably place in the air fryer and transfer the complete rice mixture into the pan.
6. Place the pan in the air fryer.
7. Set the temperature at 180 degree Celsius and timer for 20 minutes
8. Remove the pan after the set time elapse.
9. Serve hot.

NUTRITION: Calories 618 Fat 5.5g Carbs 116.5g Protein 21.5g

Air Fried Chicken Tikkas

Basic Recipe
Preparation Time: 10 minutes **Cooking Time:** 15 minutes **Servings:** 4
INGREDIENTS:
For marinade:

- 1¼ pounds chicken, bones cut into small bite size
- ¼ pound cherry tomatoes
- 1 cup yogurt
- 1 tablespoon ginger garlic paste (fresh)
- 3 bell peppers, 1ǀ cut size
- 2 tablespoons chili powder
- 2 tablespoons cumin powder
- 1 tablespoon turmeric powder
- 2 tablespoons coriander powder
- 1 teaspoon garam masala powder
- 2 teaspoons olive oil
- Salt – to taste For garnishing:
- 1 lemon, cut into half
- ⅓ cup Coriander, fresh, chopped
- 1 medium Onion, nicely sliced
- Mint leaves, fresh – few

DIRECTIONS:

1. In a large bowl mix all the marinade ingredients and coat it thoroughly on the chicken pieces.
2. Cover the bowl and set aside for 2 hours minimum. If you can refrigerate overnight, it can give better marinade effect.
3. Thread the chicken in the skewers along with bell peppers and tomatoes alternately.
4. Preheat your air fryer at 200 degrees Celsius.
5. Spread an aluminum liner on the air fryer basket and arrange the skewers on it.
6. Set the timer for 15 minutes and grill it.
7. Turn the skewer intermittently for an even grilling.
8. Once done, put into a plate and garnish with the given ingredients before serving.

NUTRITION: Calories 400 Fat 20g Carbs 17.4g Protein 46.9g

Nashville Hot Chicken in Air Fryer

Basic Recipe
Preparation Time: 10 minutes **Cooking Time:** 27 minutes **Servings:** 4
INGREDIENTS:

- 4 pounds chicken with bones, 8 pieces
- 2 tablespoons vegetable oil
- 2 cups all-purpose flour
- 1 cup buttermilk
- 2 tablespoons paprika
- 1 teaspoon onion powder
- 1 teaspoon garlic powder
- 1 teaspoon ground black pepper
- 2 teaspoons salt For Hot sauce:
- 1 tablespoon cayenne pepper
- ¼ cup vegetable oil
- 1 teaspoon salt
- 4 slices white bread
- Dill pickle, as required

DIRECTIONS:

9. Clean and wash chicken thoroughly, pat dry and keep ready aside.
10. In a bowl, whisk buttermilk and eggs.
11. Combine garlic powder, black pepper, paprika, onion powder, All-purpose flour and salt in a bowl.
12. Now dip the chicken in the egg and buttermilk and put in the second bowl marinade bowl and toss to get an even coating. Maybe you need to repeat the process twice for a better coat.
13. After that spray some vegetable oil and keep aside.
14. Before cooking the chicken, pre-heat the fryer at 190 degrees Celsius.
15. Brush vegetable oil on the fry basket before start cooking.
16. Now place the coated chicken in the air fryer at 190 degrees Celsius and set the timer for 20 minutes. Do not crowd the air fryer. It would be better if you can do the frying in 2 batches.
17. Keep the flipping the chicken intermittently for even frying.
18. Once the set timer elapsed, remove the chicken to a plate and keep it there without covering.
19. Now start the second batch. Do the same process.
20. After 20 minutes, reduce the temperature to 170 degrees Celsius and place the first batch of chicken over the second batch, which is already in the air fry basket.
21. Fry it again for another 7 minutes
22. While the chicken is air frying, make the hot sauce.
23. In a bowl mix salt and cayenne pepper thoroughly.
24. In a small saucepan, heat some vegetable oil.
25. When the oil becomes hot add the spice mix and continue stirring to become smooth.
26. While serving, place the chicken over the white bread and spread the hot sauce over the chicken.
27. Use dill pickle to top it.
28. Serve hot.

NUTRITION: Calories 1013 Fat 22.2g Carbs 53.9g Protein 140.7g

Air Fryer Panko Breaded Chicken Parmesan

Basic Recipe

Preparation Time: 10 minutes **Cooking Time:** 20 minutes **Servings:** 4 **INGREDIENTS:**

- 16 ounces chicken breasts, skinless
- 1 cup panko bread crumbs
- ⅛ cup egg whites
- ½ cup parmesan cheese, shredded
- ½ cup mozzarella cheese, grated
- ¾ cup marinara sauce
- ½ teaspoon salt
- 1 teaspoon ground pepper
- 2 teaspoons italian seasoning
- Cooking spray, as required

DIRECTIONS:

29. Cut each chicken breast into halves to make 4 breast pieces. Wash and pat dry.
30. Place the chicken in a chopping board and pound to flatten.
31. Sprits the air fryer basket with cooking oil.
32. Set the temperature of air fryer to 200 degrees Celsius and preheat.
33. In a large bowl, mix cheese, panko breadcrumbs, and seasoning ingredients.
34. Put the egg white in a large bowl.
35. Dip the pounded chicken into the egg whites and dredge into breadcrumb mixture.
36. Now place the coated chicken into the air fryer basket and spray some cooking oil.
37. Start cooking the chicken breasts for 7 minutes
38. Dress on top of the chicken breasts with shredded mozzarella and marinara sauce.
39. Continue cooking for another 3 minutes and remove for serving when the cheese starts to melt.

NUTRITION: Calories 347 Fat 15g Carbs 7.4g Protein 37g

Air Fryer Rosemary Turkey

Basic Recipe
Preparation Time: 5 minutes **Cooking Time:** 30 minutes **Servings:** 6
INGREDIENTS:

- 2½ pounds turkey breast
- 2 teaspoons fresh rosemary, chopped
- ¼ cup olive oil
- 2 cloves garlic, minced
- 1 teaspoon crushed pepper
- ¼ cup maple syrup
- 1 tablespoon ground mustard
- 1 tablespoon butter
- 1½ teaspoon salt

DIRECTIONS:

40. Combine thoroughly, minced garlic, olive oil, shredded rosemary, pepper and salt in medium bowl.
41. Rub the herb seasoning and oil all over the turkey breast loins.
42. Cover and refrigerate for at least 2 hours for better marinade effect.
43. Before cooking, allow it to thaw for half an hour.
44. Spray some cooking oil on the air fryer basket and place the turkey breast on it.
45. Set the temperature at 200 degrees Celsius for 20 minutes
46. Flip the turkey breast intermittently.
47. While cooking in progress, melt a tablespoon of butter in a microwave oven.
48. Stir in mustard powder and maple syrup in the melted butter.
49. Pour the sauce mix over the turkey breast and continue cooking for another 10 minutes
50. After the cooking is over, slice it for serving. **NUTRITION:** Calories 292 Fat 13.5g Carbs 9.5g Protein 15g

Air Fryer Lamb Chops

Basic Recipe
Preparation Time: 5 minutes **Cooking Time:** 30 minutes **Servings:** 2
INGREDIENTS:

- 4 lamb chops
- ½ tablespoon oregano, fresh, coarsely chopped
- 1½ tablespoons olive oil
- 1 teaspoon black pepper, ground
- 1 clove garlic
- ½ teaspoon salt

DIRECTIONS:

1. Set the air fryer temperature to 200 degrees Celsius.
2. Spray olive on garlic clove and place it in the air fryer basket.
3. Bake it for 12 minutes
4. Combine herbs with pepper, olive oil, and salt.
5. Rub half of the mix over the lamb chops and set aside for 3 minutes

6. Remove the roasted garlic clove from the air fryer.
7. Set the temperature at 200 degrees Celsius and preheat the air fryer.
8. Layer the lamb chops into the air fryer basket and cook for 5 minutes or until it becomes brown.
9. Do not roast the lambs altogether by overlapping one over the other. You can do the roasting in batches.
10. After finish roasting, squeeze the garlic into the herb sauce.
11. Add some more salt and pepper if required.
12. Serve the dish along with garlic sauce. **NUTRITION:** Calories 97 Fat 10.7g Carbs 1.3g Protein 0.3g

Air Fried Shrimp and Sauce

Basic Recipe
Preparation Time: 10 minutes **Cooking Time:** 20 minutes **Servings:** 4
INGREDIENTS:

- 1 pound shrimps
- ½ cup all-purpose flour
- 1 egg white
- ¾ cup panko breadcrumbs
- 2 tablespoons chicken seasoning
- 1 teaspoon paprika
- 1 teaspoon pepper
- ½ teaspoon salt
- Cooking spray, as required
- To make the sauce:
- ⅓ cup of greek yogurt, non-fat
- ¼ cup sweet chili sauce
- 2 tablespoons sriracha

DIRECTIONS:

1. Peel, devein, clean, wash and pat dry the shrimps.
2. Marinate the shrimps by using the seasoning.
3. Put egg white, all-purpose flour and breadcrumbs in three separate bowls.
4. Set the temperature to 200 degree Celsius and preheat the air fryer.
5. Dip the seasoned shrimp in flour, then in the egg white and finally dredge in the breadcrumbs.
6. Sprits cooking oil on the coated shrimp.
7. Put the shrimps in the air fryer basket and cook for 4 minutes
8. Flip the shrimps and cook further 4 minutes
9. For making the sauce, blend all the sauce ingredients in a medium bowl thoroughly.
10. Serve the shrimps along with the sauce. **NUTRITION:** Calories 318 Fat 6.7g Carbs 30.7g Protein 31.3g

Air Fryer Italian Meatball

Basic Recipe
Preparation Time: 6minutes **Cooking Time:** 15 minutes **Servings:** 6
INGREDIENTS:

- 2 pounds ground beef
- 2 eggs
- 1¼ cup bread crumbs
- ¼ cup fresh parsley, chopped
- 1 teaspoon dried oregano
- ¼ cup parmigiano reggiano, grated
- 1 teaspoon light cooking oil
- Salt to taste
- Pepper, as required
- Tomato sauce, for serving

DIRECTIONS:

1. In a mixing bowl put the meat and all ingredients except the cooking oil.
2. Hand mix all the ingredients. Once the mix blended thoroughly, make a small ball with your hand. The given quantity is enough to make 24 balls.
3. Spread a liner paper in the air fryer basket and lightly coat it with cooking oil.
4. Place the bowls in the air fryer basket without overlapping one another.
5. Set the temperature to 200 degrees Celsius and cook for 12-14 minutes until its side becomes brown.
6. Once the sides become brown, turn the balls and cook for another 5 minutes
7. Serve hot along with tomato sauce.

Nutrition: Calories 405 Fat 13.1g Carbs 16.5g Protein 52.1g

Air Fryer Coconut Milk Chicken

Basic Recipe

Preparation Time: 10 minutes **Cooking Time:** 18 minutes **Servings:** 6

INGREDIENTS:

- 1¾ pounds Chicken thighs with skin and bone -
- Marinade:
- 2 cups coconut milk
- 2 teaspoons ground black pepper
- 1 teaspoon cayenne pepper, ground
- 1 teaspoon salt
- Seasoned flour:
- 1 tablespoon baking powder
- 1 tablespoon paprika powder
- 2 cups all-purpose flour
- 1 tablespoon garlic powder
- 1 teaspoon salt

DIRECTIONS:

1. Clean, wash the chicken thighs and pat dry.
2. Combine paprika, cayenne pepper, black pepper, salt in a large bowl.
3. Put chicken into it and toss to coat the ingredients.
4. Pour buttermilk until chicken covered.
5. Refrigerate the coated chicken for a minimum of 6 hours.
6. Set the air fryer temperature to 180 degrees Celsius.
7. In another bowl combine the seasoning flour such as baking powder, paprika, all-purpose flour, garlic powder, and salt.
8. Now take out the chicken from the refrigerator and thaw it for some time.
9. Dredge the chicken into the flour and remove excess flour by shaking off it.
10. Place the coated chicken into the air fryer basket.
11. Cook it for 8 minutes
12. After 8 minutes flip the chicken pieces and cook for another 10 minutes
13. Transfer the cooked chicken onto a paper towel, so that the excess juice can dry out quickly.
14. Serve hot.

NUTRITION: Calories 384 Fat 21.7g Carbs 39.2g Protein 12.1g

Air Fryer Cauliflower Rice

Basic Recipe

Preparation Time: 10 minutes **Cooking Time:** 20 minutes **Servings:** 3 **INGREDIENTS:**

- Segment - 1
- ½ firm tofu
- ½ cup onion, chopped
- 2 tablespoons low sodium soy sauce
- 1 cup carrot diced
- ½ teaspoon turmeric powder
- Segment – 2
- 3 cups cauliflower rice
- ½ cup frozen peas
- 2 tablespoons low sodium soy sauce
- 1½ teaspoons sesame oil, toasted
- 1 tablespoon rice vinegar
- 1 tablespoon ginger, grated
- ½ cup broccoli, finely chopped
- 2 cloves garlic, minced

DIRECTIONS:

1. Crumble tofu in a large bowl. Toss the crumbled tofu with sector 1 ingredients.
2. Set the air fryer temperature to 190 degree Celsius and cook for 10 minutes. Shake the air fryer basket 2-3 times during the cooking in progress.
3. In another large bowl, combine all the ingredients mentioned in the segment 2.
4. After 10 minutes of cooking, transfer the second segment ingredients over the cooked food. Shake the air basket tray and cook for 10 minutes at 190 degrees Celsius. Make sure to shake the air fryer basket intermittently for a better baking result. When the cauliflower rice becomes tender, it is ready to serve.
5. Serve hot along with your favorite sauce.

NUTRITION: Calories 126 Fat 5g Carbs 14g Protein 7.8g

Buttery Cod

Basic Recipe

Preparation Time: 5 minutes **Cooking Time:** 15 minutes **Servings:** 4

INGREDIENTS:

- 2 tbsp parsley, chopped
- 3 tbsp butter, melted
- 8 cherry tomatoes, halved
- 0.25 cup tomato sauce
- 2 cod fillets, cubed

DIRECTIONS:

1. Turn on the air fryer to 390 degrees.
2. Combine all of the ingredients and put them into a pan that works with the air fryer.
3. After 12 minutes of baking, you can divide this between the four bowls and enjoy.

NUTRITION: Calories 232 Fat 8g Carbs 5g Protein 11g

Creamy Chicken

Basic Recipe
Preparation Time: 5 minutes **Cooking Time:** 15 minutes **Servings:** 4
INGREDIENTS:

- Pepper and salt
- 1 tsp olive oil
- 1 0.5 tsp sweet paprika
- 0.25 cup coconut cream
- 4 chicken breasts, cubed

DIRECTIONS:

1. Turn on the air fryer to 370 degrees. Prepare a frying pan that fits into the machine with some oil before adding the ingredients inside. Add this to the air fryer and let it bake. After 17 minutes, you can divide between the few plates and serve!

NUTRITION: Calories 250 Fat 12g Carbs 5g Protein 11g

Mushroom and Turkey Stew

Basic Recipe

Preparation Time: 5 minutes **Cooking Time:** 25 minutes **Servings:** 4

INGREDIENTS:

- Pepper and salt
- 1 tbsp parsley, chopped
- 0.25 cup tomato sauce
- 1 turkey breast cubed
- 0.5 lb. Brown mushrooms, sliced

DIRECTIONS:

2. Turn on the air fryer to 350 degrees. Pick out a pan and mix the tomato sauce, pepper, salt, mushrooms, and turkey together. Add to the air fryer.
3. After 25 minutes, the stew is done—divides between four bowls and top with the parsley.

NUTRITION: Calories 220 Fat 12g Carbs 5g Protein 12g

Basil Chicken

Basic Recipe
Preparation Time: 5 minutes

Cooking Time: 15 minutes **Servings:** 4 **INGREDIENTS:**

- Pepper and salt
- 2 tsp smoked paprika
- 0.5 tsp dried basil
- 0.5 cup chicken stock
- 1 0.5 lb chicken breasts, cubed

DIRECTIONS:

4. Turn on the air fryer to 390 degrees.
5. Bring out a pan and toss the ingredients inside before putting it into the air fryer.
6. After 25 minutes of baking, divide this between a few plates and serve with a side salad.

NUTRITION: Calories 223 Fat 12g Carbs 5g Protein 13g

Eggplant Bake

Basic Recipe
Preparation Time: 5 minutes **Cooking Time:** 15 minutes **Servings:** 4
INGREDIENTS:

- 2 tsp olive oil
- Pepper and salt
- 4 spring onions, chopped
- 1 hot chili pepper, chopped
- 2 eggplants, cubed
- 4 garlic cloves, minced
- 0.5 cup cilantro, chopped
- 0.5 lb cherry tomatoes, cubed

DIRECTIONS:

7. Turn on the air fryer and let it heat up to 380 degrees.
8. Prepare a baking pan that will go into the air fryer and mix all of the ingredients onto it.
9. Place into the air fryer to cook. After 15 minutes, divide between four bowls and serve.

NUTRITION: Calories 232 Fat 12g Carbs 5g Protein 10g

Meatball Casserole

Basic Recipe
Preparation Time: 5 minutes **Cooking Time:** 15 minutes **Servings:** 6
INGREDIENTS:

- 1 tbsp thyme, chopped
- 0.25 cup parsley, chopped
- 0.33 lb turkey sausage
- 1 egg, beaten
- 0.66 lb ground beef
- 2 tbsp olive oil
- 1 shallot, minced
- 1 tbsp Dijon mustard
- 3 garlic cloves, minced
- 2 tbsp whole milk
- 1 tbsp rosemary, chopped

DIRECTIONS:

10. Turn on the air fryer to a High setting and then give it time to heat up with some oil inside.
11. Add the garlic and onions and cook for a few minutes to make soft.
12. Add the milk and bread crumbs to a bowl and then mix. Then add in the rest of the ingredients and set aside to soak.
13. Use this mixture, after five minutes, to prepare some small meatballs. Add these to the air fryer.
14. Turn the heat up to 400 degrees to cook. After 10 minutes, take the lid off and shake the basket. Cook another five minutes before serving.

NUTRITION: Calories 168 Fat 11g Carbs 4g Protein 12g

Herbed Lamb Rack

Basic Recipe
Preparation Time: 5 minutes **Cooking Time:** 10 minutes **Servings:** 2
INGREDIENTS:

- 4 tbsp olive oil
- 0.5 tsp pepper
- 1 tbsp dried thyme
- 2 tbsp dried rosemary
- 0.5 tsp salt
- 2 tsp garlic, minced
- 1 lb rack of lamb

DIRECTIONS:

15. Turn on the air fryer to 400 degrees. In a bowl, combine the herbs and olive oil well.
16. Use this to coat the lamb before adding to the basket of the air fryer.
17. Close the lid, and then let this cook. Halfway through, you can shake the basket to make sure nothing sticks.
18. After ten minutes, take the lamb out and enjoy.

NUTRITION: Calories 542 Fat 37g Carbs 3g Protein 45g

Baked Beef

Intermediate Recipe Preparation Time: 10 minutes **Cooking Time:** 60minutes
Servings: 5 **INGREDIENTS:**

- 1 bunch garlic cloves
- 1 bunch fresh herbs, mixed
- 2 sliced onions
- Olive oil
- 3 lbs beef
- 2 celery sticks, chopped
- 2 carrots, chopped

DIRECTIONS:

19. Great up a pan and then add the herbs, olive oil, beef roast, and vegetables inside.
20. Turn the air fryer on to 400 degrees and place the pan inside. Let this heat up and close the lid.
21. After an hour of cooking, open the lid and then serve this right away.

NUTRITION: Calories 306 Fat 21g Carbs 10g Protein 32g

Old-Fashioned Pork Chops

Basic Recipe

Preparation Time: 5 minutes **Cooking Time:** 15 minutes **Servings:** 6 **INGREDIENTS:**

- Salt
- 0.5 tsp onion powder
- 0.25 tsp chili powder
- 0.25 tsp. Pepper
- 1 tsp smoked paprika
- 1 cup pork rind
- 3 tbsp parmesan, grated
- 5 boneless pork chops
- 2 beaten eggs

DIRECTIONS:

22. Use the pepper and salt to season the pork chops. Blend the rind to make some crumbs.
23. In another bowl, beat the eggs and then coat this onto the pork chops with the crumbs.
24. Take out the air fryer and set it to 400 degrees to heat up.
25. When this is done, add the pork chops into the air fryer and let it heat up. When this is halfway done, flip the pork chops over and cook a little more.
26. After 15 minutes of cooking, turn off the air fryer and serve.

NUTRITION: Calories 391 Fat 18g Carbs 17g Protein 38g

Turkey Pillows

Basic Recipe
Preparation Time: 5 minutes **Cooking Time:** 10 minutes **Servings:** 4 **INGREDIENTS:**

- 15 slices turkey breast
- 2 jars Cream cheese
- 1 Egg yolk
- 4 cups Flour
- 20.5 tbsp Dried granular yeast
- 2 tbsp Sugar
- 10.75 tsp Salt
- 0.25 cup Olive oil
- 0.33 cup Water
- 1 cup Milk with an egg inside

DIRECTIONS:

27. Mix the ingredients for the dough with your hands until smooth. Make it into small balls and put on a floured surface. Open the dough balls with a roller to make it square. Cut into small pieces. Fill with the turkey breast and a bit of cream cheese. Close the points together.
28. Turn on the air fryer to 400 degrees. Place a few of the balls inside and let them cook. After five minutes, take these out and repeat with the rest of the pillows until done.

NUTRITION: Calories 528 Fat 30g Carbs 23g Protein 44g

Chicken Wings

Basic Recipe
Preparation Time: 5 minutes **Cooking Time:** 25 minutes **Servings:** 2
INGREDIENTS:

- 2 tbsp chives
- 0.5 tbsp salt
- 1 tbsp lime
- 0.5 tbsp ginger, chopped
- 1 tbsp garlic, minced
- 1 tbsp chili paste
- 2 tbsp honey
- 0.5 tbsp cornstarch
- 1 tbsp soy sauce
- Oil
- 10 chicken wings

DIRECTIONS:

29. Dry the chicken and then cover it with spray. Add into the air fryer that is preheated to 400 degrees.
30. Let this cook for a bit. During that time, add the rest of the ingredients to a bowl and set aside.
31. After 25 minutes, the chicken is done. Add the chicken into a bowl and top with the sauce. Sprinkle the chives on top and serve.

NUTRITION: Calories 81 Fat 5g Carbs 0g Protein 8g

Chicken Cordon Bleu

Basic Recipe
Preparation Time: 5 minutes **Cooking Time:** 40minutes **Servings:** 6
INGREDIENTS:

- Garlic clove (1, chopped)
- Eggs (2)
- Butter (2 tsps., melted)
- Bread (1 c., ground)
- Flour (0.25 c.)
- Fresh thyme (2 tsps.)
- Swiss cheese (16 slices)
- Ham (8 slices)
- Chicken breasts (4)

DIRECTIONS:

1. Turn on the air fryer to heat to 350 degrees.
2. Flatten out the chicken and then fill with two slices of cheese, ham, and then cheese again. Roll up and use a toothpick to keep together.
3. Mix the garlic, thyme, and bread together with the butter. Beat the eggs and season the flour with pepper and salt.
4. Pass the chicken rolls through the flour, then the egg, and then the breadcrumbs. Add to the air fryer to cook.
5. After 20 minutes, take the chicken out and cool down before serving.

NUTRITION: Calories 387 Fat 20g Carbs 18g Protein 33g

Fried Chicken

Basic Recipe

Preparation Time: 5 minutes **Cooking Time:** 25 minutes **Servings:** 4

INGREDIENTS:

- Lemon (1)
- Ginger (1, grated)
- Ground pepper, salt, and garlic powder
- Chopped chicken (1 lb.)

DIRECTIONS:

1. Add the chicken to a bowl with the rest of the ingredients. Let it set for a bit to marinate.
2. After 15 minutes, add some oil to the air fryer and let it heat up to 320 degrees.
3. Add the chicken inside to cook for 25 minutes, shaking it a few times to cook through. Serve warm.

NUTRITION: Calories 345 Fat 3g Carbs 23g Protein 3g

Sesame Chicken

Basic Recipe

Preparation Time: 5 minutes **Cooking Time:** 50minutes **Servings:** 4

INGREDIENTS:

- Soy sauce
- Pepper
- Salt
- Olive oil
- Breadcrumbs
- Egg
- 1 lb. Chicken breast

DIRECTIONS:

1. Slice the chicken into fillets and add to the bowl with the sesame and soy sauce. Let this marinate for half an hour. Beat the eggs and then pass the chicken through it.
2. Add to the grill of the air fryer at 350 degrees. Let it grill for a bit.
3. After 20 minutes, take the chicken off and let it cool down before serving.

NUTRITION: Calories 375 Fat 18g Carbs 6g Protein 35g

Chicken and Potatoes

Basic Recipe
Preparation Time: 5 minutes **Cooking Time:** 55minutes **Servings:** 2
INGREDIENTS:

- Pepper and salt
- Provencal herbs
- 2 Chicken pieces
- 4 Potatoes
- Olive oil

DIRECTIONS:

4. Peel the skin from the potatoes and cut into slices. Add some pepper and place into the air fryer.

5. Preheat to 340 degrees. Cover the chicken with the herbs, pepper, salt, and oil and add it in with the potatoes.

6. Cook this until well done. After forty minutes, turn the chicken around and let it cook another 15 minutes before serving.

NUTRITION: Calories 200 Fat 4g Carbs 18g Protein 22g

Polish Sausage and Sourdough Kabobs

Basic Recipe

Preparation Time: 5 minutes **Cooking Time:** 15 minutes **Servings:** 4

INGREDIENTS:

- 1 pound smoked Polish beef sausage, sliced
- 1 tablespoon mustard
- 1 tablespoon olive oil
- 2 tablespoons Worcestershire sauce
- 2 bell peppers, sliced
- 2 cups sourdough bread, cubed
- Salt and ground black pepper, to taste

DIRECTIONS:

7. Toss the sausage with the mustard, olive, and Worcestershire sauce. Thread sausage, peppers, and bread onto skewers.
8. Sprinkle with salt and black pepper.
9. Cook in the preheated Air Fryer at 360 degrees F for 11 minutes Brush the skewers with the reserved marinade. Bon appétit!

NUTRITION: Calories 284 Fat 13.8g Carbs 16.5g Protein 23.1g

Ranch Meatloaf with Peppers

Basic Recipe
Preparation Time: 5 minutes **Cooking Time:** 30 minutes **Servings:** 5
INGREDIENTS:

- 1 pound beef, ground
- 1/2 pound veal, ground
- 1 egg
- 4 tablespoons vegetable juice
- 1 cup crackers, crushed
- 2 bell peppers, chopped
- 1 onion, chopped
- 2 garlic cloves, minced
- 2 tablespoons tomato paste
- 2 tablespoons soy sauce
- 1 (1-ounce) package ranch dressing mix
- Sea salt, to taste
- 1/2 teaspoon ground black pepper, to taste
- 7 ounces tomato paste
- 1 tablespoon Dijon mustard

DIRECTIONS:

1. Start by preheating your Air Fryer to 330 degrees F.
2. In a mixing bowl, thoroughly combine the ground beef, veal, egg, vegetable juice, crackers, bell peppers, onion, garlic, tomato paste, and soy sauce, ranch dressing mix, salt, and ground black pepper. Mix until everything is well incorporated and press into a lightly greased meatloaf pan.
3. Cook approximately 25 minutes in the preheated Air Fryer. Whisk the tomato paste with the mustard and spread the topping over the top of your meatloaf.
4. Continue to cook 2 minutes more. Let it stand on a cooling rack for 6 minutes before slicing and serving. Enjoy!

NUTRITION: Calories 411 Fat 31.4g Carbs 10g Protein 28.2g

Indian Beef Samosas

Basic Recipe
Preparation Time: 5 minutes **Cooking Time:** 30 minutes **Servings:** 8 **INGREDIENTS:**

- 1 tablespoon sesame oil
- 4 tablespoons shallots, minced
- 2 cloves garlic, minced
- 2 tablespoons green chili peppers, chopped
- 1/2 pound ground chuck
- 4 ounces bacon, chopped
- Salt and ground black pepper, to taste
- 1 teaspoon cumin powder
- 1 teaspoon turmeric
- 1 teaspoon coriander
- 1 cup frozen peas, thawed
- 1 (16-ounce) of phyllo dough
- 1 egg, beaten with 2 tablespoons of water (egg wash)

DIRECTIONS:

10. Heat the oil in a saucepan over medium-high heat. Once hot, sauté the shallots, garlic, and chili peppers until tender, about 3 minutes
11. Then, add the beef and bacon; continue to sauté an additional 4 minutes, crumbling with a fork. Season it with salt, pepper, cumin powder, turmeric, and coriander. Stir in peas.
12. Then, preheat your Air Fryer to 330 degrees F. Brush the Air Fryer basket with cooking oil.
13. Place 1 to 2 tablespoons of the mixture onto each phyllo sheet. Fold the sheets into triangles, pressing the edges. Brush the tops with egg wash.
14. Bake it for 7 to 8 minutes, working with batches. Serve with Indian tomato sauce if desired. Enjoy!

NUTRITION: Calories 266 Fat 13g Carbs 24.5g Protein 12.2g

Grilled Vienna Sausage with Broccoli

Basic Recipe
Preparation Time: 5 minutes

Cooking Time: 20 minutes **Servings:** 4 **INGREDIENTS:**

- 1 pound beef Vienna sausage
- 1/2 cup mayonnaise
- 1 teaspoon yellow mustard
- 1 tablespoon fresh lemon juice
- 1 teaspoon garlic powder
- 1/4 teaspoon black pepper
- 1 pound broccoli

DIRECTIONS:

15. Start by preheating your Air Fryer to 380 degrees F. Spritz the grill pan with cooking oil.
16. Cut the sausages into serving sized pieces. Cook the sausages for 15 minutes, shaking the basket occasionally to get all sides browned. Set aside.
17. In the meantime, whisk the mayonnaise with mustard, lemon juice, garlic powder, and black pepper. Toss the broccoli with the mayo mixture.
18. Turn up temperature to 400 degrees F. Cook broccoli for 6 minutes, turning halfway through the cooking time. Serve the sausage with the grilled broccoli on the side. Bon appétit!

NUTRITION: Calories 477 Fat 43.2g Carbs 7.3g Protein 15.9g

Aromatic T-bone Steak with Garlic

Basic Recipe
Preparation Time: 5 minutes **Cooking Time:** 15 minutes **Servings:** 3
INGREDIENTS:

- 1-pound T-bone steak
- 4 garlic cloves, halved
- 1/4 cup all-purpose flour
- 2 tablespoons olive oil
- 1/4 cup tamari sauce
- 2 teaspoons brown sugar
- 4 tablespoons tomato paste
- 1 teaspoon Sriracha sauce
- 2 tablespoons white vinegar
- 1 teaspoon dried rosemary
- 1/2 teaspoon dried basil
- 2 heaping tablespoons cilantro, chopped

DIRECTIONS:

19. Rub the garlic halves all over the T-bone steak. Toss the steak with the flour.
20. Drizzle with the oil all over the steak and transfer it to the grill pan; grill the steak in the preheated Air Fryer at 400 degrees F for 10 minutes
21. Meanwhile, whisk the tamari sauce, sugar, tomato paste, Sriracha, vinegar, rosemary, and basil. Cook an additional 5 minutes
22. Serve garnished with fresh cilantro. Bon appétit! **NUTRITION:** Calories 463 Fat 24.6g Carbs 16.7g Protein 44.7g

Sausage Scallion Balls

Basic Recipe
Preparation Time: 5 minutes **Cooking Time:** 15 minutes **Servings:** 4
INGREDIENTS:

- 1 ½ pounds beef sausage meat
- 1 cup rolled oats
- 4 tablespoons scallions, chopped
- 1 teaspoon worcestershire sauce
- Flaky sea salt and freshly ground black pepper, to taste
- 1 teaspoon paprika
- 1/2 teaspoon granulated garlic
- 1 teaspoon dried basil
- 1/2 teaspoon dried oregano
- 4 teaspoons mustard
- 4 pickled cucumbers

DIRECTIONS:

23. Start by preheating your Air Fryer to 380 degrees F. Spritz the Air Fryer basket with cooking oil.
24. In a mixing bowl, thoroughly combine the sausage meat, oats, scallions, Worcestershire sauce, salt, black pepper, paprika, garlic, basil, and oregano.
25. Then, form the mixture into equal sized meatballs using a tablespoon.
26. Place the meatballs in the Air Fryer basket and cook for 15 minutes, turning halfway through the cooking time. Serve with mustard and cucumbers. Bon appétit!

NUTRITION: Calories 560 Fat 42.2g Carbs 21.5g Protein 31.1g

Cube Steak with Cowboy Sauce

Basic Recipe
Preparation Time: 5 minutes **Cooking Time:** 15 minutes **Servings:** 4
INGREDIENTS:

- 1 ½ pounds cube steak
- Salt, to taste
- 1/4 teaspoon ground black pepper, or more to taste
- 4 ounces butter
- 2 garlic cloves, finely chopped
- 2 scallions, finely chopped
- 2 tablespoon fresh parsley, finely chopped
- 1 tablespoon fresh horseradish, grated
- 1 teaspoon cayenne pepper

DIRECTIONS:

27. Pat dry the cube steak and season it with salt and black pepper. Spritz the Air Fryer basket with cooking oil. Add the meat to the basket.
28. Cook in the preheated Air Fryer at 400 degrees F for 14 minutes
29. Meanwhile, melt the butter in a skillet over a moderate heat. Add the remaining ingredients and simmer until the sauce has thickened and reduced slightly. Top the warm cube steaks with Cowboy sauce and serve immediately.

NUTRITION: Calories 469 Fat 30.4g Carbs 0.6g Protein 46g

Steak Fingers with Lime Sauce

Basic Recipe
Preparation Time: 5 minutes **Cooking Time:** 15 minutes **Servings:** 4
INGREDIENTS:

- 1 ½ pounds sirloin steak
- 1/4 cup soy sauce
- 1/4 cup fresh lime juice
- 1 teaspoon garlic powder
- 1 teaspoon shallot powder
- 1 teaspoon celery seeds
- 1 teaspoon mustard seeds
- Coarse sea salt and ground black pepper, to taste
- 1 teaspoon red pepper flakes
- 2 eggs, lightly whisked
- 1 cup breadcrumbs
- 1/4 cup parmesan cheese
- 1 teaspoon paprika

DIRECTIONS:

30. Place the steak, soy sauce, lime juice, garlic powder, shallot powder, celery seeds, mustard seeds, salt, black pepper, and red pepper in a large ceramic bowl; let it marinate for 3 hours.
31. Tenderize the cube steak by pounding with a mallet; cut into 1-inch strips.
32. In a shallow bowl, whisk the eggs. In another bowl, mix the breadcrumbs, parmesan cheese, and paprika.
33. Dip the beef pieces into the whisked eggs and coat on all sides. Now, dredge the beef pieces in the breadcrumb mixture.
34. Cook at 400 degrees F for 14 minutes, flipping halfway through the cooking time.
35. Meanwhile, make the sauce by heating the reserved marinade in a saucepan over medium heat; let it simmer until thoroughly warmed. Serve the steak fingers with the sauce on the side. Enjoy!

NUTRITION: Calories 471 Fat 26.3g Carbs 13.9g Protein 42.5g

Beef Kofta Sandwich

Basic Recipe
Preparation Time: 5 minutes **Cooking Time:** 25 minutes **Servings:** 4
INGREDIENTS:

- 1/2 cup leeks, chopped
- 2 garlic cloves, smashed
- 1-pound ground chuck
- 1 slice of bread, soaked in water until fully tender
- Salt, to taste
- 1/4 teaspoon ground black pepper, or more to taste
- 1 teaspoon cayenne pepper
- 1/2 teaspoon ground sumac

- 3 saffron threads
- 2 tablespoons loosely packed fresh continental parsley leaves
- 4 tablespoons tahini sauce
- 4 warm flatbreads
- 4 ounces baby arugula
- 2 tomatoes cut into slices

DIRECTIONS:

1. In a bowl, mix the chopped leeks, garlic, ground meat, soaked bread, and spices; knead with your hands until everything is well incorporated.
2. Now, mound the beef mixture around a wooden skewer into a pointed-ended sausage.
3. Cook in the preheated Air Fryer at 360 degrees F for 25 minutes
4. To make the sandwiches, spread the tahini sauce on the flatbread; top with the kofta kebabs, baby arugula and tomatoes. Enjoy!

NUTRITION: Calories 436 Fat 20.5g Carbs 32g Protein 33.7g

Classic Beef Ribs

Basic Recipe

Preparation Time: 5 minutes **Cooking Time:** 30 minutes **Servings:** 4 **INGREDIENTS:**

- 2 pounds beef back ribs
- 1 tablespoon sunflower oil
- 1/2 teaspoon mixed peppercorns, cracked
- 1 teaspoon red pepper flakes
- 1 teaspoon dry mustard
- Coarse sea salt, to taste

DIRECTIONS:

36. Trim the excess fat from the beef ribs. Mix the sunflower oil, cracked peppercorns, red pepper, dry mustard, and salt.
37. Rub over the ribs.
38. Cook in the preheated Air Fryer at 395 degrees F for 11 minutes
39. Turn the heat to 330 degrees F and continue to cook for 18 minutes more. Serve warm.

NUTRITION: Calories 532 Fat 39g Carbs 0.4g Protein 44.7g

Spicy Short Ribs with Red Wine Sauce

Basic Recipe
Preparation Time: 5 minutes **Cooking Time:** 15 minutes **Servings:** 4 **INGREDIENTS:**

- 1 ½ pounds short rib
- 1 cup red wine
- 1/2 cup tamari sauce
- 1 lemon, juiced
- 1 teaspoon fresh ginger, grated
- 1 teaspoon salt
- 1 teaspoon black pepper
- 1 teaspoon paprika
- 1 teaspoon chipotle chili powder
- 1 cup ketchup
- 1 teaspoon garlic powder
- 1 teaspoon cumin

DIRECTIONS:

40. In a ceramic bowl, place the beef ribs, wine, tamari sauce, lemon juice, ginger, salt, black pepper, paprika, and chipotle chili powder.
41. Cover and let it marinate for 3 hours in the refrigerator.
42. Discard the marinade and add the short ribs to the Air Fryer basket. Cook in the preheated Air fry at 380 degrees F for 10 minutes, turning them over halfway through the cooking time.
43. In the meantime, heat the saucepan over medium heat; add the reserved marinade and stir in the ketchup, garlic powder, and cumin.
44. Cook until the sauce has thickened slightly.
45. Pour the sauce over the warm ribs and serve immediately. Bon appétit!

NUTRITION: Calories 505 Fat 31g Carbs 22.1g Protein 35.2g

Beef Schnitzel with Buttermilk Spaetzle

Basic Recipe
Preparation Time: 5 minutes **Cooking Time:** 15 minutes **Servings:** 2
INGREDIENTS:

- 1 egg, beaten
- 1/2 teaspoon ground black pepper
- 1 teaspoon paprika
- 1/2 teaspoon coarse sea salt
- 1 tablespoon ghee, melted
- 1/2 cup tortilla chips, crushed
- 2 thin-cut minute steaks
- Buttermilk Spaetzle:
- 2 eggs
- 1/2 cup buttermilk
- 1/2 cup all-purpose flour
- 1/2 teaspoon salt

DIRECTIONS:

46. Start by preheating your Air Fryer to 360 degrees F.
47. In a shallow bowl, whisk the egg with black pepper, paprika, and salt.
48. Thoroughly combine the ghee with the crushed tortilla chips and coarse sea salt in another shallow bowl.
49. Using a meat mallet, pound the schnitzel to 1/4- inch thick.
50. Dip the schnitzel into the egg mixture; then, roll the schnitzel over the crumb mixture until coated on all sides.
51. Cook for 13 minutes in the preheated Air Fryer.
52. To make the spaetzle, whisk the eggs, buttermilk, flour, and salt in a bowl. Bring a large saucepan of salted water to a boil.
53. Push the spaetzle mixture through the holes of a potato ricer into the boiling water; slice them off using a table knife. Work in batches.
54. When the spaetzle float, take them out with a slotted spoon. Repeat with the rest of the spaetzle mixture.
55. Serve with warm schnitzel. Enjoy!

NUTRITION: Calories 522 Fat 20.7g Carbs 17.1g Protein 62.2g

Beef Sausage Goulash

Basic Recipe
Preparation Time: 5 minutes **Cooking Time:** 35 minutes **Servings:** 2
INGREDIENTS:

- 1 tablespoon lard, melted
- 1 shallot, chopped
- 1 bell pepper, chopped
- 2 red chilies, finely chopped
- 1 teaspoon ginger-garlic paste
- Sea salt, to taste
- 1/4 teaspoon ground black pepper
- 4 beef good quality sausages, thinly sliced
- 2 teaspoons smoked paprika
- 1 cup beef bone broth
- 1/2 cup tomato puree
- 2 handfuls spring greens, shredded

DIRECTIONS:

56. Melt the lard in a Dutch oven over medium-high flame; sauté the shallots and peppers about 4 minutes or until fragrant.
57. Add the ginger-garlic paste and cook an additional minute. Season it with salt and black pepper and transfer to a lightly greased baking pan.
58. Then, brown the sausages, stirring occasionally, working in batches. Add to the baking pan.
59. Add the smoked paprika, broth, and tomato puree. Lower the pan onto the Air Fryer basket. Bake at 325 degrees F for 30 minutes
60. Stir in the spring greens and cook for 5 minutes more or until they wilt. Serve over the hot rice if desired. Bon appétit!

NUTRITION: Calories 565 Fat 47.1g Carbs 14.3g Protein 20.6g

Mom"s Toad in the Hole

Basic Recipe
Preparation Time: 5 minutes **Cooking Time:** 40 minutes **Servings:** 4
INGREDIENTS:

- 6 beef sausages
- 1 tablespoon butter, melted
- 1 cup plain flour
- A pinch of salt
- 2 eggs
- 1 cup semi-skimmed milk

DIRECTIONS:

61. Cook the sausages in the preheated Air Fryer at 380 degrees F for 15 minutes, shaking halfway through the cooking time.
62. Meanwhile, make up the batter mix.
63. Tip the flour into a bowl with salt; make a well in the middle and crack the eggs into it. Mix with an electric whisk; now, slowly and gradually pour in the milk, whisking all the time.
64. Place the sausages in a lightly greased baking pan. Pour the prepared batter over the sausages.
65. Cook in the preheated Air Fryer at 370 degrees F approximately 25 minutes, until golden and risen. Serve with gravy if desired. Bon appétit!

NUTRITION: Calories 584 Fat 40.2g Carbs 29.5g Protein 23.4g

Beef Nuggets with Cheesy Mushrooms

Basic Recipe
Preparation Time: 5 minutes **Cooking Time:** 20 minutes **Servings:** 4
INGREDIENTS:

- 2 eggs, beaten
- 4 tablespoons yogurt
- 1 cup tortilla chips, crushed
- 1 teaspoon dry mesquite flavored seasoning mix
- Coarse salt and ground black pepper, to taste
- 1/2 teaspoon onion powder
- 1-pound cube steak, cut into bite-size pieces
- 1-pound button mushrooms
- 1 cup Swiss cheese, shredded

DIRECTIONS:

66. In a shallow bowl, beat the eggs and yogurt. In a resealable bag, mix the tortilla chips, mesquite seasoning, salt, pepper, and onion powder.
67. Dip the steak pieces in the egg mixture; then, place in the bag, and shake to coat on all sides.
68. Cook at 400 degrees F for 14 minutes, flipping halfway through the cooking time.
69. Add the mushrooms to the lightly greased cooking basket. Top with shredded Swiss cheese.
70. Bake in the preheated Air Fryer at 400 degrees F for 5 minutes Serve with the beef nuggets. Bon appétit!

NUTRITION: Calories 355 Fat 15.7g Carbs 13.6g Protein 39.8g

Asian-Style Beef Dumplings

Basic Recipe
Preparation Time: 5 minutes **Cooking Time:** 20 minutes **Servings:** 5
INGREDIENTS:

- 1/2-pound ground chuck
- 1/2-pound beef sausage, chopped
- 1 cup Chinese cabbage, shredded
- 1 bell pepper, chopped
- 1 onion, chopped
- 2 garlic cloves, minced
- 1 medium-sized egg, beaten
- Sea salt and ground black pepper, to taste
- 20 wonton wrappers
- 2 tablespoons soy sauce
- 2 teaspoons sesame oil
- 2 teaspoons sesame seeds, lightly toasted
- 2 tablespoons seasoned rice vinegar
- 1/2 teaspoon chili sauce

DIRECTIONS:

1. To make the filling, thoroughly combine the ground chuck, sausage, cabbage, bell pepper, onion, garlic, egg, salt, and black pepper. Place the wrappers on a clean and dry surface. Now, divide the filling among the wrappers.
2. Then, fold each dumpling in half and pinch to seal. Transfer the dumplings to the lightly greased cooking basket. Bake at 390 degrees F for 15 minutes, turning over halfway through.
3. In the meantime, mix the soy sauce, sesame oil, sesame seeds, rice vinegar, and chili sauce. Serve the beef dumplings with the sauce on the side. Enjoy!

NUTRITION: Calories; 353 Fat; 16.7g Carbs; 29.5g Protein; 23.1g

Broiled Italian Chicken

Basic Recipe
Preparation Time: 5-10 minutes **Cooking Time:** 20 minutes **Servings:** 4
INGREDIENTS:

- ¾ cup shredded parmesan
- 1 cup panko breadcrumbs
- 4 chicken thighs with bone and skin
- 2 eggs, large
- 1 teaspoon Italian seasoning
- ½ teaspoon ground black pepper
- 1 teaspoon garlic powder
- ½ teaspoon kosher salt

DIRECTIONS:

71. Rub black pepper and salt over the chicken. In a mixing bowl, combine the panko breadcrumbs, Italian seasoning, garlic powder, and parmesan.
72. Beat the eggs in another bowl. Coat the chicken first with the egg, then with the crumb mixture.
73. Place Instant Pot Air Fryer Crisp over kitchen platform. Press Air Fry, set the temperature to 400°F and set the timer to 5 minutes to preheat. Press —Start‖ and allow it to preheat for 5 minutes.
74. In the inner pot, place the Air Fryer basket. In the basket, add the chicken.
75. Close the Crisp Lid and press the —Broil‖ setting. Set temperature to 400°F and set the timer to 20 minutes. Press —Start.‖ No need to flip in between.
76. Open the Crisp Lid after cooking time is over. Serve warm.

NUTRITION: Calories 577 Fat 32g Carbs 14g Protein 42g

Asian Style Chicken Meal

Basic Recipe
Preparation Time: 5-10 minutes **Cooking Time:** 30 minutes **Servings:** 2-3
INGREDIENTS:

- ¼ cup honey
- ½ cup rice vinegar
- 1-pound chicken wings
- 1 teaspoon sea salt
- 2 cloves garlic, minced
- 1 teaspoon ginger, grated
- 1 small orange, zest, and juice
- 2 teaspoons red chili pepper paste

DIRECTIONS:

77. Place Instant Pot Air Fryer Crisp over kitchen platform. In the inner pot, add 2 cups water and arrange trivet and place the chicken wings over.
78. Close the Pressure Lid and press the ―Pressure‖ setting. Set the ―Hi‖ pressure level and set the timer to 2 minutes. Press ―Start.‖ Instant Pot will start building pressure. Quick-release pressure after cooking time is over (just press the button on the lid), and open the lid. Take out the wings and empty water.
79. In a mixing bowl, combine the orange zest, orange juice, rice vinegar, honey, red pepper paste, ginger, garlic, and salt.
80. Add the sauce in the pot and place trivet; place the chicken over the trivet.
81. Close the Crisp Lid and press the ―Air Fry‖ setting. Set temperature to 390°F and set the timer to 30 minutes. Press ―Start.‖
82. Halfway down, open the Crisp Lid, shake the basket and close the lid to continue cooking for the remaining time.
83. Open the Crisp Lid after cooking time is over. Serve the chicken with the honey sauce.

NUTRITION: Calories 448 Fat 17g Carbs 41g Protein 24g

Chicken Air Fried with Pepper Sauce

Basic Recipe
Preparation Time: 5-10 minutes **Cooking Time:** 30 minutes **Servings:** 7-8
INGREDIENTS:

- 1 tablespoon Worcestershire sauce
- 1 teaspoon salt
- 1-2 tablespoon brown sugar
- ½ cup cayenne pepper sauce
- 4 pounds chicken wings

  - ½ cup butter

DIRECTIONS:

84. In a mixing bowl, add the salt, brown sugar, Worcestershire sauce, butter, and hot sauce. Combine the ingredients to mix well with each other.
85. Grease Air Fryer Basket with some cooking spray. Add the chicken wings.
86. Place Instant Pot Air Fryer Crisp over kitchen platform. Press Air Fry, set the temperature to 400°F and set the timer to 5 minutes to preheat. Press —Start‖ and allow it to preheat for 5 minutes.
87. In the inner pot, place the Air Fryer basket.
88. Close the Crisp Lid and press the —Air Fry‖ setting. Set temperature to 380°F and set the timer to 25 minutes. Press —Start.‖
89. Halfway down, open the Crisp Lid, shake the basket and close the lid to continue cooking for the remaining time.
90. Open the Crisp Lid after cooking time is over. Add it with the bowl sauce and combine; serve warm.

NUTRITION: Calories 387 Fat 15g Carbs 12g Protein 21g

Hot Buffalo Chicken

Basic Recipe

Preparation Time: 10 minutes **Cooking Time:** 12 minutes **Servings:** 6

INGREDIENTS:

- 2 lbs. chicken breasts
- 1/2 cup buffalo wing sauce
- 1/2 cup onion, chopped
- 1/2 cup celery, diced
- 1/2 cup chicken broth

DIRECTIONS:

91. Add all ingredients into the inner pot of instant pot duo crisp and stir well.
92. Seal the pot with pressure cooking lid and cook on high pressure for 12 minutes.
93. Release pressure using a quick release once done, remove lid.
94. Remove chicken from pot and shred using a fork.
95. Return shredded chicken to the pot and stir well and serve.

NUTRITION: Calories 296 Fat 11.3 g Carbs 1.3 g Protein 44.3 g

Yummy Mexican Chicken

Basic Recipe
Preparation Time: 10 minutes **Cooking Time:** 15 minutes **Servings:** 6
INGREDIENTS:

- 2 lbs. chicken breasts
- 2 tsp cumin
- 2 tsp garlic powder
- 4 oz. jalapenos, diced
- 10.5 oz. tomatoes, diced

- 1/2 cup green bell pepper
- 1/2 cup red bell pepper
- 1 onion, diced
- 1 fresh lime juice
- 2/3 cup chicken broth
- 1/2 tsp. chili powder
- 1 tbsp. olive oil
- 1/4 tsp. salt

DIRECTIONS:

96. Add oil into the inner pot of instant pot duo crisp and set pot on sauté mode.
97. Add onion, bell peppers and salt and sauté for 3 minutes.
98. Add remaining ingredients and stir well.
99. Seal the pot with pressure cooking lid and cook on high pressure for 12 minutes.
100. Release pressure using a quick release once done. Remove lid.
101. Remove chicken from pot and shred using a fork.
102. Return shredded chicken to the pot and stir well.
103. Serve and enjoy.

NUTRITION: Calories 347 Fat 14.2 g Carbs 7.8 g Protein 45.7 g

Balsamic Chicken

Basic Recipe
Preparation Time: 10 minutes **Cooking Time:** 17 minutes **Servings:** 6
INGREDIENTS:

- 2 lbs. chicken breasts
- 1/3 cup balsamic vinegar
- 1 onion, chopped
- 1/2 cup chicken broth
- 1 tbsp.Dijon mustard
- 1/2 tsp. dried thyme
- 1 tsp. garlic, chopped

DIRECTIONS:

1. Mix together Dijon, chicken broth, and vinegar and pour into the inner pot of instant pot duo crisp.
2. Add chicken, thyme, garlic, and onion and stir well.
3. Seal the pot with pressure cooking lid and cook on high pressure for 12 minutes.
4. Release pressure using a quick release once done. Remove lid.
5. Remove chicken from pot and shred using a fork. Pour the leftover liquid of pot over shredded chicken.
6. Line the air fryer basket with foil.
7. Add shredded chicken to the air fryer basket and place basket in the pot.
8. Seal the pot with air fryer lid and select broil mode and cook for 5 minutes.
9. Serve and enjoy.

NUTRITION: Calories 303 Fat 11.4 g Carbs 2.3 g Protein
44.5 g

Italian Chicken Wings

Basic Recipe

Preparation Time: 10 minutes **Cooking Time:** 15 minutes **Servings:** 4 **INGREDIENTS:**

- 12 chicken wings
- 1 tbsp. chicken seasoning
- 3 tbsp olive oil
- 1 tbsp. garlic powder
- 1 tbsp basil
- 1/2 tbsp. oregano
- 3 tbsp tarragon
- Pepper
- Salt

DIRECTIONS:

10. Add all ingredients into the mixing bowl and toss well.
11. Pour 1 cup water into the inner pot of instant pot duo crisp then place steamer rack in the pot.
12. Arrange chicken wings on top of the steamer rack.
13. Seal the pot with pressure cooking lid and cook on high pressure for 10 minutes.
14. Release pressure using a quick release once done. Remove lid.
15. Remove chicken wings from the pot. Dump leftover liquid from the pot.
16. Add chicken wings into the air fryer basket then place a basket in the pot.
17. Seal the pot with air fryer lid and select broil mode and cook for 5 minutes.
18. Serve and enjoy.

NUTRITION: Calories 588 Fat 29.6 g Carbs 2.6 g Protein 74.6 g

Yummy Hawaiian Chicken

Basic Recipe

Preparation Time: 10 minutes **Cooking Time:** 12 minutes **Servings:** 6 **INGREDIENTS:**

- 2 lbs. chicken breasts, skinless, boneless, and cut into chunks
- 2 tbsp cornstarch
- 1 cup chicken broth
- 20 oz. can pineapple tidbits
- 1 tbsp. garlic, crushed
- 2 tbsp brown sugar
- 6 tbsp soy sauce
- 1/2 tsp. ground ginger
- 1/2 tsp. salt

DIRECTIONS:

1. Add all ingredients except cornstarch into the inner pot of instant pot duo crisp and stir well.
2. Seal the pot with pressure cooking lid and cook on high pressure for 10 minutes.
3. Release pressure using a quick release once done. Remove lid. In a small bowl, whisk together 1/4 cup water and cornstarch and pour into the pot.
4. Set pot on sauté mode. Cook chicken on sauce mode until sauce thickens.
5. Serve over rice and enjoy.

NUTRITION: Calories 377 Fat 11.5 g Carbs 18.7 g

Protein 46 g

Dijon Chicken

Intermediate Recipe Preparation Time: 10 minutes **Cooking Time:** 50 minutes
Servings: 4 **INGREDIENTS:**

- 1 1/2 lbs. chicken thighs, skinless and boneless
- 2 tbsp Dijon mustard
- 1/4 cup French mustard
- 4 tbsp maple syrup
- 2 tsp. olive oil

DIRECTIONS:

1. In a large bowl, mix together maple syrup, olive oil, Dijon mustard, and French mustard.
2. Add chicken to the bowl and mix until chicken is well coated.
3. Transfer chicken into the instant pot air fryer basket and place basket in the pot.
4. Seal the pot with air fryer lid and select bake mode and cook at 375 f for 45-50 minutes.
5. Serve and enjoy.

NUTRITION: Calories 401 Fat 15.3 g   Carbs 13.8 g
Protein 49.6 g

Mango Chicken

Basic Recipe
Preparation Time: 10 minutes **Cooking Time:** 15 minutes **Servings:** 2
INGREDIENTS:

- 2 chicken breasts, skinless and boneless
- 1 ripe mango, peeled and diced
- 1/2 tbsp turmeric
- 1/2 cup chicken broth
- 2 garlic cloves, minced
- 1/2 tsp. ginger, grated
- 1 fresh lime juice
- 1/2 tsp. pepper
- 1/2 tsp. salt

DIRECTIONS:

1. Add chicken into the inner pot of instant pot duo crisp and top with mango. Add lime juice, broth, turmeric, pepper, and salt.
2. Seal the pot with pressure cooking lid and cook on high for 15 minutes.
3. Once done, allow to release pressure naturally. Remove lid.
4. Shred chicken using a fork and stir well.
5. Serve and enjoy.

NUTRITION: Calories 407 Fat 12.1g Carbs 30 g Protein 45.3 g

Honey Cashew Butter Chicken

Basic Recipe
Preparation Time: 10 minutes **Cooking Time:** 7 minutes **Servings:** 3
INGREDIENTS:

- 1 lb. chicken breast, cut into chunks
- 2 tbsp rice vinegar
- 2 tbsp honey
- 2 tbsp coconut aminos
- 1/4 cup cashew butter
- 2 garlic cloves, minced
- 1/4 cup chicken broth
- 1/2 tbsp. sriracha

DIRECTIONS:

1. Add chicken into the inner pot of instant pot duo crisp. In a small bowl, mix together cashew butter, garlic, broth, sriracha, vinegar, honey, and coconut aminos and pour over chicken.
2. Seal the pot with pressure cooking lid and cook on high for 7 minutes.
3. Release pressure using a quick release once done. Remove lid.
4. Stir well and serve.

NUTRITION: Calories 366 Fat 2.1 g Carbs 20.7 g Protein 36.4 g

Sweet & Tangy Tamarind Chicken

Basic Recipe

Preparation Time: 10 minutes **Cooking Time:** 15 minutes **Servings:** 4

INGREDIENTS:

- 2 lbs. chicken breasts, skinless, boneless, and cut into pieces
- 1 tbsp. ketchup
- 1 tbsp. vinegar
- 2 tbsp ginger, grated
- 1 garlic clove, minced
- 3 tbsp olive oil
- 1 tbsp. arrowroot powder
- 1/2 cup tamarind paste
- 2 tbsp brown sugar
- 1 tsp. salt

DIRECTIONS:

1. Add oil into the inner pot of instant pot duo crisp and set the pot on sauté mode.
2. Add ginger and garlic and sauté for 30 seconds.
3. Add chicken and sauté for 3-4 minutes.
4. In a small bowl, mix together the tamarind paste, brown sugar, ketchup, vinegar, and salt and pour over chicken and stir well.
5. Seal the pot with pressure cooking lid and cook on high for 8 minutes.
6. Release pressure using a quick release once done. Remove lid.
7. In a small bowl, whisk arrowroot powder with 2 tbsp water and pour it into the pot.
8. Set pot on sauté mode and cook chicken for 1-2 minutes.
9. Serve and enjoy.

NUTRITION: Calories 598   Fat 27.6 g   Carbs 18.9 g
Protein 66.4 g

Korean Chicken Wings

Basic Recipe
Preparation Time: 5 minutes **Cooking Time:** 10 minutes **Servings:** 8
INGREDIENTS:

- Wings:
- 1 tsp. Pepper
- 1 tsp. Salt
- 2 pounds chicken wings
- Sauce:
- 2 packets splenda
- 1 tbsp. Minced garlic
- 1 tbsp. Minced ginger
- 1 tbsp. Sesame oil
- 1 tsp. Agave nectar
- 1 tbsp. Mayo
- 2 tbsp. Gochujang
- Finishing:
- ¼ c. Chopped green onions
- 2 tsp. Sesame seeds

DIRECTIONS:

1. Ensure instant crisp air fryer is preheated to 400 degrees.
2. Line a small pan with foil and place a rack onto the pan, then place into instant crisp air fryer.
3. Season the wings with pepper and salt and place onto the rack.
4. Lock the air fryer lid. Set temperature to 160°f, and set time to 20 minutes and air fry 20 minutes, turning at 10 minutes.
5. As chicken air fries, mix together all the sauce components.
6. Once a thermometer says that the chicken has reached 160 degrees, take out wings and place into a bowl.
7. Pour half of the sauce mixture over wings, tossing well to coat.
8. Put coated wings back into instant crisp air fryer for 5 minutes or till they reach 165 degrees.
9. Remove and sprinkle with green onions and sesame seeds. Dip into extra sauce.

NUTRITION: Calories 356 Fat 26g Carbs 21g Protein 23g

Paprika Chicken

Intermediate Recipe Preparation Time: 10 minutes **Cooking Time:** 30 minutes

Servings: 4

INGREDIENTS:

- 4 chicken breasts, skinless and boneless, cut into chunks
- 2 tsp. garlic, minced
- 2 tbsp smoked paprika
- 3 tbsp olive oil
- 2 tbsp lemon juice
- Pepper
- Salt

DIRECTIONS:

1. In a small bowl, mix together garlic, lemon juice, paprika, oil, pepper, and salt.
2. Rub chicken with garlic mixture.
3. Add chicken into the instant pot air fryer basket and place basket in the pot.
4. Seal the pot with air fryer lid and select bake mode and cook at 350 f for 30 minutes.
5. Serve and enjoy.

NUTRITION: Calories 381 Fat 21.8 g Carbs 2.6 g Protein 42.9 g

Garlic Lemon Chicken

Intermediate Recipe Preparation Time: 10 minutes **Cooking Time:** 40 minutes **Servings:** 4 **INGREDIENTS:**

- 2 lbs. chicken drumsticks
- 4 tbsp butter
- 2 tbsp parsley, chopped
- 1 fresh lemon juice
- 10 garlic cloves, minced
- 2 tbsp olive oil
- Pepper
- Salt

DIRECTIONS:

1. Add butter, parsley, lemon juice, garlic, oil, pepper, and salt into the mixing bowl and mix well.
2. Add chicken to the bowl and toss until well coated.
3. Transfer chicken into the instant pot air fryer basket and place basket in the pot.
4. Seal the pot with air fryer lid and select bake mode and cook at 400 f for 40 minutes.
5. Serve and enjoy.

NUTRITION: Calories 560 Fat 31.6 g Carbs 2.9 g Protein 63.1 g

Flavorful Herb Chicken

Intermediate Recipe Preparation Time: 10 minutes **Cooking Time:** 4 hours
Servings: 6 **INGREDIENTS:**

- 6 chicken breasts, skinless and boneless
- 1 onion, sliced
- 14 oz. can tomato, diced
- 1 tsp. dried basil
- 1 tsp. dried rosemary
- 1 tbsp. olive oil
- 1/2 cup balsamic vinegar
- 1/2 tsp. thyme
- 1 tsp. dried oregano
- 4 garlic cloves
- Pepper
- Salt

DIRECTIONS:

1. Add all ingredients into the inner pot of instant pot duo crisp and stir well.
2. Seal the pot with pressure cooking lid and select slow cook mode and cook on high for 4 hours.
3. Stir well and serve.

NUTRITION: Calories 328 Fat 13.3 g Carbs 6.3 g Protein
43.2 g